Geometries of Experience

Geometries of Experience

Thinking with Remo Bodei

Edited by

MASSIMO CIAVOLELLA, EFRAÍN KRISTAL,
HEATHER RENEE SOTTONG

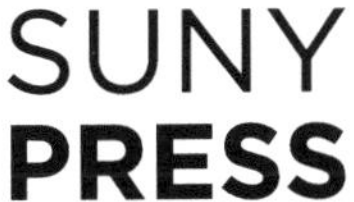

EU GPSR Authorised Representative:
Logos Europe, 9 rue Nicolas Poussin, 17000, La Rochelle, France
contact@logoseurope.eu

For information, contact State University of New York Press, Albany, NY
www.sunypress.edu

Library of Congress Cataloging-in-Publication Data

Names: Ciavolella, Massimo, 1942– editor. | Kristal, Efrain, 1959– editor. | Sottong, Heather Renee, 1983– editor.
Title: Geometries of experience : thinking with Remo Bodei / edited by Massimo Ciavolella, Efrain Kristal, Heather Renee Sottong.
Description: Albany : State University of New York Press, [2025]. | Series: SUNY series in contemporary Italian philosophy | Includes bibliographical references and index.
Identifiers: LCCN 2025014360 | ISBN 9798855804577 (hardcover : alk. paper) | ISBN 9798855804591 (ebook) | ISBN 9798855804584 (pbk. : alk. paper)
Subjects: LCSH: Bodei, Remo, 1938–
Classification: LCC B3613.B5254 G46 2025 | DDC 195—dc23/eng/20250505
LC record available at https://lccn.loc.gov/2025014360

Contents

Introduction

Heather Renee Sottong

This volume, which I coedited with Massimo Ciavolella and Efraín Kristal, is a collection of essays in honor of the life, friendship, and intellectual achievements of Remo Bodei. Bodei is undeniably one of Italy's most influential and prolific contemporary philosophers, and his extensive bibliography and the sheer number of reprints and translations of his books testifies to this fact. In total he published hundreds of articles and twenty-eight books:[1] *Letteratura e psicoanalisi* (Literature and Psychoanalysis), 1974; *Sistema ed epoca in Hegel* (System and Epoch in Hegel), 1975, reworked and republished with the title *The Owl and the Mole* in 2014; *Multiversum: Tempo e storia in Ernst Bloch* (Multiversum: Time and History in Ernst Bloch), 1979, revisited and republished in 1983; *Scomposizioni: Forme dell'individuo moderno* (Breakdowns: Forms of Modern Individualities), 1987, German translation in 1996, expanded and republished in 2016; *Hölderlin: La filosofia y lo trágico* (Hölderlin: Philosophy and the Tragic), 1990; *Geometria delle passioni* (Geometry of the Passions), 1991, Spanish translation in 1995, French translation in 1997, and English translation in 2018; *Ordo amoris: Conflitti terreni e felicità celeste* (The Order of Love: Earthly Conflicts and Heavenly Happiness), 1991, German translation in 1993, Spanish translation in 1998, French translation in 2015; *Le forme del bello* (The Forms of the Beautiful), 1995, Spanish translation in 1998, Portuguese translation in 2005, Turkish translation in 2008, new editions in 2005 and 2017; *Le prix de la liberté* (The Price of Freedom), 1995; *Libro della memoria e della speranza* (Book of Memory and Hope), 1995, Spanish translation in 1998; *La filosofia nel Novecento* (Philosophy of the Twentieth Century), 1997, Spanish and

French translations in 1999, Portuguese translation in 2000, new edition in 2006, Vietnamese translation in 2011; *Se la storia ha un senso* (If History Makes Sense), 1997, Portuguese translation in 2001; *Il noi diviso: Ethos e idee dell'Italia repubblicana* (We, the Divided: Ethos, Politics and Culture in Post-War Italy, 1943–2006), 1998, English translation in 2006; *Le logiche del delirio: Ragione, affetti, follia* (Logics of Delusion: Reason, Affects, Madness), 2000, French and Spanish translations in 2002, new edition in 2005, English translation in 2006; *I senza Dio. Figure e momenti dell'ateismo* (I Without God. Figures and Moments of Atheism), 2001; *Il dottor Freud e i nervi dell'anima. Filosofia e società a un secolo dalla nascita della psicoanalisi* (Doctor Freud and the Nerves of the Soul), 2001, Spanish translation in 2004 and 2006; *Destini personali: L'età della colonizzazione delle coscienze* (Personal Destinies: The Age of the Colonization of Consciousness), 2002, Spanish translation in 2006, new edition in 2008; *Una scintilla di fuoco. Invito alla filosofia* (A Spark of Fire: Invitation to Philosophy), 2005, Spanish translation in 2006; *Ospiti della vita* (Guests of Life), 2006; *Piramidi di tempo: Storie e teoria del déjà vu* (Pyramids of Time: Stories and Theories of the Déjà Vu), 2006, French translation in 2007, Spanish, Turkish, and Romanian translations in 2010; *Paesaggi sublimi: Gli uomini davanti alla natura selvaggia* (Sublime Landscapes: Man in front of Wild Nature), 2008, Spanish and Croatian translations in 2011, new edition in 2013; *La vita delle cose* (The Life of Things), 2009, Spanish translation in 2013, new Italian edition and English translation in 2014, French translation in 2017, German translation in 2019; *Ira: La passione furente* (Wrath: Raging Passion), 2011, Hungarian translation in 2013; *Immaginare altre vite: Realtà, progetti, desideri* (Imagining Other Lives. Realities, Projects, Desires), 2013, Spanish translation in 2014; *Generazioni: Età della vita, età delle cose* (Generations: Ages of Life, Ages of Things), 2014, Spanish translation in 2016; *Limite* (Limits), 2016; and *Dominio e sottomissione: Schiavi, animali, macchine, Intelligenza Artificiale* (Domination and Subordination: Slaves, Animals, Machines, Artificial Intelligence), 2019; *Leopardi e la filosofia* (Leopardi and Philosophy), 2022 (published posthumously).

Of these, arguably the most influential are *Scomposizioni. Forme dell'individuo moderno* (1987); *Destini personali: L'età della colonizzazione delle coscienze* (2002); and *Geometria delle passioni: Paura, speranza e felicità: Filosofia e uso politico* (1991), from which this volume takes its name. Each article herein addresses one of his key works and the influence it had both in Italy and beyond. While Bodei's initial interests were in classical German philosophy, namely, the Weimar Classicism period (1770–1830), he has written on a vast array of topics, from the utopian thought of the twentieth century, to questions of aesthetics, to memory and collective identity, to the conflict of passion and reason. In what follows, prominent scholars consider many of Bodei's most important contributions and ensure that his legacy lives on.

Efraín Kristal's article "Things, Landscapes and Wrath: The Philosophical Investigation According to Remo Bodei" opens the volume. Kristal begins with useful reflections on Bodei's unique philosophical approach, which involves "rigor and specificity" (p. 10); a consideration of the interplay between passion and reason; a synthesis of philosophy, literature, and history; and a trajectory from antiquity to the present. Kristal then discusses how this approach plays out in three of Bodei's smaller books that address a specific concept or theme: *La vita delle cose* (On the Life of Things); *Paesaggi sublimi* (Sublime Landscapes); and *Ira: La passione furente* (Wrath: Raging Passion).

In his article "The Owl and the Mole: Remo Bodei's Hegel," Alfredo Ferrarin provides us with a firsthand account of how Bodei's scholarship profoundly marked his generation's reading of Hegel. It is, as he explains, difficult even to overestimate the importance of Bodei for Hegel studies in Italy. Ferrarin begins by outlining the trajectory of how Bodei became a leading expert, from his *tesi di laurea*, to his translations, to his book, to his introductory essays to the works of other important nineteenth- and twentieth-century Hegel scholars—and all before the age of forty. His groundbreaking book *Sistema ed epoca in Hegel* was first published in 1975. Thirty-nine years later, Bodei rewrote this book, nearly doubling its length, and retitling it *La civetta e la talpa* (The Owl and the Mole, Bologna: Il mulino, 2014). Ferrarin unpacks this metaphor, explaining its significance to Bodei and pinpointing that objectivity of reason is the true heart of Hegel's thought in Bodei's interpretation. Furthermore, he underscores the great privilege that Italians take for granted—being able to read Bodei's scholarship on Hegel in his original elegant prose, so rich with metaphor and idiomatic figures of speech that it is "untranslatable" (p. 38). Indeed, the English language, fit for plain and linear argumentation cannot quite encompass Bodei's sophisticated sentences and implicit references to works of literature as well as to a vast array of both humanistic and scientific scholarship.

It is a nearly insurmountable feat to translate Bodei, but one that the next contributor to this volume, Gianpiero W. Doebler, has bravely taken on. It is thanks to his great dedication and linguistic finesse that Bodei's *Geometria delle passioni: Paura, speranza, felicità: filosofia e uso politico* is available in English. In his essay "*Paura, speranza, felicità*: Translating Remo

Bodei's Geometry of the Passions," Gianpiero walks us through his five-year journey of translation, from fear, to hope, to happiness. This essay is a gem for anyone familiar with Bodei's prose who wants a deeper consideration of the challenges involved in transforming his very long and poetic Italian sentences with their multiple subordinate clauses, parenthetical comments, series, and incorporated quotes into fluid, intelligible English. As Doebler explains, "to parse these periods into accessible English, it was necessary to sometimes derive three or four (and in some cases five) sentences from one symphonic Italian construction" (p. 47). Not only that, but the project also required painstaking bibliographical research to locate appropriate editions of the myriad sources quoted by Bodei in at least seven languages. Gianpiero reveals the unexpected challenges arising in the translation of part 4 and recalls his experience consulting with Bodei personally to settle on the best English counterparts to various philosophical phrases. It was a labor of love that has made one of Bodei's most important works more accessible to the world.

In my own article, I discuss Bodei's book *Ordo Amoris: Conflitti terreni e felicità celeste* (The Order of Love: Earthly Conflicts and Heavenly Happiness), which has not yet been translated into English (perhaps another job for Gianpiero). Fortunately, however, it is available in German, Spanish, and French. In this text Bodei engages in a rich discussion of divine love, which unlike romantic love, is characterized by constancy, coherency, and order. Bodei considers Augustine's concept of the order of love versus the disorder of evil; the eschatological differences between political states and religions; and love and memory. What I find most interesting about this book and what I focus on in this essay is how Bodei discusses Augustine's theories on love in relation to modernity, which he points out has dismantled the belief in *ordo amoris*. The globalization of markets and communication have stirred up the painful sensation of an uprooting of traditions and a sensation of disorientation in a world that is more and more vast and unfamiliar. The book is relevant for those interested in St. Augustine's vision of divine love and for all scholars investigating the philosophical tradition that stems from him, which has influenced contemporary thinkers including Heidegger, Jaspers, Wittgenstein, Arendt, and Jonas.

Peter Carravetta's article is on Bodei's book *The Life of Things*, in which he explores the multilayered meanings of "things," which he distinguishes from mere material objects. Indeed, a main focus of the book is the process by which an object becomes a "thing," which, as Carravetta explains, is a "significant cultural referent, at times a social force impacting on values, beliefs, habits, and eventually choices" (p. 64). Things factor into one's identity, create continuity among generations, and connect individual and collective histories. Bodei argues that by a certain focusing of our attention, we can confer a sense to an object that can transform it into a thing, thereby enriching our lives. Carravetta comments on some of Bodei's considerations in light of his own research in postmodernity, rhetorical hermeneutics, and migration. Particularly interesting is how this process of transformation from object to thing might play out for migrants who must reorganize their existence in a new space in which they themselves are considered "other."

Olimpia Pelosi takes on the question of corporality, that is, the evolution of the Western construction of the body from Plato to Bodei and Foucault. After reflecting on how Plato's statement "the body is the tomb of the soul" (*Cratylus*) has indelibly influenced Western philosophical views on the body since Late Antiquity, she lucidly sums up major Christian contributions to the discourse (St. Paul, Tertullian, Augustine, and Thomas Aquinas), followed by corporeal perceptions in the modern era (namely, Descartes and Spinoza), to then arrive at the body of the paper: Bodei and Foucault's views, which are strikingly parallel but yet critically unexplored in any comparative study. Neither Bodei nor Foucault see the body as the grave of the soul; instead, they view it as a container of *Erlebnis* (or lived experience). Even more thought provoking than the similarities between Bodei and Foucault's visions are Pelosi's reflections on the subtle differences. This essay is well documented and incredibly useful to any scholar interested in the body/soul dichotomy in Western thought.

Christoph Wulf sheds light on how perceptive Bodei's reading was of the German poet, Friedrich Hölderlin. While over the years various political and social groups (including the National Socialists during the Second World War) forced and promoted their own one-dimensional reading of Hölderlin to suit their own ends, Bodei drew attention to the contradictory and ambiguous nature of Hölderlin's poetry, which gives it its high aesthetic quality while making it open to multidimensional interpretations. Wulf is particularly interested in the oscillation between the *utopian* and the *tragic* that characterizes Hölderlin's work. In much of his poetry he longs for a utopian world, which he associates with the world of the Greek gods, but the imagined mythical space is nonexistent and therefore inaccessible. This is what Bodei aptly recognizes as "tragic" in his book *Hölderlin: La filosofía y lo trágico*" (1990). As Wulf explains in the final section of this essay, the irreconcilable dichotomy between the longed-for divine world and harsh human reality is beautifully and metaphorically expressed in

Hölderlin's epistolary novel, *Hyperion*, when Hyperion says, "What do I care about the shipwreck of the world, I know nothing other than my blissful island."

In "Torquato Tasso and His 'Virtù Eroica' as a Passion of the Will," Paolo Cherchi reconstructs the history of discussions on "heroic virtue," beginning with Aristotle's *Nicomachean Ethics*. When researching this topic for his book *Il tramonto dell'onestade* back in 2016, Cherchi was surprised by the paucity of information available. He turned to Bodei, whose *Geometry of the Passions* had left a lasting impression and an extensive bibliographic archive. In this article he revisits his investigation in order to explain why this particular virtue/passion had difficulty "finding a stable place in the geometry of any moral system" (p. 122). He begins by making a useful distinction between two notions of "heroic virtue"—that of saints and that of secular heroes—so that the two can be followed in parallel. The article culminates in a discussion of Torquato Tasso's 1583 essay, *Discorso sulla virtù eroica e sulla carità*, which was intended as a companion essay to the poem *Gerusalemme Liberata*, published in 1581. In it Tasso seeks to elucidate the nature of this special and difficult to define virtue in relation to his quest for a new hero.

Andrea Borsari focuses on *Destini personali* (*Personal Destinies*), which he views as part of a "triptych," along with *Geometria delle passioni* (Geometry of the Passions) and *Scomposizioni* (Decompositions). Written and published in 2002, *Destini* deals with theories of individuality, beginning with Locke's and Schopenhauer's, and continuing with discussions of ideas of self in Ribot, Janet, Binet, Nietzsche, Bergson, Proust, Pirandello, Simmel, and beyond. Bodei's knowledge on this topic is vast and complex, and Borsari clearly traces his thinking while making important connections between the other two books in the "triptych," while outlining the development of similar themes in Bodei's later work. It is a revelatory piece for those interested in evolving ideas on individuality, from the idea of *Bildung* in the Goethezeit to the fragmentation of the individual into multiple selves in the twentieth century. Following in the path of Spinoza who sought to get rid of the reductive binary Reason/Passion, Bodei considers the vital role that passions play in our personal growth. Borsari concludes the essay with some open questions posed in response to Bodei's work, questions that "are still there for the philosophical enterprise of those who remain" (p. 167). And our hope with this volume is just that, that the questions remain open, the dialogue alive.

Note

1. Thirty-four if you consider the books he coauthored: *Hegel e l'economia politica* (Hegel and Political Economy) with R. Racinaro and M. Barale in 1975; *Hegel e Weber: Egemoni e legittimazione* (Hegel and Weber: Hegemony and Legitimacy) with F. Cassano in 1977; *Politica e felicità* (Politics and Happiness) with L. F. Pizzolato in 1997; *Mitezza e coraggio* (Meekness and Courage) with S. Givone in 2013; *La nuova fisica delle particelle e i segreti dell'universo: Un dialogo tra filosofia, scienza e religione* (The New Particle Physics and the Secrets of the Universe: A Dialogue Between Philosophy, Science, and Religion) with G. Tonelli in 2017; and *Le virtù cardinali* (The Cardinal Virtues) with G. Giorello, M. Marzano, and S. Veca in 2017.

1

Things, Landscapes, and Wrath

The Philosophical Investigation
According to Remo Bodei

Efraín Kristal

Remo Bodei wrote over thirty books that make up one of the most impressive monuments of both contemporary Italian and European philosophy. Some of these books are indispensable pillars of his thought, they are major works that make important statements about the personal and political dimension of the contemporary Western individual. These include *Scomposizioni* (decompositions), *Geomettria delle passioni* (Geometry of Passions) and *Destini personali* (personal destinies), in which he explores the predicaments of the contemporary individual in the vicissitudes of personal, institutional and historical experience. These books address the breakdown of the contemporary individual, the essential role of human passions and emotions in understanding any human situation be it personal or collective, and the mistake of trying to understand human predicaments by appealing to reason alone. As he once put it,

> È [. . .] sbagliato contrapporre ragione e passioni come logica e assenza di logica. Si tratta di due logiche diverse [. . . .] Queste due logiche, da un lato collaborano e, dall'altro, si contrappongono. Con Ovidio, si potrebbe dire di loro: *nec sine te, nec tecum vivere possum.* Non possiamo vivere né senza razionalità

e con passioni né con razionalità e senza passioni. Anche nella conoscenza vi è, infatti, una tonalità affettiva, così come nelle passioni vi è una peculiare forma di conoscenza, paradossalmente proprio nei loro eccessi, nel loro stravedere.[1]

It is [. . .] a mistake to oppose reason and passion as an opposition of logic and absence of logic. They are logics of different kinds [. . . .] On the one hand, these two kinds of logics collaborate, and on the other hand they are opposed to each other. With Ovid's assistance one could say of them: *nec sine te, nec tecum vivere possum*. We can neither live without reason and with passions, nor with passions without reason. Even in knowledge, there exists an affective tonality, and in the same way in the passions there exists a peculiar form of knowledge, paradoxically, in its own excesses, in its own blindness.

One of the most fascinating aspects of Bodei's philosophical approach involves the rigor and specificity with which he is able to tease out the logic of realms of human experience where—for better and for worse—reason is always a partner to passion, and not the partner who is necessarily playing a dominant role. In *Destini personali* (personal destinies), Bodei explores a weighty idea, the "colonization of consciousness," which is a way to signal how contemporary politics can commandeer the consciousness of individuals and derail their humanity. Another concept of this type that matters to Bodei—and he acknowledged the investigations of the Frankfurt School when he discusses it—is the role that desires generated by consumer culture play in undermining the humanity of individuals and communities.

These three books (*Scomposizioni, Geomettria delle passioni*, and *Destini personali)* are also pillars of Bodei's philosophical project and they embody one of his major contributions to philosophy, which is a keen exploration of the role of the emotions and the passions in the vicissitudes of the lives of individuals, communities, and in political affairs. The second of these books, a real centerpiece, is arguably the most important book of Bodei's oeuvre, and thanks to Gianpiero W. Doebler's splendid translation published in 2018 by University of Toronto Press, it now exists in English with the title: *Geometry of the Passions: Fear, Hope, Happiness: Philosophy and Political Use*. In this book Bodei fully develops an idea that is essential for the understanding of his entire oeuvre, namely, that the emotions, both simple and morally complex, are not merely a helpful support to understanding political and historical situations. They are indispensable to do so. And he has also argued that a neglect of the emotional constellations of individuals is a disturbing political indicator of an undesirable political state of affairs. The book includes meditations on Spinoza's *Ethics*, its most illustrious antecedent in the history of philosophy, but if Spinoza is squarely in the tradition of philosophical rationalism when he teases out an array of human emotions, Bodei will always insist on the complex dynamics of reason and passion, which is why Bodei's titles very often include a term such as *geometry* that alludes to rationality, and another term such as *passion* that names or alludes to the irrational side of human experience.

If these three books (*Scomposizioni*, *Geomettria delle passioni*, and *Destini personali*), generously discussed in this volume, are the ones in which Bodei's major philosophical project is laid out with a commanding grasp of the philosophical underpinnings of his concerns, Bodei has also written important books on politics, such as *Il Noi diviso* (*We, The Divided*), in which his general ideas about the human passions and politics are explored with nuance and informed detail in the context of the Italian historical and political situation. Bodei has also written important books that address the significance, within the broad outlines of his philosophical interests, of major intellectual figures in the area of philosophy, psychology, and the arts. These can be towering figures in the history of philosophy, such as Hegel, but they can also be poets, such as Hölderlin, or the founder of contemporary psychology, Sigmund Freud.

There are also books in which Bodei addresses the history of philosophy, such as his *Filosofia del Novecento*, a seminal account of twentieth-century philosophy; or *Le Forme del Bello*, his book on aesthetics, originally published in 1995, and reissued with substantial additions in 2017, to account for developments in aesthetics since it was first published. Bodei has also published books addressing specific themes or concepts, such as his book on the experience and theory of the déjà vu (*Piramidi di tempo: Storie e teoria del déjà vu*), his book on the logics of delirium (*Le logiche del delirio: Ragione, affetti, follia*), his book on the concept of limits (*Limite*), his book in which he explores the concept of wrath (*Ira: La passione furente*), his book on landscapes (*Paesaggi sublimi: Gli uomini davanti alla natura selvaggia*), and his book on lives of things (*La vita delle cose*).

Each of Remo Bodei's books are intended to be read, and can be read, as self-contained works; but when one begins to realize that they belong to a vast intellectual network of communicating vessels, they take on new levels of significance; and the whole is greater than any of its parts. It is also the work of an indefatigable and generous philosopher—with a prodigious memory and a breathtaking level of erudition—whose guiding light, and core contributions, have always been in his exploration of the vicissitudes and tensions between rational and irrational aspects of human experience, in order to understand the role that the philosophy writ large, from antiquity until the present, can play a role in diagnosing the most urgent predicaments of humanity in our time, sometimes with the assistance of other disciplines and the arts—for Bodei never limits his investigations to the philosophical literature that is its spinal cord. Like Hegel, a philosopher to whom he consecrated one of his earliest books (*La civetta e la talpa: Sistema ed epoca in Hegel*), and significant sections of *Scomposizioni*, Bodei has always been sensitive to the importance of engaging philosophy and history (including the historical moment in which Bodei himself is philosophizing); and like Hegel, Bodei has always sought to develop philosophical approaches to engage terms that are or appear to be antithetical until they can be resolved, and perhaps even reconciled, in the unfolding of human history. That being said, unlike the more progressive and optimistic Hegel of the *Phenomenology of Spirit* who was persuaded that philosophers can trace a distinct teleological process that should be obvious for anyone to see once it is reasoned through a dialectical process ending in a kind of absolute philosophical knowledge and political enlightenment for humanity; or the late, and more conservative, circumspect Hegel who reconciled himself with the provisional truths of the Prussian state and those of its political and religious authorities, Bodei does not give an apodictic tone to his philosophical meditations. Instead, he studies historical processes to understand and come to terms, as best he can, where humanity finds itself; and he is also interested in philosophical thinking to help humanity understand some of its own predicaments, in order to shed light on the way out of those very predicaments, which require the agency and responsibility of others, rather than to presume that philosophy has all the answers, and is there to dictate its solutions. There is clearly an anti-authoritarian sentiment at the core of Bodei's philosophical approach.

A Question of Method

In this essay, I would like to pay homage to Remo Bodei's inspiring project by exploring some of the books that address a specific concept or a theme. I offer some observations on his book on the life of things, his book on the sublime landscape, and his book on wrath. I intend to underscore some of Bodei's insights, aperçus, and illuminating observations about each of these particular themes, but I would also like to discuss these three books to say something about Bodei's philosophical approach, given that a similar method is at play in each of the books. Bodei has a unique ability to map out a philosophical territory, and with a Socratic impulse in which he puts the ideas of the philosophical tradition and of his contemporaries to a test, as he works with some ideas, shows the limits of others, and even puts his own initial impressions to the same kind of test. Drawing on his astonishing combination of erudition, memory, and power of synthesis, he is able to identify dead ends and false starts, in order to clear a field of inquiry that clarifies urgent human predicaments without prescribing easy answers. His inquiries are all the more complex when he offers historical accounts of how a term that is central to his discussion—and this point will be particularly salient in our analysis of the book on wrath—can be interpreted in contradictory and even irreconcilable ways over different historical periods, or even in the same historical period. This is not to say that Bodei lacks clarity, as he is very careful in his analysis of contested terms, or that he does not have personal inclinations and preferences, as he is also clear about his own tendencies. But he does not want his readers to follow precepts, even when he might feel partial to them after an arduous investigation in which a myriad of positions and arguments are presented with care. Ultimately, Bodei would like his readers to participate in a collective task, allowing them to break away from dogmatic ways of thinking, and from the imposition of ideological positions, while taking personal responsibility for the contingencies of their own thoughts and lived experience. As he has put it himself: "The principal task of philosophy is to critically redraw the variations in the maps of meaning, reorienting individuals with respect to continuous mutations in the balance of ideas and values, and to destroy and to expose ill-equipped, sectarian, or untruthful modes of thought."[2]

All his books share a perspective Bodei himself summarizes in several places: a desire to avoid philosophical formulas or slogans, and a will to make his readers think for themselves as they engage in a process in which questions are raised, speculations are both considered and tested, and illuminations come about in a process of discovery that the reader is invited to consider. One of the remarkable features of Bodei's approach to philosophy is his gentle generosity and his ability to share his vast erudition and considerable power of synthesis: in his books he lays out on a silver platter the history of a problem, he summarizes the insights that various philosophical traditions have to bear on the matter at hand; as he gently presents his own original insights, and opens the door for his readers to come up with their own. There is always an open-ended feel to Bodei's philosophical investigations that has underpinnings in his personal humility and intellectual generosity, even when his own positions and recommendations are part of the mix.

Bodei's philosophical project has a pedagogical dimension as well in as much as his readers are exposed to the depth and breadth of a set of questions to such a degree that they can no longer make naive or uninformed judgments about the topic at hand, and this is also a sign of Bodei's generosity as a thinker because the groundwork he sets up in each of his books could allow readers to come to different conclusions than those he articulates once he has taken the reader on an intellectual odyssey of sorts.

In *Personal Destinies* he gives a hint about his philosophical approach, in which his disdain for consumerism is evident in his mention of "intellectual *fast food*."

> Contro il diffondersi del *fast food* intellettuale, ho cercato di comporre un'opera che non sia di rapido consumo, ma di meditata, graduale e, possibilmente, sapida e non penitenziale riflessione, che poggi su idee e analisi *thick*, dotate cioè di spessore teorico e storico, e non su nozioni sottili, *thin*, su dati esili e su generalizzazioni avventate.[3]

> Against the dissemination of intellectual *fast food*, I've decided to compose a work that is not intended for fast consumption, but a work that requires a reflection that requires a slow meditation, hopefully enjoyable and not particularly painful, grounded in ideas and a thick analysis, that is to say endowed with theoretical and historical density, and not on thin notions, on thin data and hasty generalization.

In his books Bodei also finds a fine balance between his desire to avoid jargon and facile claims, while at the same time doing a considerable amount of ground work for his readers, including a thorough canvassing of what philosophers of a wide range of traditions have to say about a particular topic—for Bodei is as home in the Germanic traditions in which he was originally trained, as he is in the philosophical traditions of France and Italy. But he is equally at home in the contributions of the Anglo-American tradition. Bodei will sometimes make a note at the beginning of a book in which he lets his readers know that his books can be read in several ways, and from this perspective his approach to footnotes is instructive. In several books Bodei alerts his readers that they are welcome to read the work without looking at a single footnote, because the book is designed to be read without them. This kind of observation is again a sign of his generosity, for it is true that he has designed some of his books to be read without the footnotes, so that the reader can appreciate and meditate on the broad outlines of the argument, including the texts by other thinkers Bodei tends to include. That being said, Bodei's footnotes invariably offer an impressive array of nuance: they give relevant bibliographical references, contextual and technical indications, invitations to explore some points in more depth, and clarifications on books and traditions in which some of his points are grounded. In his typical modesty Bodei says in one of his footnotes that his footnotes are intended to give voice to "those who have participated in the shared enterprise represented in each book."[4]

In Italy he has educated two generations of both specialized and general readers; as his books are intended to educate the readers of goodwill who may not have formal philosophical training; but the considerable amount of groundwork he offers is also helpful, and even empowering, to students of philosophy who are given the necessary tools and guidance to tackle important philosophical issues with a deeper understanding of their contexts. Only now, and thanks to the excellent translation of *Geometry of Passions* by Gianpiero Doebler, and perhaps also to this volume, the English-speaking world might begin to better profit from the Bodei's contributions not only to philosophy but also to philosophical pedagogy.

But at the moment Remo Bodei, whose work is widely known in Europe, is not known in the Anglo-Saxon philosophical contexts—with the exception perhaps of specialists in Italian studies. One of the challenges of Bodei's approach in the Anglo-Saxon context, admittedly, is that most of his books are intended to be explorations of a subject matter in which Bodei rarely announces his main thesis or his provisional conclusions, and he sometimes alerts his readers of this way of writing, as in the opening pages of *Logics of Delusion*:

I shall not divulge the contents of what is to follow. I want the itinerary to be a surprise, a voyage of discovery also for the reader, who is invited to examine the question [. . .] from many angles, with no initial preference or bias. Only at the end, when the concatenation of sectorial hypothesis, deliberately presented in the form of exercises in perplexity, will have led to conclusions that retrospectively illuminate premises left in shadow, will the circle be closed, and the journey concluded.[5]

When in the midst of a philosophical investigation Bodei sometimes raises a series of questions rather than conclusions, he is not being rhetorical: he is underscoring the perplexities that require meditation, and he is training his readers to develop their own thought processes as much as is helping them to overcome received ideas and clichés.

In each of his books about a specific theme Remo Bodei engages in a productive dialogue with the philosophical past, with the most recent developments in contemporary philosophy, but his is just as interested in what literature and the other arts may have to contribute to the discussion. He will invariably begin any one of his discussions with an engagement with the classics of antiquity, and given that Gabriella Giglioni, Remo Bodei's wife is a distinguished professor of Classics at the University of Pisa; Bodei could not have a better interlocutor in his engagements with these topics. Bodei will also frame his arguments in the context of European history and philosophy from antiquity until the present. Most of his books will seriously engage with the philosophy of antiquity, the Christian Middle Ages, the early modern period, the modern period, and with contemporary philosophy. Since he is ecumenical he will address German, French, and Anglo-American philosophical traditions, and he will always summarize the contributions of Italian philosophy to a problem and engage in a constructive dialogue with his contemporaries. There are few books by Bodei that do not at some point make an apposite reference or commentary to Dante, who is a paradigm and model for Bodei in as much as Dante will also address the entire range of historical, philosophical, and fictional works at his disposal in order to explore issues of personal and political urgency. And, as in Dante, the most urgent reflections on contemporary predicaments live happily with relevant reflections from a catholicity of sources from many traditions and genres.

On the Life of Things

To offer a sense of his approach in the smaller books that address a specific theme I'd like to make some observations about three of his books: his book on the life of things (*La vita delle cose*), his book about sublime landscapes (*Paesaggi sublimi*), and his book about the concept of wrath (*Ira: La passione furente*). In the book on the life of things Bodei writes about nonhuman objects that are within the grasp of human beings and pregnant with humanity so that to engage with them means to come in contact with the human experience that informs the qualities that define them as things; in the book on sublime landscapes he discusses nonhuman objects that are too overwhelming for humans to fully grasp as a way to offer a meditation on humanity's connection to nature and to the ways culture has reconfigured that relationship for better and for worse; and in the book on wrath he explores an extreme human passion with the potential to defy and overcome reason's ability to control it if it is not attended to with thoughtful care. By the time you finish reading any one of these works, you have explored the themes in antiquity, in the Christian Middle Ages, in the transition from the early modern to the modern period; and you have been exposed to a wide range of philosophical interlocutors, and just as many writers of literary works: Bodei is as comfortable discussing Proust, the poetry of Leopardi or Carducci, the poetry of Pablo Neruda or Jorge Luis Borges, as he is with the philosophical tradition or cultural manifestations from around the globe; and the visual arts will often also play a significant role.

The main theme of his book on the life of things is the process whereby an object becomes a thing, and the book begins with a critique of the conflation of the two terms, which, in Bodei's view, have confused philosophy as much as it has confused common sense. Bodei makes the bold claim that there are ways in which our lives will be enriched with what amounts to a thought experiment, that is to say, if we imagine *the life of things*, the possibility that "inanimate objects can have an autonomous life, can move, feel or even think and act" (gli oggetti inanimati possono avere una vita autonoma, muoversi, sentire o addirittura pensare ed agire).[6] This way of thinking presupposes a distinction Bodei thinks worth making between an object, as something that is in front of us or that can even confront us, as opposed to the "thing" as something that can only be understood as an element in a web (*un nodo*) of human relationships, as part of the texture of human life. As Bodei argues,

> La cosa non è l'oggetto, l'ostacolo indeterminato che ho di fronte e che devo abbattere o aggirare, ma un nodo di relazioni in cui mi sento e mi so implicato e di cui non voglio avere l'esclusivo controllo.[7]

> The thing is not an object, an indeterminate object I have in front of me that I must bring down or evade, but a web of relationships in which I'm implicated, and from which I don't want to have exclusive control.

Adding one of Bodei's characteristic philosophical moves, which is to search for a specific kind logic that is not necessarily the logic of reason, Bodei points out that none of the words Aristotle, Hegel or Husserl use to talk about things apply to objects, but each of them point us "to the logic, the investigation or the praxis of human relations" (alla logica, alla ricerca, alla prassi o ai rapporti umani).[8]

Bodei begins his philosophical meditation on the thing with a philosophical call to a return to things themselves, which he identifies as understandable, in turning points, or moments of crisis, in the history of philosophy, in which philosophers from antiquity until the present have called for an urgent return to things themselves: from Aristotle to Hegel, Husserl, Heidegger, and Blumenberg. Bodei quotes a text from the *Metaphysics* in which Aristotle argues that "when men came to this point the things themselves opened the way and obliged them to pursue with the investigation" [quando gli uomini furono giunti fino a quel punto, le cose stesse aprirono loro strada, e li costrinsero a proseguire la ricerca].[9] In the same spirit, Bodei quotes a passage from Hegel's *Phenomenology of Spirit*—which give the title to Bodei's book—in which Hegel argues that "philosophical knowledge requires us to abandon ourselves [*sich übergeben*] to the *lives of objects*, that they become present and express their interior needs" (Il conoscere filosofico esige che ci si abbandoni [*sich übergeben*] alla vita dell'oggetto o, che è lo stesso, che se ne abbia presente e se ne esprima l'interiore necessità).[10]

Aristotle, Hegel but also Husserl, Blumenberg, and even Dante, help Bodei to point out the extent to which we are mistaken when we think of things as if it, they were either components of a natural environment, or inorganic, lifeless elements. Things are things we understand because they are pregnant with humanity. The philosophy of Vico is also clearly in the offing because, for Bodei, the world of things is conditioned by a world of human experience, activity, and history. Vico's notion that we are better suited to understand the products of the human spirit than we are able to understand an external nature is a guiding idea for Bodei in this and other works.

Bodei points out that Theodor Adorno is thinking along these lines, namely that things should not be naturalized, in his critique of a conformist consumer society of mass culture when the founder of the Frankfurt School argues that an exploration of subjective experience can break through the clichés and facades of received modes of classification. In a nod to Adorno, Bodei argues that whenever objects become things informed by human experience, they cannot be reduced to mere merchandise or to their functions, or to exchange value. Objects become things when they are associated to our ideas, activities, passions, and fantasies; when they are invested with our affects and are framed in the contexts of our relationships; when we include them in the narratives we tell about ourselves and our relationships.

In Bodei's argumentation literature invariably plays a significant role, so he quotes Fernando Pessoa in a text in which the Portuguese writer explores his human attachment to things.

> Abbandono sempre ogni cosa con esagerate commozione. La povera stanza d'affitto dove ho passato alcuni mesi, il tavolo dell'albergo di provincia dove sono stato sei giorni, perfino la triste sala d'attesa della stazione dove ho speso due ore aspettando il treno: sì le cose buone della vita mi fanno male in modo metafisico quando le abbandono e penso, con tutta la sensibilità dei miei nervi, che non le vedrò né le avrò mai più.[11]

> It hurts when I leave certain things behind and I think that I'll never see them or have them again. The poor rented room where I spent a few months, the table of the provincial inn where I spent six days, even the sad waiting room of the station where I spent two hours waiting for the train: yes, the good things in life hurt me in a metaphysical way when I abandon them and I think with all the sensibility of my nerves, that I don't see them or have them anymore.

To give historical dimension to this thought process according to which one can attach human feelings to things, Bodei relies on Benedetto Croce when he argues that things are links in a chain of being between generations. Bodei is not as explicit, but it is clear he feels clear affinities with Croce's view according to which "things are not very different from people or animals. They have a soul and I feel a need to protect them from too much of a dire destiny" (le cose non sono molto diverse dalle persone o dagli animali. Hanno un'anima, e io mi sentivo in dovere di proteggerli da un destino troppo funesto).[12]

These preliminary observations are the antecedents to Bodei's discussion of the early Husserl's *epoché*, his attempt to bracket the natural attitude toward objects; and while Bodei appreciates Husserl's gesture to decouple the notion that things are part and parcel of a natural world, he thinks that the early Husserl is too sanitized to fully take advantage of his own philosophical insights. In other words, Husserl does is not willing to go as far as Croce in attributing a humanity of sorts to things. This is why Bodei prefers the post-Husserlian insights of thinkers such as Simmel, Bloch, and Heidegger, all of whom are able to identify a world of human interiority in our conception of exterior things, moving away from a conception of objects based on mere perception to one based on relationships, use, and human affect.

In his exegesis of Simmel, Bloch, and Heidegger, Bodei makes the point that the objects that surround us are part of "a human world that is the work of thousands of people (dead and alive) who have left traces that survive their work and their physical disappearance" (il mondo umano è opera di miliardi di persone [i morti e i vivi] che hanno plasmato la realtà lasciandovi tracce che sopravvivono al loro lavoro e alla loro scomparsa fisica).[13] It is in this spirit that Bodei also argues that the humanity of objects are part and parcel of our intersubjective experience in the present, of the past, and potentially of the future, as things of the past are to us what things of the present might be to the future. In this spirit, the life of things requires care and attention that cannot be reduced to their mere sensory or objective qualities; and Bodei cites the poetry of Pablo Neruda, who was keenly attentive to the humanity of objects throughout his entire poetic career, particularly in his *Elemental Odes*, featuring poems about objects of everyday life, redolent of lived experience.

In the spirit of the Adorno-Horkheimer critique of consumer society, Bodei argues that the reduction of objects to commodities can blind us to the kind of humanity in objects that Pablo Neruda and other poets are able to discern with such force. The drive to consume superfluous objects and search for the banality of status symbols is especially blinding to the "life of things." In an observation that underscores Bodei's political commitments, he asks if it is inevitable "to accept the destiny an economic system based on the waste of resources while more than a third of humanity suffers from a painful lack of primary goods" (un destino inesorabile che ci obbliga ad accettare la permanenza di un sistema economico basato sullo spreco di risorse propio mentre più di un terzo dell'umanità soffre di una straziante penuria di beni primari).[14]

Bodei underscores the nostalgia for pre-industrial objects by individuals and groups such as the Arts and Crafts movement, as an understandable response to the dehumanization of industrial society, and a way of high-lighting the notion that we might be better able to appreciate the charge of affect on unique objects that are made by human hands as opposed to those that are manufactured by machines, but while he appreciates the desire to return to the human, the nostalgia for pre-industrial forms of life misses an important point, namely, that the practices with which some objects are manufactured and the humanity attached to things are not the same, and an object manufactured by a machine may have profound human association. That being said, Bodei appreciates the apprehensions of the Arts and Crafts movement regarding the dehumanization that can take place in the context of industrial society, and he links it to a broader fear he shares, namely, that the humanity of objects might remain hidden to many and might even become dissipated to a great degree. In this context Bodei references Wilhelm Dilthey's fear that "individuals in the present might lose touch with the meaning of messages from the past, and that historical experience might become impoverished or indecipherable, in a process that would also impoverish our experience of the present" (Il timore del filosofo tedesco era, infatti, che agli individui finisse per sfuggire il senso dei messaggi del passato e che l'esperienza storica tendesse perciò a rendersi povera o indecifrabile, contagiando il presente degli stessi mali).[15]

For Bodei, a work of art can be a corrective to the dehumanization of objects precisely because works of art can serve as an antidote to the banalization of objects that are isolated from their utilitarian purposes for the purpose for contemplation and meditation, and he offers a moving investigation of Dutch Still Life painting, which separates objects from their original context that included a human presence to endow them with a human presence of sorts. As Bodei argues, an object in a still life painting can become a protagonist, can have pathos, can be contemplated for itself, and is pregnant with humanity because it is endowed with traces and evidence of human experience.

In the provocative final chapter of the book Bodei calls for a project to make things *speak*, and in the spirit of his analysis of the still life he says: "Paradoxically, things speak all the more about us about what constitute us, the more we let them speak in their own language" (Paradossalmente, le cose parlano tanto più di noi, di ciò che ci costituisce, quanto più le lasciamo esprimere nel loro linguaggio),[16] and he concludes that "our relationship to things is like, in a minor key, a love relationship between two human beings: to love someone the other must be like and unlike me, to the extent that the other completes me with what I lack" (Il nostro rapporto con loro somiglia, in tono minore, a quello dell'amore tra persone: per amare qualcuno, l'altro deve essere un altro me stesso, uguale a me per sentirmi in sontonia con lui, ma, contemporaneamente, anche diverso da me, affinché mi completi in ciò di cui sono carente).[17] Bodei concludes his book with the thought that the brevity of life makes it so that we can only have contact with a limited number of things and he says the following:

> La decisione di conoscere e aver cura di alcuna, senza precludersi la comprensione delle altre, implica non solo un atteggiamento di costante attenzione al mondo e alle persone, una volontà di sapere e un desiderio di "amare," ma anche un ethos (e perfino una presa di posizione politica) per contribuire a fare una *respublica* della società toccataci in sorte.[18]

> The decision to know and to take care of some without precluding the understanding of others, does not only imply an attitude of constant attention to the world and to people, a will to know and a desire to love, but also an ethos (and even a political parti pris) to contribute to make into a republic (a public object in its Latin etymology) the society in which we happen to be.

On the Sublime Landscape

If the *Life of Things* is a book about the process whereby objects become things through human agency; *Sublime Landscapes*, is book about humanity and nature, or more precisely, about how humanity has shifted its perceptions regarding its relationship to nature. Bodei is interested in a particular kind of natural feature (the mountain, the forest, the ocean, the dessert, the volcano, etc.) that has undergone a transformation in the history of Western consciousness, namely, spaces that can be perceived as powerful and threatening, but that can also remind us of our precarious existence in the world, in a way, paradoxically, that can help us affirm our humanity, and transform our sense of fear into a feeling of admiration and respect for nature. Although, characteristically, Bodei explores concepts of nature and of the sublime going back to antiquity, he is primarily interested in a moment in the history of philosophy, literature, and the arts when the two concepts (nature and the sublime) are conceived in relation to each other, which is not the case in the earliest conceptions of the sublime, starting with Longinus, that don't involve nature. The philosophical tradition that matters most to Bodei is, in this regard, a recent one, featuring the ideas of Addison, Kant, Schiller, Burke, and others, in which the concept of the sublime is inextricably linked to humanity's relation to nature. Bodei is particularly interested in the experience of the sublime as an experience in which the power of nature underscores the limits of a humanity. But hanging over this reflection is the sense of a lost opportunity, that is, the views that followed this moment in which modernity has both alienated itself, and lost its fear of nature, transferring those feelings toward political and historical events.

In the book Bodei underscores that until the end of the seventeenth century, threatening places, spaces, and natural features (such as the ocean, the forest, and the dessert) were feared and shunned; but at the beginning of the eighteenth century, the same places were frequented and called sublime, and that this was the case for a good part of the century, until technological developments gave many the illusion that humanity could become more powerful than nature—and this is one of the underlying motivations of the book—that both nature and human survival are under threat. The point invites readers in our present moment to look back unto a moment in which human fears and anxieties about nature gave way to the possibility of better understanding the individuality of humans, thanks to the challenges that nature brings to bear. Bodei also makes the point that in our time, those sublime feelings have shifted from feelings about nature to feelings about history and politics.

The initial move from the fearful and horrible to the sublime as ways to experience nature, for Bodei is not just a metamorphosis of ideas, but also of perceptions. For Bodei a painted landscape should not be thought of as a copy of nature, but as culture projected on nature, and here we find a parallel between this book and the book on things; because things, like sublime landscapes are not autonomous entities, but products of human experience.

The book begins with a brilliant exegesis of classical and Christian antecedents, and explores to a point in the history of Western consciousness in which the sense that humans are at the center of the universe, as well as the assurances of an afterlife, are challenged by the uncertainties generated by the Copernican revolution, or by Giordano Bruno's bold insights, including his unambiguous affirmation of the earth as a planet among others, or to the imperatives that led to the advent of a more secular world, all of which characterize modernity. As Bodei puts it, "modernity first appears as a cosmic exile of man expelled from the consoling and ordered center of the universe, an epoch in which the fear and bewilderment regarding the spectacles in which nature exhibits its excessive greatness and its destructive potential, humiliates and threatens us" (La modernità appare dapprima come un esilio cosmico dell'uomo dal consolante e ordinato centro dell'universo, un'epoca in cui cresce la paura e lo sconcerto dinanzi agli apettacoli in cui la natura esibisce la sua smisurata grandezza e la sua distruttrice potenza, avvilendo e minacciando la piccola e indifesa 'canna da pesca'.)[19]

The paradox of this situation is that the encounter with the sublime—that which can potentially intimidate, threaten, and humiliate humanity—is a way to affirm a superior kind of humanity, able to challenge what is threatening and potentially humiliating. Facing up to the sublime is also a way—according to Bodei—of affirming the human will to triumph over nature.[20] The sublime landscape becomes a place in which humans attempt to address and perhaps to tame their own anxieties. In his book Bodei rehearses the well-known positions on the sublime by Addison, Burke, Kant, and Schiller, with elegance and acumen, and he underscores the significance of the poet Giacomo Leopardi, who did not read Kant even though his poetry, Bodei argues, offers analogues to Kant's notions of the mathematical sublime, or the experience with nature that is beyond our conceptual possibilities to grasp; and the dynamical sublime, or the experience with that threatens us. Bodei cites Leopardi because the poet offers salutatory insights that are not to be found in Kantian philosophy and that can help us think beyond Kant. The most important of these insights is that the sublime can be an antidote to human anxiety and humiliation with respect to our relationship to the power of nature. Bodei also argues that the poetry of Leopardi captures the essence of the concept as it also anticipates the end of a period in which Western culture could have been enthralled by the sublime as what we can now call consumer culture, and its vacuous imperatives, entered human experience.

> Come già aveva intuito Leopardi, le esigenze dell'umanità civilizzata, la quale pretende che sia finita la lotta contro la natura sopraffatrice, convengono nell'immediato non solo nella volontà di dare soddisfazione a bisogni elementari di cibo o abitazione a lungo penalizzati, ma anche nel perseguimento del superfluo, del *comfort*.[21]

> As Leopardi had grasped the demands on civilized humanity, which pretends to put an end to the struggle against nature, converge not only in the will to satisfy the basic human needs of food and shelter, but also the search of the superfluous and of comfort.

Bodei argues that this move from its coming to terms with the power of nature to the pretense that nature can be controlled and managed by humanity was missed by Hegel who had an insufficient grasp of the significance of the sublime, even though his philosophy is emblematic of humanity's shift from its preoccupations with nature to its preoccupations with history and politics: "With Hegel, the sublime begins thus migrate from nature to history. One must look for it in the destinies of humans and in the complementary obligation of reason to find in them an adequate meaning" (Con Hegel il sublime comincia così a emigrare dalla natura alla storia. Bisogna cercarlo nei destini umani e nel complementare compito della ragione di trovare in essi un senso adeguato).[22]

This shift takes place for several reasons: nature no longer elicits fears because the period of circumnavigation and exploration of the globe has come to an end, because of developments in science, the rise of consumer society, the failures of humanism to capture the experience of humanity at large, which is thematized by the advent of Nietzschean philosophy: "Nietzsche's Übermensch is not concerned about his own conservation, lacks any desire of transcendence towards god, or legitimation of his own superiority with a moral law" (questo oltreuomo è in Nietzsche significativamente privo non solo di paure per l'autoconservazione, ma anche di qualsiasi desiderio di trascendenza verso Dio o di legittimazione della propria superiorità grazie alla legge morale.)[23]

In this process the feelings of fear, intimidation and the like that used to be associated to nature, have not disappeared, they have rather moved from nature to history and to politics. Hegel thematized this turning point in the concluding pages of his *Phenomenology of Spirit* with an image Bodei considers to be an application of the sublime to politics, namely, the sublime image of Napoleon as "the spirit of the world on a horse," as in the famous painting by Jacques-Louis David, *Napoleon Crossing the Alps*, in which the French general appears to tower over the small mountains in the background, so that the power of destruction that moves us is no longer nature's but the power of our technological tools and the related power of modern warfare. In this process, Bodei makes many powerful observations, including the rise of a militaristic sublime in the ideologies of fascism and national socialism, in which the virtues of war and militarism can transform civil life as well, and he also points to a new banality that has undermined and downgraded the sublime associated with nature in some experiences of tourism, for which Bodei has a nuanced response, typical of his philosophical instincts, because for him the banality of many experiences of tourism is symptomatic of the need, "felt by millions to elevate themselves for a little while over the mediocrity and fatigue of the everyday towards a better life they vaguely perceive" (sentita da milioni di persone, di sollevarsi per qualche tempo al di sopra della mediocrità e della fatica del quotidiano in direzione di una vita migliore oscuramente avvertita).[24]

Bodei's book moves from ominous and fearful nature as the source of the sublime, to ominous and fearful humanity as the source of the sublime, particularly when humanity becomes stronger and potentially more destructive than ever with our new arsenals of weapons and our technologies that threaten the survival of the planet. In this context, "it is man himself that for his own eyes has become sublime: he infuses upon himself a terror for his own exterminating violence" (è l'uomo a essere diventato, ai suoi propri occhi, sublime al quadrato: da un lato incute terrore a se stesso per la propria violenza annientatrice).[25]

On Wrath

The third topic I'd like to address is the title of Bodei's book, *Wrath*. In line with his investigations on the human passions and his attempt to define the logic of what is not normally considered logical, he defines *wrath* as a loss of reason and self-control born out of an offence or an affront that one considers unfair or unjust, or a blow to one's self-esteem. Bodei argues that "wrath is an ambivalent indicator of the degree of vulnerability of the ego and at the same time, of his will to assert itself" (L'ira è un indicatore ambivalente del grado di vulnerabilità del proprio io e, insieme, del suo desiderio di assertività).[26] In the early sections of the book, Bodei offers an investigation of the notion in the Homeric world, in the biblical world, and in the Christian world. He then explores the notion of a just wrath in some religious and philosophical traditions, the philosophical traditions that condemn wrath, the exploration of female wrath in the Medea story from its expressions in Greek tragedy until modern feminist expressions that explore the exclusion of women and emigrants from contemporary European society. Bodei then explores the philosophical traditions that offer cures for wrath from Aristotle until Nelson Mandela. After this initial survey, Bodei investigates the role of wrath in political movements and popular indignation from the French Revolution.

Bodei shows that wrath is inevitably linked to power relations and that it involves the protection of physical or psychic spaces. Wrath is a passion that is affirmed when human beings protect their mental and physical milieus to avoid feeling assaulted, humiliated, or insulted. They are the result of the feeling that one's needs have been insufficiently addressed. Bodei concludes that wrath, like other human passions, ought not to be repressed but understood as they are a thermometer of sorts, of social situations that ought to be understood in order to be addressed to reach an equilibrium in which it is possible to respond in a measured way to the harm one has suffered, as opposed to the disproportionate sense—fueled by insecurity—that a particular grievance has threatened the totality of one's being. It is an extreme passion that can overturn reason's ability to control it, and that must be respected to gain the balance and reconciliation that Bodei always sought between the logic of reason and the logic of passion.

As Bodei mentions in the introduction to the book, his approach to the topic of wrath is "genealogical," to the extent that he offers an account of the term that is as much historical as it is theoretical. In the earlier chapters he offers a contrast between the Greek notions of "wrath" going back to the first lines of the *Iliad*, which famously begins with the "wrath" of Achilles, and contrasts the wounded pride of the Homeric hero, grounded in a culture of shame, with notions of "wrath" inspired by the attempts of some Christian theologians to reconcile "justice" with "mercy." In this context Bodei underscores that "Agostino approva l'ira contro i peccatori per le stesse ragioni per cui la ammette contro se stesso, ossia affinché ciascuno si rinnovi"[27] (Saint Augustine approves of wrath against sinners for the same reasons why he approves of wrath against himself, which is to say, for the purpose or renewal).

A significant aspect of Bodei's genealogical investigation involves the notion of a wrath that might be considered "just" when inspired by a sense of outrage at an injustice. Bodei cites Aristotle's views that wrath is a desire for vengeance accompanied by pain for an undeserved offense against ourselves; and he shows how this Aristotelian view is nuanced in the Middle Ages by Saint Thomas Aquinas when he argues that wrath should be condemned when it is disproportionate or misguided, but permissible when it is directed toward just objectives; and he also points out that this view by Aquinas helps to understand why some of those who expressed a "just wrath" or a wrathful indignation against evil or injustice are praised in Dante's *Paradise*. In a striking section of the book, Bodei argues that Michelangelo was well versed in these views on wrath, and that they inform his sculpture of Moses, intended to honor the character of Pope Julius II, in as much as it captures the biblical figure, that prefigures Christ, "nel momento in cui sta per cedere all'ira e spezzare le valore delle leggi"[28] (in the moment in which he is about to give into wrath and break the tables of the law). This view is also in line with another component of Bodei's genealogy of the notion of wrath, when he points out that, "Il 'dolce Gesù' non esiste. L'ira è parte integrante della sua figura ed è segno della natura umana e non solo divina del Cristo"[29] (The "sweet Jesus" does not exist. Wrath is part and parcel of his figure, and a sign of the human, and not just the divine nature of the Christ). Bodei adds that in the protestant tradition, there is also a sense of a justified wrath with antecedents in Martin Luther himself who also was in line with notions of this kind of wrath.

> Di questa santa ira, intesa come un tonificante dell'anima, era consapevole anche . . . Martin Lutero (che nel 1510, per inciso, aveva visto Giulio II a Roma, nel suo unico soggiorno in quella città). Egli sosteneva, infatti, che quando era irato poteva scrivere, pregare e predicare meglio, perché il suo animo e il suo intelletto diventavano più agili ed acuti.[30]

> Luther (who had seen Julius II in Rome in 1510, in his only stay in that city) was conscious of the fortifying of this saintly wrath. In fact, he maintained that when he was irritated he could write, pray and preach better because his spirit and intellect were more agile and were sharper.

After exploring Classical and Judeo-Christian views of wrath, Bodei returns to modern and secular versions of the notion. While the notion that there are contemporary philosophical and political positions, for which wrath can be justified, there are also other positions with antecedents in epicurean and stoic philosophical views that condemn it, and develop "terapie dell'anima miranti, soprattutto, alla cura di questa passione"[31] (therapies of the spirit intended to cure that passion). The former can justify revolutionary action, while the later inform the positions of Desmond Tutu and Nelson Mandela in their advocacy for truth and reconciliation.

In terms of modern philosophy, Bodei distinguishes two fundamental positions in contemporary philosophy regarding the passion of wrath. On the one hand, he cites the position of Descartes and Spinoza—a position that is also the antecedent to his own views on the moral emotions—according to which this kind of passion cannot be abolished by will or reason, but instead must be respected, understood, and channeled. Bodei contrasts the former two positions, with a different kind of position, inspired by Kant's

Pragmatic Anthropology, according to which passions of this kind are a "'cancro della ragione,' un tumore da estirpare senza esitazioni"[32] ("cancer of reason," a tumor that must be extirpated without hesitation).

Bodei considers Kant's position to be noble, but misguided. He also knows that energies that can be unleashed by wrath have been manipulated by populist and totalitarian regimes, even if those regimes pretend to address injustices. In the concluding sections of the book Bodei argues, in line with his fundamental view that the logic of passions must not be denied, that wrath is symptomatic of "un intralciato, combattuto et inappagato bisogno di felicità"[33] (a complicated, fraught or frustrated desire for happiness)—suggesting that its root causes must be respected in order to decouple the narcissistic aspects of the emotion from the ones that are justified. And Bodei concludes the book with a message of particular relevance to the present moment: "Per conseguire una maggiore armonia con noi stessi, conservando la nostra umanità e le nostre passioni, queste non devono, dunque, essere represse, ma sapientemente elaborate et indirizzate, intrecciando affetti et conoscenza" (To achieve a greater harmony with ourselves, preserving our humanity and our passions, these do not have to be repressed, but wisely elaborated and channeled, interweaving affections and knowledge).[34]

In each of these three books that I have glossed, Bodei's readers are exposed to the exploration of a theme, as much as they are exposed to the philosophical method of a great thinker, as generous in his ability to tease out a problem in its historical and philosophical dimension as he is able to dialogue with philosophers and artists of an impressive number of traditions. In the process one is inspired, and edified, even as one is also invited to explore the perils of the human situation.

Notes

1. Bodei, Remo, *Ira: La passione furente* (Il Mulino, 2010), 11–12.

2. Bodei, Remo, *We, the Divided: Ethos, Politics and Culture in Post-war Italy, 1943–2006,* translated by Jeremy Parzen and Aaron Thomas (Agincourt Press, 2006), 181.

3. Bodei Remo, *Destini personali: L'età della colonizzazione delle coscienze* (Feltrinelli, 2002), 18.

4. Bodei, *La vita delle cose,* 13.

5. Bodei, Remo, *Logics of Delusion* (The Davies Group, translated by Giacomo Donis), xvi.

6. Bodei, Remo, *La vita delle cose* (Editori Laterza, 2009), 12.

7. Bodei, *La vita delle cose,* 20.

8. Bodei, *La vita delle cose*, 20.

9. Aristotle, quoted by Bodei, *La vita delle cose*, 14.

10. Hegel, quoted by Bodei, *La vita delle cose*, 15.

11. Pessoa, quoted by Bodei, *La vita delle cose*, 24.

12. Croce, quoted by Bodei, *La vita delle cose*, 27.

13. Bodei, *La vita delle cose*, 51–52.

14. Bodei, *La vita delle cose*, 66.

15. Bodei, *La vita delle cose*, 81.

16. Bodei, *La vita delle cose*, 115.

17. Bodei, *La vita delle cose*, 116.

18. Bodei, *La vita delle cose*, 119.

19. Bodei, Remo, *Paesaggi sublimi: Gli uomini davanti alla natura selvaggia* (Bompiani, 2008), 29.

20. Bodei, *Paesaggi sublimi*, 38.

21. Bodei, *Paesaggi sublimi*, 158.

22. Bodei, *Paesaggi sublimi*, 79.

23. Bodei, *Paesaggi sublimi*, 148.

24. Bodei, *Paesaggi sublimi*, 167–77.

25. Bodei, *Paesaggi sublimi*, 179.

26. Bodei, Remo, *Ira: La passione furente* (Il Mulino, 2010), 10.

27. Bodei, *Ira*, 49.

28. Bodei, *Ira*, 66.

29. Bodei, *Ira*, p. 45.

30. Bodei, *Ira*, 66.

31. Bodei, *Ira*, 71.

32. Bodei, *Ira*, 99.

33. Bodei, *Ira*, 116.

34. Bodei, *Ira*, 118.

Bibliography

Bodei, Remo. *Destini personali: L'età della colonizzazione delle coscienze*. Feltrinelli, 2002, 18.

Bodei, Remo. *Ira: La passione furente*. Il Mulino, 2010.

Bodei, Remo. *La vita delle cose*. Editori Laterza, 2009.

Bodei, Remo. *Logics of delusion*, translated by Giacomo Donis. The Davies Group, 2006.

Bodei, Remo. *Paesaggi sublimi: Gli uomini davanti alla natura selvaggia*. Bompiani, 2008.

Bodei, Remo. *We, the Divided: Ethos, Politics and Culture in Post-war Italy, 1943–2006*, translated by Jeremy Parzen and Aaron Thomas. Agincourt Press, 2006.

2

The Owl and the Mole

Remo Bodei's Hegel

Alfredo Ferrarin

It was during my freshman year at the University of Bologna that I first saw Remo Bodei at a conference on what was then a hotly debated topic, the so-called crisis of reason. The book by that very title edited by Gargani had just come out (*Crisi della ragione*, Einaudi, 1979), and Bodei was one of the invited speakers, as well as one of the participants in that collection of essays. I was frustrated in Bologna at the lack of interest in what at the time I took to be the pivotal figures around which my interests revolved, from Hegel and Nietzsche to Wittgenstein, Benjamin, and Adorno. When I transferred to Pisa, I found that Bodei had announced a class on Hegel's lectures on the philosophy of history at the Scuola Normale Superiore. It was a turning point in my education. I discovered that studying philosophy could be a feast—the fun of learning and establishing unexpected connections married to the curiosity and desire to assimilate more of the treasures that Bodei, in his boundless erudition, lavished on us.

At the time, Pisa was an unparalleled center for Hegel studies: after Gentile and Scaravelli, Massolo and Luporini, who had been among Bodei's teachers, had taught there (after his return from Berkeley, Enrico de Negri lived in Pisa until he passed away in 1990). We students enjoyed the fruitful aftermath of that phase: In the early 1980s in the Philosophy Department courses on Hegel were regularly offered not only by Bodei but also by Badaloni, Barale, and others. In 1982 Claudio Cesa joined the Scuola Normale Superiore of Pisa. This institution, a one-of-a-kind institution of higher learning in Italy, had ties with several prestigious universities in Europe (for the case in point, German idealism, let me mention the Hegel-Archiv in Bochum and the University of Munich), and hosted outstanding scholars and philosophers. As students, we were exposed to an international array of visiting professors teaching courses; so it was that I sat in on brilliant seminars (I especially remember one by Adriaan Peperzak) and went on to pursue my research in Bochum (though not with Meist and Pöggeler, as Bodei had encouraged me to, but with Jaeschke) and in Munich (with Henrich, who had been one of Bodei's teachers in Heidelberg, and Horstmann). To name a few of my classmates, in the same three to four years I was sitting side by side with Giovanna Pinna, Angelica Nuzzo, Giuseppe Varnier, and Vladimiro Giacché both in Bodei's classes and in Bochum to study Hegel.

If I begin with personal memories, it is not to speak of myself, but because I want to draw on a memory I share with my generation to frame a picture of Bodei and the influence he had on a wider public in Italy and beyond. We debated German idealism from many angles, but our Hegel was invariably marked by Bodei's groundbreaking book, *Sistema ed epoca in Hegel* (Il Mulino, 1975). It is difficult to overestimate the importance of Bodei for Hegel studies in Italy, and it is likely no less hard for younger students, let alone for non-Italians, to imagine what that cultural climate meant and how rich, articulate, diverse, and conflictual it was. Let me illustrate a few points to make readers perceive it more fully.

Strictly speaking, *Sistema ed epoca* was not Bodei's first book. In 1974 he had edited *Letteratura e psicanalisi* (Zanichelli). *Sistema ed epoca*, in turn, came as the provisional conclusion of a long trajectory. In 1962, a journal recently founded by Lugarini, *Il pensiero*, had published (in two separate issues) a ninety-page article by the twenty-three-year-old student Bodei on intellectuals, the historical world and the *Constitution of Germany*, which was actually the topic of his *tesi di laurea* (at the time Italy did not have a PhD program, so that a *tesi di laurea*, as the top title in individual education, was in many cases considered the equivalent of a doctoral dissertation). The young Bodei went on to publish on Solger, Isaak von Sinclair, Hölderlin, Bloch, and Gramsci, but his parallel work as a translator was both hugely important and little short of incredible. Hegel's major works were available in Italian, but almost nothing from his Jena years was. In 1971 Bodei published his translation of the *Differenzschrift* and *Glauben und Wissen* (*Faith and Knowledge*) together in a volume by the title *Primi scritti critici*; in the same year Cantillo made available to Italian readers parts of Hegel's system projects from 1803 to 1806, and in 1972 Cesa published a choice of Hegel's early political writings. What is remarkable is that Bodei not only knew deeply many of the more meaningful figures for Hegel scholarship in the nineteenth and twentieth centuries; he also translated or edited them and wrote meticulous introductory essays on each one of them. He published Karl Rosenkranz's *Hegel's Life* (Vallecchi, 1966, then Mondadori, 1974, later reprinted with a new introduction by Bodei in 2012, Bompiani); he edited Adorno's *Three Studies on Hegel* (Il Mulino, 1971); in 1975 he translated Ernst Bloch's *Subjekt-Objekt* (Il Mulino), and in 1976 Franz Rosenzweig's *Hegel and the State* (Il Mulino). If you feel you miss Kojève, not to worry: in 1991 the publisher Einaudi of Turin asked Bodei to edit and introduce his famous lectures on the *Phenomenology of Spirit*. Each one of these introductions is a short book in itself. Bodei loved translating and making available philosophical works of thinkers he respected and valued, and in later years he edited several other works by Hegel, Hölderlin, Adorno, Bloch, and Rosenkranz, but also Blumenberg, Kracauer, Matte Blanco, Pirandello, Szondi, Foucault, and Ricoeur. What bears stressing is that all those editions and essays appeared before he reached the age of forty. Not only was he a very hard-working and productive scholar, but he was also an uncannily prolific writer (in 1975 he also published an exceptional essay, "Hegel e l'economia politica," with another booklet on "Dialettica e controllo dei mutamenti sociali in Hegel" to follow).[1]

He had taken classes with Ernst Bloch, Eugen Fink, and Eric Weil, but he always recognized gratefully his teachers in Pisa, in particular Arturo Massolo. *Sistema ed epoca* is dedicated to him, and it is to his course that Bodei became an assistant along with Gargani, Barale, and Cristofolini in the 1960s. Finally, it is important to stress that Bodei took to heart his responsibility as a committed intellectual and public figure to the point that he tirelessly promoted culture at all levels, in lectures around the globe, interviews, philosophy festivals, and even television appearances. He thereby inspired generations of students and auditors in ways that an academic philosopher hardly could, and this is why with Bodei's death it is not only Italy that loses, and will sorely miss, a unique figure.

Until *Sistema ed epoca* it was commonplace to approach Hegel by preliminarily separating the wheat from the chaff. It was not just Croce who intended to sever what is alive from what is dead, even Marxism lived off oppositions such as the one between system and dialectic, or (think of Lukacs and Adorno) the youthful Hegel enamored with the French Revolution and political economy and the mature, successful, supposedly reactionary thinker in Berlin, the defense of the right of the negative and nonidentical versus the apology of the whole and the false. Bodei's operation was strategically complex. In those very ideological years in which it was all-important to know what side one was on, he diverted attention from the exclusive relation between Hegel and Marx to burst all the more trite and widespread bubbles: the legends and myths regarding panlogism, the end of history, the idolatry of the State, especially a self-enclosed system pretending to resolve into itself all aspects of reality. It was salutary to study Hegel in his context anew and with fresh eyes. Bodei avoided reading Hegel through Nietzsche's perspective like Löwith, stayed away from all the preconceptions of the so-called schools of suspicion and eschewed the self-appointed "negative thought" of those years—which took progressively a hold of much Italian philosophy by turning to the thread weaving together the legacy of the late Schelling, Nietzsche, Heidegger, and Schmitt—to take up Hegel's writings again with an amazingly detailed and grounded historical knowledge and an expertly encompassing philosophical dexterity. *Sistema ed epoca* is so comprehensive and ambitious precisely because it does not begin by taking apart Hegel's system but follows it in all its more minute details. This is why Bodei pays such close attention to the Heidelberg and Berlin lecture courses, to the additions to the *Encyclopaedia*, and to Hegel's knowledge and discussion of the sciences of his time, whether it is Bopp and Schlegel on comparative linguistics at its inception, Spallanzani and the physiology of digestion as a model for assimilation of externality in thinking, Carnot and Lagrange on calculus and a new way to frame the notion of infinite.

I suggest that Ernst Bloch, from whom Bodei had several reasons to mark his distance, was helpful in this move (Bodei had studied with him in Tübingen, and later edited in Italian not just *Subject-Object*, but also *Karl Marx, Philosophy of the Renaissance*, and *The Principle Hope*; Bodei's first book after *Sistema ed epoca* was *Multiversum: Tempo e storia in Bloch*, Bibliopolis, 1979). Bloch approached Hegel wholesale, not by dividing his progressive and reactionary sides. Also, Bloch delved into specific aspects that proved important for Bodei, from time to matter. The present is for Bloch pregnant with the future, and the future is a hunger for being. Bloch saw matter, in turn, through the lenses of Leibniz as germinal, that is, as the potential of becoming and as *conatus* (it is through this notion that Bloch read Aristotle's matter in biology, as well as Avicenna as the champion of a supposed Aristotelian left).[2]

The premise of Bodei's Hegel is the critique of the dichotomy theory-practice. Doing/making and seeing are not opposed, but rather enliven and promote one another. The owl of Minerva does not limit itself to grasping what has been without having a say on it; nor does the mole, inspired by Shakespeare's *Hamlet* and later celebrated by Marx as the genuine revolutionary subject, work unconsciously and underground at an enterprise whose meaning is doomed to escape us. Like a mole, Bodei loved digging in the remotest archives and libraries he could get access to, and so it was that he discovered that the owl, as described by Hegel, is inspired by a journal edited by Achenholz, on whose front page an owl is drawn accompanied by a motto from Leibniz, "Die Gegenwart ist schwanger mit der Zukunft" (the present is pregnant with the future). This has the effect of removing the weight of balance from the ratification of historical time legitimizing what happens to the interpretation of history as drawn irresistibly toward a future that is still for us partly impenetrable. And the mole stands indeed for an unconscious relentless work, but one aimed at appropriating the world and destroying tradition insofar as it stands in spirit's way. The owl then finds in the mole at once its antagonist and its collaborator. It accelerates the mole's work by gaining consciousness of the internal contradictions of a dying world and helps the gestation of a new age that breaks the old chains and emancipates us from the burden of a no longer lively past. In other words, philosophy's owl is not simply the Greek *glaukopis* taking flight at dusk and photographing in hindsight what is by now gone but favors spirit's unconscious work precisely inasmuch as spirit digs underneath the surface, and collapses edifices that no longer hold, in directions that are unknown to contemporaries, but which will eventually prevail and will help to shape the future. Likewise, the concept of system is not a straitjacket aimed at arresting movement and enclosing in rigid boundaries what risks evading it. Bodei takes his bearings from biology, economics, mathematics, theory of complexity, and theory of systems (Bertalanffy is a case in point), rather than from the criticism of a self-contained and self-enclosed architectonic construction in Feuerbach, Kierkegaard, Schopenhauer, and Nietzsche, as he introduces a concept of a system that he uses to understand the relation between logical categories and historical movement and to counter what he calls a "spineless historicism" (*storicismo invertebrato*) dominant, now and then, in the history of philosophy (and in much Italian philosophical historiography, in particular).

In the Introduction to the second edition of *Scomposizioni* (Il Mulino 2016, 15), one of Bodei's latest self-presentations, by way of commentary on the major books he published after the 1980s he writes: "In my intentions, each one of them should have represented an integral part of the constellation of themes which still guides me: individuality, personal identity, passions, rationality, consciousness, contradictions, temporal structures, expectations of change, flights from the world towards interiority, religious dimension." Bodei published, as I said, twenty-eight books, and quite naturally not all of them have to do with Hegel. And yet, all of these are themes that Bodei found in Hegel, and he was perfectly right in doing so. As Bodei himself reminded us, it is Hegel who quotes Aristotle on passion as the moving force of action; it is Hegel who quotes Goethe's maxim according to which nothing great in history has been accomplished without passion. Put succinctly, passion does not blur the clarity of the mind but is the indispensable thrust of all thought that does not remain abstract. Likewise, contradiction in the *Science of Logic* is the vitality of all change and is thus far more important than the so-called dead identity. As Bodei wonders what it means that philosophy is its own time grasped in thought, he comes to realize that the system is not alternative to becoming and history but is the best way to understand movement as an internally articulated whole, in the logical categories pervading and animating it. As a result, we could say that Bodei's Hegel is the thinker of the unity of *logos* and *polemos*, reason and conflict. Dialectic in turn is not an argumentative procedure or a determinate kind of logic (think of the traditional opposition, revived in Kant's *Critique of Pure Reason*, between analytic and dialectic as, respectively, the logic of truth as opposed to the logic of illusion). For Bodei's Hegel, dialectic is rather a method of construction of individual and collective identity in their mutual relation, the thought of the I and the We as they jointly configure themselves as correlative terms and determine one another. For us, who come after Feuerbach, but also Trendelenburg, the late Schelling, and Nietzsche, dialectic has the irenic ringtones of conciliation and totalization; for Bodei's Hegel, dialectic is the negative-rational moment that recognizes contradiction in difference, so that identity is inert and abstract if it is not run through by alterity, negativity, and conflict. Bodei's Hegel wages a never-ending war against the abstractions of theory. He invites us to return, after the crises that push us to find comfort in interiority, in utopias, in contemplation, to the intimate link between system and method, between history and reason, between *logos* and *polemos*, between the negative-dialectical and the positive-speculative moments. The objectivity of reason is the true heart of Hegel's thought in Bodei's interpretation.

⌁

There is a striking, highly unusual practice in Bodei's last years. He reprinted many of his books, but every time he substantially altered the contents by reshuffling or rewriting sections and adding large parts from scratch. To limit ourselves to Hegel-related works, *Sistema ed epoca* came out in 1975, went immediately out of print, and was rewritten by Bodei in 2014 to reach almost twice the original length. The title is also new, *La civetta e la talpa* (*The Owl and the Mole*, Il Mulino, 2014). The same happens with *Scomposizioni*, originally published by Einaudi (1987), recently re-edited by Bodei (Il Mulino, 2015) with 180 new pages added, with Adorno (a new introduction, "Strappare il vero dal falso," to a new translation of the same title, *Three Studies on Hegel*, Il Mulino 2014, 7–26), and with Rosenkranz (*Hegels Leben* is reprinted with a new introduction in 2012, Bompiani, 5–32). Every time Bodei repeats he has been working by alternating new blocks and minute inlays (*intarsi*, as in fine woodwork on antiques). Correspondingly, variations may include anything from updated bibliographies, minor changes, and new footnotes to whole unprecedented chapters.

I believe Italians hardly realize the privilege and unique advantage they enjoy by knowing this kind of Hegel. Especially from a comparative point of view, knowing the intricacies and details of such an amazingly far-reaching philosophical ambition grants us access to a complexity that is largely ignored elsewhere. From this point of view, I beg to differ with Bodei's unwarranted—indeed unintelligible—optimism as he salutes with a degree of enthusiasm what in his latest years he called the Hegel renaissance in the US (*La civetta*, op. cit., 14–15). It seems to me that a neopragmatist, antimetaphysical view of Hegel, equally recalcitrant to history, system, religion, and the actuality of thought, runs counter not only to Hegel, but more pertinently to the Hegel Bodei never grew tired of exploring, valuing, and teaching.

Speaking of Hegel and traditions alien to Italian cultural attitudes and styles, let me recall one of the most frustrating efforts I ventured to make. When I taught Hegel in a seminar at Boston University, I tried to make Bodei's scholarship available to anglophone circles. As I mentally tried to translate excerpts from *Sistema ed epoca*, I soon ran up against insurmountable obstacles. Simply put, Bodei's language is untranslatable. It would be worthwhile to study thematically Bodei's rich, brilliant, and highly sophisticated prose. Bodei, as I mentioned, translated Bloch, who wrote that "there are precious gems that are not transparent" (*undurchsichtige Edelsteine*) (*Subjekt-Objekt*, op. cit., 20). Bloch was describing Hegel's prose and recommending a sustained effort at finding precious gems where most readers, too impatient to find the struggle with Hegel's convoluted language worth its while, are simply thrown off. This does not apply to Bodei's language, which is fine, elegant, beautiful; yet it is the opposite of syntactical forms such as the plain, clear, linear argumentation and the descriptive terminology required by English philosophical prose. Bodei's language is so forbiddingly cultivated because it exudes implicit references to the most diverse cultural scopes (classical literature, mythology, but also phrases coming from chemistry, biology, economics, medicine, psychoanalysis, etcetera, adapted to the context at hand), and this may cause difficulties for someone who is not as well-versed in all scientific and literary-humanistic fields of the knowable. But it is untranslatable because it does not occasionally recur to metaphors, it is indeed built on analogies, and sometimes on proverbs and idiomatic figures of speech. To name two examples, respectively, at the beginning of *Destini personali* Bodei speaks of the formation of the I, first through images from the vegetable realm (among others, coral formed by colonies of coelenterates) and progressively to other analogies (psychological, political, and parliamentary in nature: the I abdicates before the mob, or the federation of souls finds new unity, or the exiled Is return and take hold of power, or the Is painstakingly negotiate their distribution of tasks). It is significant from this point of view that a descriptive title such as *Sistema ed epoca* is later transformed into *The Owl and the Mole*, as if erudite references, figures, formulae, images, even rhetorical tropes came more and more to the front over the years (incidentally, Bodei loved Gerard Genette's books). To mention now an example of idiomatic phrases, to refer to the self-enclosed system Bodei speaks of a Procrustean bed, a straitjacket, and other variously colorful vernacular expressions (*mettere le brache al mondo* is another one, something like "forcing trousers on the world"). The argumentative procedure of Bodei's language is also remarkable. It is as if he wanted to make a mockery of the seeming cogency of a self-appointed rigorous logical argument and efface all traces of a linear, demonstrative, syllogistic exposition. It is not only apophantic logos that is depreciated, even only a simply assertive prose is put in question. In his last book, *Dominio e sottomissione* (Il Mulino, 2019), there is one chapter that is made entirely of questions. It is stunning to read in chapter 6 fifteen pages of question marks. It is as if Bodei wanted to stress one more time that you can write philosophy through something like Condorcet's *tableaux* (*Scomposizioni*, op. cit., 324–31), and as if in the vivid brushstrokes on a canvas the devil (beginning with the sudden breaks in a continuous tradition) had to be sought for in the detail. To philosophize with a hammer is definitely not Bodei's style. Rather, the chisel is his tool, and the microscope is his lens, and jointly they serve as his instruments to paint a synoptic, encompassing view.

Now, it seems to me that Bodei is not thereby inventing anything new. On many of these aspects, he is heir to the highest forms of German philosophical prose, especially the *Goethezeit* and later Simmel, Benjamin, Adorno, and Bloch. In this sense, many of Bodei's phrases can be found in the philosophers he loved. Among these, famously the "diamond-net of categories" comes from section 246 of Hegel's *Encyclopaedia*, the empty glass bowl of the I is drawn from Schopenhauer, the constellation of meaning is distinctly Benjamin's jargon. During a eulogy I pronounced at his funeral, I said that there is a Stendhalian elegance to some of his phrases. I had in mind especially the title he had chosen for the collection of essays in which we celebrated his eightieth birthday, *Cristalli di storicità* (op. cit.). Like much else in Bodei, I meanwhile discovered that this phrase is to be found already in his earliest writings (for example, in *Scomposizioni*).[3]

Bodei's language exemplifies one the key themes of Hegel's philosophy. There is an objective reason, working underground and mostly unbeknownst to us, and sometimes it just so happens that we have assimilated Bodei's teaching and language unwittingly. For example, in my latest book, *Thinking and the I*, I wrote that in the same years in which Hegel spoke of objectivization and reification, Stendhal, in *De l'amour* (1823), spoke of a crystallization by which a lover projects onto the beloved an image until eventually the act of this projection effaces itself and results in the shining salt crystals that a lover is so keen on admiring as if they were natural diamonds.[4] Naturally, Hegel speaks of thought's reification, not of an illusory projection or sublimation, and yet the emphasis is the same, on a past activity (on thought's part), which exercises its power because we have forgotten about it and it is unconscious to us. And this is what sometimes happens to readers of Bodei. It is inevitable that we will assimilate his brilliant phrases, which may then be taken up again as if they were our coinage. So, this thought gave me pause, in fear that I had stolen this reference to Stendhal from Bodei without remembering he had called our attention to it.

Strangely, there is no trace of it in Bodei's writings that I have been able to verify. But widening the scope of this instance allows me to stress one last point. I have learned so much from Bodei's inspiration and example that sometimes I wonder if it is not just phrases and styles but theses I have come to formulate in my own research that do not owe him more than I realize. Such are the multifarious ways of the unconscious cunning of reason and of a tradition in which almost everything has already been thought—as Hegel wrote in the Preface to the *Phenomenology*, learning comes down to dismantling and taking apart what appears as a uniform given to appropriate and inwardize what initially seems foreign. For example, the couple of correlative and yet quite distinct terms through which Kant describes reason in the Architectonic of the first *Critique*, the organism and the architect as models of knowledge, or the unconscious logos and the culmination of reflection in a self-conscious spirit in Hegel's logic, on which I have built my two latest books, are not so far from the essential traits defining the mole and the owl.[5]

If for Stendhal it is the lover's eros that moves him or her to crystallize, Bodei's passion is that of understanding. He writes that in his work he has been trying to define his crystals of historicity as those "conceptual formations in which events and ideas have deposited and structured themselves in time—they do modify themselves, but according to determinate formal modalities."[6] Nobody has taught us to fluidify historical sediments as he has. His infinite curiosity and will to understand are reflected in a motto he often quoted in class, Spinoza's "nec ridere, nec lugere, sed intelligere" (neither laugh nor cry but understand). Yet, if we wanted to identify the spirit of Bodei's research fully, I believe we should integrate that motto with Heraclitus's suggestion as reported by Aristotle: to his visitors who had come to hear about lofty things and showed disdain for what is humble, Heraclitus said, do not be intimidated, there are gods here, too (kai theous entautha).[7]

Notes

1. Respectively in S. Veca, ed., *Hegel e l'economia politica*, 29–78, and R. Bodei and F. Cassano, *Hegel e Weber: Egemonia e legittimazione*, 21–193. For a select bibliography of Bodei's works, including twenty-eight books and almost 1,000 articles, see the appendix to E. C. Corriero and F. Vercellone, eds., *Cristalli di storicità. Saggi in onore di Remo Bodei* 203–34.

2. See *Avicenna und die Aristoteliche Linke*.

3. This holds of so much in Bodei's production: almost everything was there at the beginning. His last book, *Dominio e sottomissione*, is largely anticipated in the essay I quoted earlier, the 1977 "Dialettica e controllo dei mutamenti sociali in Hegel"; some of his considerations on politics in Hegel throughout the years take

up themes and suggestions to be found in the first of all his articles, "La funzione della filosofia e degli intellettuali nel mondo storico hegeliano" (op. cit., *Il pensiero*, 1962).

4. "Leave a lover with his thoughts for twenty-four hours, and this is what will happen: At the salt mines of Salzburg, they throw a leafless wintry bough into one of the abandoned workings. Two or three months later they haul it out covered with a shining deposit of crystals. The smallest twig, no bigger than a tom-tit's claw, is studded with a galaxy of scintillating diamonds. The original branch is no longer recognizable. What I have called crystallization is a mental process which draws from everything that happens new proofs of the perfection of the loved one" (*Love*, trans. G. and S. Sale, 2004, 84).

5. *The Powers of Pure Reason: Kant and the Idea of Cosmic Philosophy* and *Thinking and the I: Hegel and the Critique of Kant*.

6. In "A un altro me stesso," in *Filosofi italiani contemporanei*, G. Riconda and C. Ciancio, eds., 85.

7. "Every realm of nature is marvelous: and as Heraclitus, when the strangers who came to visit him found him warming himself at the furnace in the kitchen and hesitated to go in, is reported to have bidden them not to be afraid to enter, as even in that kitchen divinities were present, so we should venture on the study of every kind of animal without distaste; for each and all will reveal to us something natural and something beautiful" (*De partibus animalium*, I 5, 645a 17–23.

Bibliography

Aristotle. *De partibus animalium*. Translated by A. L. Peck. Harvard University Press, 1937.

Bloch, Ernst. *Avicenna und die Aristoteliche Linke*. Suhrkamp, 1963.

Bodei, Remo. *Dominio e sottomissione. Schiavi, animali, macchine, Intelligenza Artificiale*. il Mulino, 2023.

Bodei, Remo, *Economia politica e tempo della storia*. Edited by Alfredo Ferrarin, Istituto Italiano di studi filosofici, 2024.

Bodei, Remo. "A un altro me stesso," in *Filosofi italiani contemporanei*. Edited by Giuseppe Riconda and Claudio Ciancio, 77–90. Mursia, 2013.

Bodei, Remo, and Franco Cassano. *Hegel e Weber. Egemonia e legittimazione*. De Donato, 1977.

Bodei, Remo, Paolo Cristofolini, Giorgio Guzzoni, et al. *Il pensiero*. Inschibboleth Edizioni, 1962.

Bodei, Remo, Roberto Racinaro, and Massimo Barale. *Hegel e la Economia Politica*. Edited by Salvatore Veca. Gabriele Mazzotta Editore, 1975.

Corriero, Emilio Carlo, and Federico Vercellone, eds. *Cristalli di storicità: Saggi in onore di Remo Bodei*. Rosenberg & Sellier, 2019.

Ferrarin, Alfredo. *The Powers of Pure Reason: Kant and the Idea of Cosmic Philosophy.* University of Chicago Press, 2015.
Ferrarin, Alfredo. *Thinking and the I: Hegel and the Critique of Kant.* Northwestern University Press, 2019.
Stendhal. *Love.* Translated by Suzanne Sale. Penguin, 2004.

3

Paura, speranza, felicità

Translating Remo Bodei's *Geometry of the Passions*

Gianpiero W. Doebler

Paura, speranza, felicità—Italian terms that translate as "fear, hope, happiness." I have taken the liberty of appropriating the subtitle of Remo Bodei's *Geometria delle passioni: Paura, speranza, felicità: Filosofia e uso politico* (1991) as my title here—albeit in a clearly more lighthearted manner than Bodei explores those phenomena in his book—because fear, hope, and happiness characterize what many translators go through when we tackle a book-length work of such erudition. And all three of those responses certainly applied to the process of creating the first English translation of Bodei's volume, which was published in 2018 by University of Toronto Press, as *Geometry of the Passions: Fear, Hope, Happiness: Philosophy and Political Use.*

In 2011, Remo Bodei, Massimo Ciavolella, and Luigi Ballerini were kind enough to approach me about the possibility of preparing the first English translation of this work. Having worked with them previously on other translations of an academic nature—and as a former doctoral student of each—I was honored and intrigued by the possibility of becoming absorbed in the intricacies of such a major philosophical tome. What I never expected was that it would be as rewarding and engaging an endeavor as it turned out to be. And inasmuch as reading *Geometria delle passioni* already requires considerable intellectual attention and effort (in any language!), it poses additional challenges and questions for a translator. It is precisely some of those challenges and rewards that I briefly touch on here.

This journey of translation was an effort that would take, between other professional commitments, five years—longer than any of us expected at the outset. The goal, however, was always a volume that does justice both to the erudition of Remo's argument and the unmistakable elegance of his prose. But my aim here is not to discuss the result. What I would most like to share are some of the challenges that execution of this project presented, because it is here that Remo's rubric of *paura, speranza e felicità* comes into play.

Early in the book, Bodei cites Spinoza's definitions of hope and fear: "Hope is 'inconstant pleasure, arising from the image of a thing future or past, of whose outcome we are in doubt.' Fear is 'inconstant pain, likewise arising from the image of a thing in doubt.'"[1]Although completing the translation was never in doubt, both inconstant pleasure and inconstant pain certainly accompanied me from time to time on this journey. The fear (if I might call it that) accompanied three particular challenges.

Challenge 1: The Length of the Work

In addition to the text's inherent sophistication, the Italian edition contains approximately 209,000 words and hundreds of footnotes and internal references. While Bodei, Ciavolella, and Ballerini were generous and trusting in encouraging me to make minor abridging edits to the text as I went along, the newness of the material to me and my absorption in the detail of the discussion's structure and language made that an extra challenge. It was helpful to have another set of eyes look at the text with editing in mind, and I am thankful to Efraín Kristal of UCLA for having gone through and marked suggested abridgments before I even started my work. As I worked my way through the manuscript, I also evaluated the sections he had marked for deletion, and I found his suggestions to be consistently excellent, abridging certain sections without compromising the integrity of the narrative. These frequently included, for example, passages that referenced Italian texts or commentators that would be unfamiliar to English-speaking readers and whose removal would not substantively distract from the overall discussion. The final translation came in at approximately 192,000 words, so although these edits may have resulted in some streamlining, they did not constitute a major reduction of the volume.

Challenge 2: Learning as You Go and
Applying What You've Learned

My past translations have included such texts as poetry and recipes. These genres are as different from one another as they are from philosophy, but all three require considerable parsing of a text and the interplay and nuance of its vocabulary. Although my background was invaluable, Bodei's work required its own level of focus and attention to detail. I had not read *Geometria* before I took on the assignment, so in addition to being a translator, I was also Remo's student on the adventure through which he guides his readers. My understanding of Bodei's philosophical argument and narrative arc increased so much during my first pass through the manuscript that I realized it was necessary to apply that knowledge in more extensive revisions than usual during subsequent, careful editorial passes through the book. Where the first pass took approximately two years, the stage of cleanup, revision, and true-up of quotations (which I will discuss next) required a similar period. Naturally, this extended the project over a longer period than we intended, and I was thankful both for the continued encouragement of Bodei and Ciavolella and for their forbearance.

Challenge 3: The Mountain of Primary Texts and
Secondary Citations with which Bodei Supports His Discussion

Those familiar with Bodei's text as it was originally published in Italian, or in its translation into French or Spanish (in the latter case, twice), are aware that his discussion relies heavily on quotation of, and reference to, dozens of writers. In the realm of philosophy, this notably includes Spinoza, of course, as well as Seneca and Descartes. But in addition to these principal figures, he brings in support of many other works ranging from antiquity to the years very close to the time of the volume's first publication.

To present the words of these other authors correctly, it was necessary to find authoritative English translations of their works and locate the passages within them corresponding to the text that Bodei cites in the original (in which he sometimes cites text in the original languages and, at other times, in Italian translation). This required months of rather painstaking bibliographical research to locate appropriate editions, find the quoted passages within them, insert the passages into the text, and reconstruct the footnotes and bibliography. It was a two-step process, working backward from the (usually Italian) translation in the original edition, then finding the corresponding text in the original or in an English translation. For some original texts that are organized clearly—Spinoza, for example—this is relatively straightforward. For others, where Italian and English editions are organized, labeled, or indexed differently, this can become time-consuming.

To give you an idea of the magnitude of this undertaking, the final manuscript submitted to the publisher, with 600 double-spaced pages, included approximately 840 single-spaced footnotes, citing scores of authors whose work originally appeared in at least seven languages. And many of those authors are represented by reference to multiple works—twenty-two by Seneca alone, for example, ten by Plato, nine by Plutarch, eight by Hobbes, seven by Aristotle, and of course extensive samplings of numerous works by Spinoza and Descartes. To be sure, it was a library sleuth's dream (albeit a rather long one, as dreams go). It is here, of course, that I was blessed by our association with UCLA and the breadth of resources to which one has access there. It appears that a large number of works that Bodei cites, when they are consulted by scholars in the twenty-first century, are consulted in their original languages, because a great many of the existing translations had to be recalled from the University of California's long-term storage facility.

Although time-consuming, this work proceeded well. There were, however, occasional surprises, such as the challenges posed by translating what, in my opinion, is the most exciting part of *Geometria*—part 4, the culmination of Bodei's discussion, concerning events of the French Revolution and, in particular, the Terror. This section quotes extensively from publications of the Revolutionary period, some of them of an ephemeral nature, and particularly from the extensive writings of Robespierre and Saint-Just.

I expected that good English translations of these figures' writings would be easy to locate. As it turns out, this is not always the case. English translations of Revolutionary pamphlets and newspapers are often quite incomplete, very poorly organized or indexed, and in many cases—to the extent Bodei's quoted passages were translated at all—they were clumsily rendered into early-nineteenth-century English.[2] Incorporating stilted, 200-year-old translations into the modern edition was not an option, and in order to have these quotes read properly in modern English, I ultimately chose to produce my own fresh translation from the French for these passages. Consequently, I am indebted to the translator of the French edition of *Geometria*, Marilène Raiola, for having done the work to retrieve the original French text for these passages.[3]

This brings us to the element of *hope*. For this project, this involved hope that the result would not only cogently reflect Bodei's content but justly reflect the style with which he relates what is ultimately a gripping story. And this brings me to the next challenge.

Challenge 4: The Elegance of Remo Bodei's Prose

Every translator faces the challenge of not only accurately representing an author's words, but adequately reflecting—to the extent possible in a different idiom—the elegance with which the original author expresses it. In the case of Remo Bodei, whose styling is as sophisticated and expressive as it is erudite, that task is considerable.

Bodei is a master of both sentence and paragraph construction. As many readers of Italian know, the syntax that is often prized in Italian intellectual writing (when it is done well, as in Bodei's case) often employs very long, carefully constructed sentences with multiple subordinate clauses, parenthetical comments, series, and incorporated quotes. Although standard in Italian academic prose, this type of expository styling does not, of course, transfer readily into good English written argumentation, with its preference for shorter periods and more declarative phraseology.

Despite the complexity of Remo's constructions, however, he consistently infuses his paragraphs with form and rhythm that are nearly poetic. He fills his sentences with a lexical and syntactic beauty that can leave admirers of the Italian language shaking our heads in admiration of his wordcraft alone. I say this not as flattery, but from deep admiration of his style.

The translator, however, does not have the luxury of simply sitting back and enjoying the melody; there is the very real task of converting that text into something that flows well in the target language. Since Italian-style constructions do not always lend themselves to fluid, intelligible English, some careful deconstruction and reordering was necessary to achieve this.

Many of Bodei's paragraphs follow a similar pattern. He will open with a thesis or introductory sentence that may be long by English standards but reasonable by Italian. Frequently, this will be followed by a second, even longer expository sentence with quotations, asides, and qualifications—the longest I observed was on the order of 150 words. To parse these periods into accessible English, it was necessary to sometimes derive three or four (and in some cases five) sentences from one symphonic Italian construction.

I will give but one example here to illustrate the challenge, in Italian and in English, in the hope of providing an idea of both the beautiful construction of Bodei's prose and the challenge it presents to the translator. The following is the single opening sentence, 102 words long, of one paragraph in part 3 of the book:

> Dinanzi allo scambio razionale di equivalenti tra gli uomini (misura per misura) o al voler donare senza ricevere—atteggiamento tipico del magnanimo aristotelico, che sottolinea così la propria superiorità nei confronti degli altri—prevale in Spinoza un proprio *ordo amoris*, il concedersi gioioso del saggio non solo al *nos*, agli altri uomini, bensì anche all'intera natura, in una crescita del suo intelletto e dei suoi affetti (il comprendere non è in Spinoza, come nella moderna ermeneutica, una pura modificazione di prospettiva intellettuale, ma, indissolubilmente, una capacità di trasformare se stessi e il mondo godendone, senza violare le leggi della necessità).

This was not even one of the longer examples! In English, this necessarily became two sentences, although even this required a fair amount of subordinate clause construction:

> Ahead of the rational exchange of equivalents between men (measure for measure) or the wanting to give without receiving—an attitude typical of the Aristotelian magnanimous man, who highlights his own superiority with respect to others—a real *ordo amoris* prevails in Spinoza, the joyful yielding of the wise man not only to *nos*, to other men, but to all of nature, in a growth of his intellect and feelings. (In Spinoza, understanding is not, as in modern hermeneutics, a pure modification of the intellectual perspective, but an indissoluble capacity to transform oneself and the world by enjoying it, without violating the laws of necessity.)

After dealing with sentences, it was necessary to move down another level.

Challenge 5: Bodei's Careful, Exacting Vocabulary

As one might expect with a philosopher as insightful and precise as Bodei, the manner in which he uses terms is not always the first, second, or even or third standard meaning or *accezione* of a term, and it was ever a challenge to ascertain that I understood the original text well enough to choose the proper corresponding English. In a number of cases, Bodei himself was generous in serving as a resource in my evaluation of alternatives. There are few neologisms in this text, but some terms that seemed natural when rendered in Italian required discussion to settle on an appropriate English counterpart. One of these terms was *ulteriorità*, which comes into play in the discussion within the introduction, in the phrase *logica dell'ulteriorità*. Working with Bodei, we ultimately decided on *logic of furthering*, a term not as immediately understandable, or nearly as mellifluous, but one that seemed the closest approximation of the principle being described. Another term of even greater importance, because it occurs several dozen times throughout the book, is one deriving from Spinoza, which in Italian is rendered *potere di esistere*. This became "power of existing," in consultation with Bodei himself.

Although it cannot be characterized as something arousing either fear or hope, I do want to mention a few things about my process on this project.

All translators have their own methods for doing their best work and stories about how they sometimes need to adapt those procedures to suit the material at hand. In the case of *Geometria's* intensity and density, my pattern was somewhat different from other translation commissions. I found the language and the subject so absorbing and exacting that, on the first pass, after about two to three hours of work on the raw translation, I had become absorbed to the point that I would begin to lose track of the English. I would see Remo's text and understand it, but I would start to lose my way back to the corresponding English terms. I learned to trust this as an important signal to take a break.

Further, in order not to disrupt the flow of my translation on a project with so many internal quotations, I did not stop every time I encountered quoted material, but my initial renderings included "dummy quotes"—that is, I would create a placeholder quote (carefully marked by a separate color, so that none would go into the final translation), based on the quote as it had appeared in the Italian edition. I then went back and replaced those temporary quotes with either an authoritative English translation from the original language, my own translation where required, or in some cases—Shakespeare and Hobbes, for example—with the original English text.

Finally, a few words about *happiness*. In this case, it is not just the happiness of having completed the book (although that certainly was real), but the happiness of having had such an engaging—I would even say, exciting—volume to work with. I can add to this the happiness of having been able to work with the late Remo Bodei personally as a resource and sounding board, the happiness of having the research resources available through UCLA, and the patient and encouraging support of Massimo Ciavolella and his association of University of Toronto Press in bringing this book forward to English readers.

Bodei's discussion in *Geometry of the Passions* is thoughtful, engaging, and important, and it is my hope that this edition not only closes a long-standing gap in the body of Remo Bodei's work available in English but that readers find within it both a clear expression of his argument and a worthy echo of his distinctive voice.

Notes

1. It is important to note that the translations of Spinoza's words throughout the completed book—and in the present discussion—are not my own, but from Samuel Shirley's editions of Spinoza.

2. Interest in English translations of lesser-known writings of the French Revolutionary period seems to have waned in the first half of the nineteenth century. Once again, those who wish to study these writings probably do so in the original French.

3. In the original Italian edition of *Geometria*, Bodei quotes Italian translations of these French texts.

Bibliography

Bodei, Remo. *Geometry of the Passions: Fear, Hope, Happiness: Philosophy and Political Use.* Translated by Gianpiero Doebler. Edited by Luigi Ballerini and Massimo Ciavolella. University of Toronto Press, 2018.

4

Ordo amoris

Bodei on Augustine's Concept of Love and Beyond

Heather Renee Sottong

Ordo Amoris: Conflitti terreni e felicità celeste is one of Remo Bodei's smaller, but no less influential books, first published in Italian in 1991 and subsequently translated into German, Spanish, and French (*Ordo amoris: Augustinus, irdische Konflikte und himmlische Glückseligkeit*, Passagen Verlag, 1993); Spanish (*Ordo amoris: Conflictos terrenos y felicidad celeste*, Cuatro, 1998); and French (*Ordo amoris: Conflicts terrestres et bonheures célestes*, Les Belles Lettres, 2015). In this rich and dense book, Bodei discusses, among other things, Augustine's concept of the order of love versus the disorder of evil; questions of the divided will; the eschatological differences between political states and religions; and connection between love and memory. In the present essay, I will provide an overview of these main themes and discuss how Bodei relates Augustine's theories on love to modernity and secular belief structures.

To begin, I will provide a brief summary of Augustine's concept of love and its relationship to order, which, as Bodei points out, contrasts strikingly with modern ideas regarding romantic love. Unlike the volatile *amour passion* of the romantic age that pulls one back and forth on a terrestrial plane, *ordo amoris* is a celestial kind of love that allows one to leave behind sin and the past and rise toward a future in which the soul will find peace with God. Also, unlike romantic love, this divine love is characterized by constancy, coherency, and order. In Augustine love is synonymous with renewal and the resolution of conflict. It has the power to dissolve the bonds that block the will, relieve the weight of the past, and permit each of us to reformulate and begin our lives anew. Love opens us not only to the future, but also to the past. Through love we can release the harm that we have committed and endured. And this leads to order, both in the sense of a free disposition of the soul and of an obedient response to an external and divine command.

But how can love become "order" in the double sense of both the free will of the soul and an obedient response to an external commandment? For our modern sensibility, we think of love as something spontaneous and transgressive rather than something we associate with routine and authority. For Augustine, however, love has everything to do with authority.

Understanding Augustine's notion of order requires understanding the Christian belief in a hierarchy of beings that descends from God to the angels, to humans, all the way down to the smallest worm. Love for Augustine is the highest command, and the "weight" that helps the spirit rise to its proper origin. To explain this, Augustine appropriated the metaphor of gravity from Plato's vision of the soul's journey and maps it to the Christian desire for God. He writes in the *Confessions*,

> A body inclines by its own weight towards the place that is fitting for it. Weight does not always tend towards the lowest place, but the one which suits it best, for though a stone falls, flame rises. Each thing acts according to its weight, finding its right level. If oil is poured into water, it rises to the surface, but if water is poured on to oil, it sinks below the oil. This happens because each acts according to its weight, finding its right level. When things are displaced, they are always on the move until they come to rest where they are meant to be. In my case, love is the weight by which I act. To whatever place I go, I am drawn to it by love. (XIII.9)[1]

Augustine makes a few adjustments to the metaphor. Rather than the body acting as a weight upon the soul, the soul's love is one's weight. Furthermore, love determines the center of gravity or the point of attraction for the soul. Gravity is comparable to desire, the force that propels the soul forward toward its end. If the soul loves God, the gravity of desire draws the soul upward until finding perfect rest in Him.

As Bodei explains, the order of love is the committing of oneself consciously to this hierarchy in hopes of reaching God: "In fact, *ordo amoris* designates, strictly speaking, the conscious adhesion of the will, strengthened through love, to the rigorous hierarchy of good that culminates in the enjoyment of God" (*L'ordo amoris* designa infatti, in senso stretto, l'adesione consapevole della volontà, potenziata in amore, alla struttura rigorosamente scalare del bene che culmina nella fruizione di Dio).[2]

While Augustine associates love with order, evil is the reversal or disruption of the order decreed by God. It is derivative of the chaos introduced into the world by the fall of Satan. Because of the fall from grace, Augustine believed that humans can easily resort to evil because of weakness, lack of commitment, or perverse orientation of human will. Therefore, he advocates for strong government to hold the corruptible nature of human beings in check. He was, as many have pointed out, perhaps the first political realist.[3]

He does not lean toward utopia nor sanction tyrannical governments; rather, he believes that the only way for human beings to become better while on this earth is to convert and receive God's grace. While the political state will never fully satisfy the needs of people, in *civitas Dei*, all needs will be satiated for all eternity. This makes the Christian not a citizen of this world, but a pilgrim in transit.

Augustine's injection of religion into political theory has several clear benefits, which will become important later when we discuss the aspects of his thinking that Bodei feels are worth regaining. First, it is important to note that Augustine was first and foremost a philosopher—indeed he went through philosophy to get to his Christian conversion. Having done so, he realized the drawbacks of relying on reason alone. Philosophy does not give us one clear, unified, and simple response when trying to answer difficult questions about human existence. To illustrate this point, in Book 19 of *City of God*, Augustine sets out to showcase the "diverse" and "empty dreams" of the philosophers when it comes to earthly happiness (XIX: 1).[4] He refers to the work of Marcus Varro, a Roman philosopher who in his *De Philosophia* tried to compile philosophical arguments about what makes people happy. Varro found 288 different answers to this basic question. The varied responses created by human reason are not very reassuring. How can philosophy be the path to truth if it creates more confusion than clarity? Faith is a surer foundation for certainty, and therefore philosophy is subordinate to faith, although not to be excluded from it.

The idea in the *City of God* is that Christianity is more reasonable than the life of pure philosophizing. It answers questions more simply. Very importantly, it takes into account all aspects of human nature instead of just one part: reason. Thinkers who solely rely on reason are likely to develop theories that are unrealistic, overly hopeful, and overconfident about what we can accomplish in this life. From the Christian perspective, this overestimation of self is a sin—pride. Furthermore, as Bodei explains, the pagans that Augustine opposes are negating deep-rooted aspects of human existence that cannot be explained via *logos*. Blinded by the pride of their own rationale, these thinkers limit themselves to what can be explained by logic and write off everything else as "miraggi della fantasia" (mirages of the imagination) and the "prodotto di passioni ed attese surriscaldate" (product of passions and overheated waiting).[5] Unlike the *sophia* of the pagans, the Christian faith does not try to hide its contradictions but rather attempts to openly grapple with paradoxes such as the suffering of the righteous and the conflict between free will and divine omniscience. Bodei perceives this acknowledgment of paradoxes as a strength rather than a weakness.[6]

Furthermore, reason alone does not help people to weather the terrible calamities of life that inevitably avail them. Following the Sack of Rome, Augustine wrote the *City of God* to defend against accusations that Christianity was responsible for the decline of Rome. Early in the text, he demonstrates that calamity is nothing new, nor is Christianity the cause of calamity. Human life is often miserable, and misery does not respect goodness or wisdom. The Stoics counseled persevering and retreating into the mind, but Augustine did not condone what he considered detachment. By renouncing the fullness of life, they reduced man to a mere "rational animal." Furthermore, he was unsatisfied with the arguments the stoics put forth that the ultimate good was to be found in this life.

For Augustine, life on earth is inevitably fraught with famine, war, and illness; bliss is to be attained only in paradise. This way of thinking allows Christians to accept what is bad in this world as a means to a better end. Suffering can be perceived positively because it testifies to the good that has been taken away here on earth, but will be restored in heaven. In fact, Christianity gives people the wherewithal to survive horrific suffering (like during the Sack of Rome) and come out of said suffering strengthened.

The Christian promise of eternal happiness contrasts strikingly with pagan ideas of cyclical patterns of eternal return, reincarnation, or of a definitive dissolving into nothingness. Although the concept of reincarnation does suggest an orderly and hierarchical progression (depending on the moral quality of the previous life) to a higher form of being in the next, the most that believers of reincarnation can aspire to is a full stop to the cycles of suffering. Christians, on the other hand, await eternal bliss after the moral efforts of just one lifetime. Furthermore, the religious structure of the Church provided individuals with community and a surrogate family. The role of the Church, as sinners grapple with earthly conflicts, is to correct its sons and daughters, even if strictly. Faith provides an unwavering framework and a morality that can be relied on in inevitable moments of uncertainty.

But while Augustine's stable and orderly worldview influenced philosophers for centuries to come, it does not hold much weight in the present. Modernity dismantled the belief in *ordo amoris*. Or rather, as Bodei explains in an extended metaphor,

> Quando le nuvole del dubbio si addensano proprio sulla vetta, avvolgendo quasi completamente il vertice della gerarchia cosmica (Dio, quale "sommo bene" e fonte perenne di suprema beatitudine), tutti i gradini della scala divengono allora sostanzialmente impercorribili e il concetto stesso di "ordine dell'amore" viene deligittimato.

> When the clouds of doubt gather right on the summit, almost completely enveloping the top of the cosmic hierarchy (God, as the "supreme good" and perennial source of supreme bliss), all the rungs of the ladder then become substantially impassable and the very concept of "order of love" is delegitimized.[7]

Without the rungs of reason going up the ladder of faith, the potential believer is asked to take a giant leap rather than a simple step.

Instead of any one predominant religious worldview, in the modern age a particular secular worldview prevails for some time—until the unrest over failed promises leads to the violence of revolution. During revolutionary periods, society seeks to construct a more just version of itself, emboldened by the promise of future solutions. Indeed, the modern age is characterized by cycles of changes of direction that promise to bring about renewal and develop more morals, catechism, or even the secular bigotry of civic virtues. The values most commonly invoked in the last centuries for the edification of a new world are *liberty* and *equality*; *democracy* and *communism*; *reason*, *science*, and *progress*. The way these words are invoked, and the reassuring function they assume, Bodei argues, is not far off from the reassurance provided by religious sentiment. However, not all political projects, morals, and philosophies of history contain substantial spiritual aid to help individuals deal with the hardship, trauma, and fatigue of social and individual life by giving them a sense of purpose and a goal.

Furthermore, in the present era, the globalization of markets and communication have stirred up for millions of humans the painful sensation of an uprooting of traditions and a sensation of disorientation in a world that is more and more vast and unfamiliar.[8] No less than other eras, there is extreme inequality between higher social classes and the poor. For the latter, this world is one of privation, suffering, humiliation, and poverty with little amusement. Some turn to drugs as a temporary paradise. Secular philosophy does not offer much consolation for those enduring poverty and constant struggle.

When for hundreds of millions of men and women the primary search for meaning is no longer to be found on the historical-political plane to the same extent, we start to witness a schism—a bifurcation of our singular human history. As Bodei explains, secular thought had, until recent centuries, precariously managed to prevent against this potential schism; but now the theoretical forms that held things together (the "invisible hand" of the economy, sociological systems, philosophies of history, and the ideologies that incessantly reproposed and legitimized it) have become incoherent. History as conscious and successful planning and history as an uncontrollable event have never coincided well in any theory, but their relationship has now become even more uncertain and opaque.

What's even more alarming, according to Bodei, is that this multi-millennial process of "disenchantment" with the world operated by Western rationalism has led to a return to "obscurantism," driven by faiths that base themselves on a revelation.[9] In places where economic growth is limited, and suffering is the only present, the power of messages of otherworldly salvation cannot be denied. Bodei writes as follows:

> Quando questi uomini disperati non hanno da perdere che le catene che li tengono avvinti al mondo, il messaggio religioso tocca corde profonde e riesce più persuasivo di un diagramma economico corretto, di tecniche di contraccezione ragionevoli o di qualsiasi teoria vera ma remota dalla loro esperienze.

> When these desperate men have nothing to lose except the chains that keep them fettered to the world, the religious message strikes a profound chord and is ultimately more persuasive than a rational and technical economic diagram or any theory which may be true but which is remote from their experience.[10]

Some people are turning back to faith to find sense in the world and to redeem themselves from the desperation of facing a reality that is disturbing. Some of the largest monotheistic religions (in particular, Christianity and

Islam), have, in the last two decades, began to reestablish their hegemony over this segment of the population, which finds modernity unfulfilling. But the abandonment of the idea that there is a sense, a logic to human events does come at a cost.

> Abbandonare alle chiese i progetti e gli ideali di libertà terrena, di effettivo pluralismo della verità, di raggiungimento potenziale della maggiore età della specie umana, significa per lo spirito laico regredire all'ascolto della parola solenne, autoritaria, despositaria di verità che dispensa soltanto a chi, con atto di umile obbedienza, compie il primo passo in direzione del credere. Significa convertire di nuovo—con un movimento di "desecolarizzazione"—valori e significati "immanenti" in "trascendenti."

> To abandon to the churches the projects and ideas of earthly freedom, of real plurality of truth, of potential achievement of the greatest age of the human race, signifies for those of a secular spirit to regress to listening to solemn and authoritarian words, custodians of a truth that is accessible only to those who, with an act of humble obedience, take the first step in the direction of faith. It signifies converting once again—with a movement of desecularization—"inherent" values and meanings into "transcendent" ones.[11]

While those of a "secular spirit" cannot accept dogmas, the religious cannot accept atheism, individualism, and earthly logic. Bodei finds it unlikely (and perhaps not even desirable) that an irenic compromise between secular and religious values be attempted, nor a spiritual hegemony of religion over politics.[12] Instead he proposes that we reflect on the areas of friction and agreement in order to safeguard common values in moments of crisis. Instead of speaking of "tolerance," which is a word that indicates a condescending attitude toward that which is not held in common, he proposes the word "respect."

Although Christianity, as an institutionalized religion became extremely intolerant over time, the Christian love at its basis was not. According to Bodei, Christian love "instituted by the Lamb of God" interrupted "the perverse game of the 'victim mechanism' accustomed to institutionalizing intolerance by identifying a 'scapegoat.'"[13] Christ accepted "hate without reason" on the part of his persecutors, renouncing vengeance, and thereby setting the example of turning the other cheek. It was only later that Christianity became intolerant. Why? Perhaps because any religion that wants to achieve staying power needs a nucleus of infallibility. And because the negation of eternal salvation to nonbelievers is a great way to incentivize potential believers—a sort of "ricatto spirituale" (spiritual blackmail).

But now perhaps the aforementioned problem of incommensurability can be resolved through said "respectful" consideration of common values. This is precisely where Augustine comes into play. The Christian *civitas Dei peregrinans*, which unites and separates the city of God from the earthly city, but which has now overcome the reaction of total rejection of the modern world, is currently part of the Church's discourse with regained authority. With two millennia of experience, the Catholic Church can attempt to take charge of some problems of common interest which, precisely because of their magnitude and nature, are not able to be resolved by states or international organizations. The Church has mobilized itself to replace the fragments of values expressed by secular politics and ethics, offering an alternative not only to the atheism of a god who failed, but also to the disastrous effects of an overinsistence on human freedoms in democratic societies, or hedonistic philosophy, detached from God. What we find in Augustine is an admittance of contradictions and a toning down of overly optimistic theories of what is possible on earth.

> Amplificando e approfondendo i conflitti, per poi provvisoriamente risolverli, la fede si arricchisce e si diversifica, spiega paradossi quali il potere e l'impotenza del libero arbitrio, il volere a ritroso che modifica il peso del passato, la gratuità e il merito nel ricevere la grazia, la convivenza in se stessi di una felicità "così antica e così nuova," il significato positivo e negativo del dolore e del male per affermare o confutare l'esistenza di Dio.

> By amplifying and studying in-depth conflicts, in order to temporarily resolve them, faith enriches and diversifies itself. It explains paradoxes such as the power and impotence of free will; the retroactive desire to change the weight of the past; the gratuitousness and merit in receiving grace; the coexistence within oneself of both an ancient and new happiness; the positive and negative significance of grief and evil in order to assert or refute the existence of God.[14]

Some of Augustine's ideas on the inevitability of earthly conflicts proved influential, in various ways, to thinkers such as Luther, Jansenius, Dostoevsky, Lukacs, and Sartre, who all countered what appeared to be an excess of optimism in regard to the possibilities of reality. Augustine was convinced that there is no peace in this world. Hence, the first part of the title of this book, "Earthly Conflicts." He did not intend to annul or repress desires (in particular fear and hope), and he did not intend to rationalize them either. He did not aspire to the tranquility of the soul, but rather to the sweet and tormenting anxiety that leads to salvation.

Love and Memory

Following the copious introduction, Bodei considers a number of important themes such as the divided will, happiness, and the desire for immortality. Since it will not be possible to relate all the rich content of the book here, I will simply close with a few comments on one of the many themes discussed—love and memory, or love in relation to the past. In Augustine's view, love doesn't take away the memories of the past, but it takes away their burden. Indeed, love, forgiveness, and memory are the remedies for the irreversibility and weight of the past and the eternal return. Hope and freedom are derived from love's power to provide closure with the past so that we may proceed toward the future, committed to the path of *ordo amoris*. Love has the power to forgive not just individual sins committed during one's lifetime, but also original sin, innate in man since Adam's fall.

Augustine is against the pagan belief in *fatum*, which looks at the past as something that cannot be changed. Love and Christian forgiveness, on the other hand, invite people to reevaluate the past on a different plane of meaning. *Amore-memoria* (we can re-remember) times which isolation or desperation rendered particularly bitter.

> La memoria non falsifica o ripudia ciò che è stato: lo ritraduce
> di continuo, orientandolo secondo l'ampiezza del presente, con-
> nettendolo a contesti più vasti (in quanto solo nel presente si
> ha il ricordo di altri presenti).

> Memory does not falsify or reject what has occurred. Rather
> it retranslates it continuously, reorienting it according to the

> present, connecting it to a vaster context. Only in the present
> does one have a memory of other presents.[15]

In order to better clarify how Augustine conceives of love's effect on past memories, Bodei quotes a phrase (out of context) from Baudelaire's poem *Un fantôme* (II, 20): love produces, *"dans le présent le passé restauré."*[16] I very much appreciate the fact that Bodei colors his clarifications of Augustine's theories with lines of modern poetry. Bodei's particular style of writing and teaching synthesized literature and philosophy, which he never saw any reason to separate. And this makes a great deal of sense. Why should we perpetuate the rigid demarcations between the two fields when a lot can be gained from considering them simultaneously? Similarly, what Bodei appreciates about Augustine is his ability to synthesize religious thought and philosophy. Just as religion should not be without reason, reason need not be devoid of spiritual sustenance.

Furthermore, the references to modern literature in Bodei's reflections help us get a sense of where traces of Augustine's thought persist, and from which lines of thinking it is entirely absent. In another section of the book, he includes a poem of Bertolt Brecht titled "Gegen Verführung," in order to contrast Augustine's consoling and soothing vision of the afterlife with Brecht's warning against the temptation of believing in the eternal. The poem ends with the line: "Ihr sterbt mit allen Tieren / Und es kommt nichts nachher" (You die like all the animals / And nothing comes after).[17]

In Augustine, on the other hand, death marks the beginning of the true life and the fulfillment of our hope: "Incipit vita nova." In the Heavenly City Christians are promised two main sources of happiness—one anthropocentric, and one theocentric. First, those in heaven will be reunited with family members and loved ones; second, they will derive joy from the vision of God. While still on the earthy plane, believing in life after death has certain psychological implications: it makes misery and suffering in this world more bearable; it means that we were not born in vain; and it indicates that the world has a sense that we will understand afterward. In this mindset, the city of God and the idea of God as a best friend who never fails takes precedence over social and political relationships.

Bodei's juxtaposition of modern and Augustinian ideas is not presented as a battle between the secular and the religious. To oppose reason to tradition, liberty to servitude, modernity to obscurantism, he clarifies, does not help us to pinpoint the problem. The goal is to better understand through investigation and reflection, what mixture of ideas happened in different "subsystems" of society and to identify possible combinations of both secular and religious systems of thought that, although operant, might not yet be explicitly explored.

Notes

1. Saint Augustine, *Confessions*, translated and with an Introduction by R. S. Pine-Coffin, Book XIII 9, 317.

2. Remo Bodei, *Ordo amoris: conflitti terreni e felicità celeste*, 10. All English translations of *Ordo amoris* are mine.

3. See, for example, Reinhold Niebuhr, 1953, "Augustine's Political Realism." In *The Essential Reinhold Niehbur: Selected Essays and Addresses.*, Edited by Robert McAfee Brown, 123–41.

4. Saint Augustine, *The City of God,* trans. Marcus Dods Book XIX, 1, 818.

5. Bodei, *Ordo amoris*, 17.

6. Bodei, *Ordo amoris*, 14.

7. Bodei, *Ordo amoris*, 25.

8. Bodei, *Ordo amoris*, 33.

9. Bodei, *Ordo amoris*, 37.

10. Bodei, *Ordo amoris*, 35.

11. Bodei, *Ordo amoris*, 38.

12. Bodei, *Ordo amoris*, 38–39.

13. Bodei, *Ordo amoris*, 40.

14. Bodei, *Ordo amoris*, 14.

15. Bodei, *Ordo amoris*, 131.

16. Qtd. in Bodei, 130.

17. Bertolt Brecht, *Gegen Verführung* (1918), in *Gesammelte Werke*, vol. III (Suhrkamp Verlag, 1967), 260. Quoted in Bodei, 159.

Bibliography

Augustine. *The City of God.* Translated by Marcus Dods. Modern Library, 2000.

Augustine. *Confessions.* Translated and with an Introduction by R. S. Pine-Coffin. Penguin Books, 2000.

Bodei, Remo. *Ordo amoris: conflitti terreni e felicità celeste.* Il Mulino, 2005.

Brecht, Bertolt. *Gesammelte Werke*, vol. III. Suhrkamp Verlag, 1967.

Niebuhr, Reinhold. *The Essential Reinhold Niehbur: Selected Essays and Addresses.* Edited by Robert McAfee Brown. Yale University Press, 1986.

5

Things: Bodies: Moving

Reflections on the Thought of Remo Bodei

Peter Carravetta

Dripping water hollows out stone,
not through force,
but through persistence.

—Vittorio De Sica, Bicycle Thieves, 1948

In *La vita delle cose* (2009), Remo Bodei undertakes a multipronged exploration of the "contents," so to speak, of our perceived reality. Leaving aside momentarily the question of the status and apparatus of the sentient consciousness, the main focus of the project is to determine (1) when whatever we touch, use, or generally what is not in me, or part of me, we call "objects," and (2) when these same entities make up a fluid dimension that constitutes "things," typically involving more complex semantic/symbolic dimensions, something that consciousness does not relate to casually and mindlessly, but has meaning, "makes sense," in several more specific environments. This raises at least the possibility that *objects can become things* (and thus expand our emotional and cognitive reference points in our immediate world). At the same time, *things become greater than (even distanced from) the objects* they may originate in or refer to, and for the multitude transform themselves into symbols, icons, emblems, and *topoi*—in short,

63

a significant cultural referent, at times a social force impacting on values, beliefs, habits, and eventually choices. An exploration and assessment of *the dynamics of things*—what Bodei calls the *life* of things—becomes crucial to an understanding of the very society in which we live.

I want to comment on some of Bodei's considerations in view of other areas of research in which I have been involved, mainly explaining postmodernity, developing a rhetorical hermeneutics, and the study of migration in its broad range of interdisciplinary and transactional dynamics, as well as its philosophical import. The aspects that Bodei with his usual acumen tackles in *The Life of Things* illustrates a general philosophy of our existence mired in a fractured subjectivity and a reality of incessant commodity exchanges (where commodities include not only "objects," or merchandise, of course, but also services, those "things" we need, want, and do, like online shopping, banking, voting, and so on). This is also the background panorama for an understanding of the migrant, in several aspects, from the anthropological to the metaphysical, to the psychological constitution of an "I" and the relationship self-other/s. For the migrant, typically considered a subject that is de jure outside, or on the *other* side, of a given community, city-state, or nation, not legit in some manner, has been characterized (in both practice and theory) as a being intrinsically marginal, suspect, often demonized, at times forced to find and accept an identity imposed from the members of the commune, according to its laws of acceptance and incorporation, or else assigned an identity that is more like a moniker, an armband, a shibboleth of untrustworthiness or unacceptable sociality. The very existence of the migrant, I claim, challenges the very idea of a definite, legitimate, lasting incorporation (as citizenship), and with that discloses a different sociocultural dimension still awaiting a fuller philosophical recognition.[1] But I will return to this later in this chapter.

At the beginning of the book Bodei parses some of the meanings of the word *cosa*, thing. In the Italian and cognate Romance languages, the word is a contraction of the Latin *causa*, "that which we consider so important and involving as to summon us to defend it"[2] (as in "standing up for a/your cause," or "fight for the cause"). As *res*, the word, retains the root of the Greek *eiro*, to speak, as in the Latin *rhetor*, and points to what interests us because we discuss it. Conceptually, says Bodei, *cosa* is related to the Greek *pragma*, to the German *Sache* (from the verb *suchen* to search), entailing *discourse around what matters*, and having little to do with the definition and ontology of mere physical objects. Though of course at some point in the culture, objects often do become things, and vice versa. But before elaborating on that, let us recall that in the philosophical tradition, *pragma* is given theoretical cogency by Aristotle, in the expression *auto to pragma*, "the thing itself" (*la cosa stessa*), which is made to designate how things actually stand (independently of their names as used in argumentation, as discussed in the *Topics*), as well as the process (and means) one engages in reaching a truth. The expression, as is well known, has had a rich and tumultuous life, being redefined or better reconceptualized in the Modern Age by Hegel (*die Sache selbst*) and by Husserl (*Zu den Sachen selbst*). A development that I consider consistent with the Post-Modern Age properly understood, basically as a loosening and relativizing of hierarchies and stable structures, is suggested by Hans Blumenberg, not by chance a theoretician of mythology, whereby the expression should now become: *"Zu den Sachen und zurück,"* from his 2002 book by the same title (14).

We have just enough now to move on to how all this actually plays out in the culture. It soon becomes evident that the return to the things themselves will entail some form of appropriation, a conscious competing and taking away (from someone else) within the given polis, valorizing oneself through one's external corelations, often transforming the individual (who is not, like bees or ants, pre-ontologically, genetically, keyed to the survival and flourishing of society) into *a symbol that extends its grasp and influence in the body of the society*. In this dynamic, the very objects possessed by a powerful individual—say, Louis XVI, Theodore Roosevelt, or Queen Elizabeth II—acquire the status of a "thing" (mythic, monumental, ideological, fashionable) to be treasured, paraded, traded, and respected. How this comes about concretely, sociology has already explained to us. The question is problematized further if we ask: What does the varying cultural dynamic between objects and things do in relation to a self, the consciousness of one's identity and sovereignty? What I'd like to draw attention to, here, is Bodei's recovery of a passage in *The Phenomenology of Spirit*, where Hegel writes about the cofounding givenness of subject-object, but with this crucial modification: "everything depends upon understanding and expressing the true not as *substance*, but rather decisively as *subject*" (16). In other words, there is an entreat to consider the other (that which is outside of me, and therefore a priori foreign), in its multifarious determinations, *not as* object empirically understood (and whereby humans would be just finite bodies, manipulable, object of study as in the physical sciences), *but as* a life-form imbued with the same basic apparatus of other members in the group, suggesting a *relational existence* on the basis of which we can *go beyond the subject-object opposition and explore the subject-to-subject exchange*. This requires a methodic weighing in of the available evidence, the above-mentioned "things themselves," and then *a return to the self-consciousness*, here clearly understood in a phenomenological way, of having to commit to a position, a discourse, an idea, but still something that is of relatively major interest in the polis and therefore, depending on personal or political orientation, "worth fighting for." Matters can get complicated when, going beyond Edmund Husserl (28–29), intentionality is now also grounded on the body, on the sentient person. The recurring references to Maurice Merleau-Ponty support this. This brings us back to objects, the material side of existence.

Bodei here opens up to the various ways in which *attention*, the art of knowing how to focus, what to see, when to be receptive, *can confer a sense to an object as to transform it into a "thing"* of more profound (even though perhaps amorphous or elusive) significance. In any case, it entails an "opening up to the world" (chapter 2), and with that a reckoning of the myriad objects we are surrounded by and the perplexing sensation that much is actually indifferent (to us, to everyone! That is, objects are inert, or merely mechanical). The invitation here is to "look for" hidden meanings, "listen to" and "for" narratives, perhaps long-gone or re-exhumed (reliving in the *echo of* the past), recalibrate our sensorial/sensuous inputs (some form of education, or training, here helps), elaborate connections and values as if to create a mental map of things.

And things have a history. The relations we have with things—especially understood as impactful common structures, *res publica*—impact directly on our values, our behavior, and how we shape our discoursing with others. Things rise and decline in history. Bodei returns to this topic very often in the book. *Re-semanticizing, altering the value of the symbols embodied in our preferences and dislikes, our upholding the value of specific symbol-things or at times destroying them, is the warp and woof of social and cultural interpretation* (55–56). This discloses venues for an understanding of how our relationship to the world about us changes over time, as well as show that, within that dynamic, there is potential for each individual to intervene, rethread the habit, modify the traditions that otherwise tend to rigidify, and reset them in motion in order to better embody and represent changing mores. We are placing the me/others dialectic across the object/thing relation. Bodei did not call it so, but we have here a sort of epistemic-social hermeneutics.

Thus, things, we learn, have in many ways defined our very sense of time. We can immediately think of how specific personal effects, such as photographs, amulets, jewelry, tools, old hats and scarves, etcetera are jealously protected by each of us, and particularly the different kinds of migrants.[3]

Sometimes, our sense of temporality—something other than Cartesian time—is directly linked to our experience of these possessions, what we discover *in* them, what we attribute *to* them, and how in the broader society they are concretized (a Gadamerian word), induce us to see innumerable objects as "things," as if they had a life of their own. Almost. This is so that both empiricist and transcendental idealists can relate. But through the emergence of modern (self-)consciousness, we have understood that even *things*, alas! *are not forever.* The permanence of something—buildings, monuments, paintings, poems, fame, social order, mythology, theology—is not guaranteed by any Supreme Being or Primal Quantum: things age and decline. Sometimes, through a rhizomatic effect, they resurface elsewhere or at other times. But in general, we should understand the proverbial phrase "sculpted in stone" as a metaphor, a conceptual catachresis, for whatever the object (theory, monument, feeling), it bore a resemblance to something real, as when writing the emperor's name in marble was a quintessentially human attempt at immortality, an intersection, but also a coagulation, of symbol and desire, ritual, and fear. But in recent, late Modernity—say, from the post–World War II period—we know that marble ain't cutting it anymore.[4]

Bodei goes through a panoply of cases (*casi, cose*)—drawn from literature, mythology, philosophy, political science—while questing after big metaphysical questions: Is the investment in attributing value to objects, to the point of changing them into specific yet prismatic symbols, topoi, and rituals in the realm of beliefs, fueled by a need to cover up an emptiness, a fear that things do end, that humans too are temporally defined, indeed highlighting the finitude of existence? Beyond that, reaching into the late nineteenth and early twentieth century, we learn that "sensible qualities" are corralled under the aesthetic, the sensible qualitative experience of the beautiful,[5] or alternatively reduced to the *qualia* of personal, psychological states (85). He cites Jean Baudrillard on this context, reminding how we have, in the techno-oppressive and now digital age, become simulacra of ourselves, where even we, humans in the flesh, can enter the domains of signification and social action mostly as *media*ted agents, a priori deterritorialized and electronically transient. What's added here is also that we are influenced to accept the "violent" loss of formerly long-lasting, affective things.

A brief reminder of Bodei's previous work should suffice to grasp by broad strokes how he arrived at this quest to recover and tune into the silent discourse of our experience. In two early papers (1978, 1982) the philosopher sought to identify shifts in our understanding of the past through close readings of Max Weber and Walter Benjamin, pointing to a changing sensibility about the comprehension of temporality. Yet he doesn't believe, like Jean-François Lyotard, that the great Enlightenment-inspired *metarécits* of emancipation, idealism, and progress itself are now discredited ideologies and that everything is over.[6] He turns to Hegel to find a space from where to investigate the lives of these forms of discourse when they do not adhere to or fall neatly into the historiographic categories and institutional classifications that we automatically use to ground our deliberations. The issue is to go beyond contradiction as the axiom of logical thinking[7]: Bodei claims that (social, symbolic) life is not enslaved to logic, and that there might well be expressions of the discourse of philosophy that reveal other realities, often accessible if we dare enter the thicket of paradoxes that life in Modernity has displayed, "macroscopic transformations and disagreements [dissidi]" that show, through a series of close readings gathered in *Scomposizioni* (1987), the search for outer limits, for the unknown, and for "linee di fuga," in authors such as Kant, Novalis, Hölderlin, Rousseau, Goethe, and Hegel. By the end of that volume, he observes that the modern ego took forms such as "knots," (R. D. Laing), or had become "modular" (Paul Berg), or floating prefabricated shards that no longer need "unity" (245), and that the traditional ethical imperatives—family, class, state, church—themselves having significantly evolved, it became onerous for the free individual to construct themselves an identity: "In a polycentric world, the reference points and the links to loyalty multiply themselves and become diverse, forcing the individual to divide and subdivide themselves and constantly adjust or modify the map of their identity" (246). The ego is uprooted, deprived of or forced to detach itself from traditions, induced to burn their *Erlebnisse*, travel with a light memory, and worry not about the future.

This is of preeminent importance to the migrant. Except for that last phrase, worry not about the future? How would that be even conceivable? Already fractured in its putative identity and statutorily defined as someone between (at least) two places, characterized by their moving *between* these places, should not the preoccupation with the destination, and thus the future, be foremost in their deliberations? But if from all sides the news is really bad, that "the I," "*l'io*," the "*moi*," "*das Ich*," is no longer the one defined and consolidated through long historical periods with reference to values that become a superstructure (again: state, church, but also economies, laws, and various canons), and is now incomplete, splintered, in a riddled and uncertain Age of the Persistent Distortion, and time itself is now lodged in the networks, then what hope is there for the migrant?

That the social conditions of the individual agent are undergoing epochal alterations is confirmed in Bodei's more traditional historiographical volume, *La filosofia del Novecento* (1997), where again he underscores that individuals have lost their "social placenta," citing Robert Nozick, experiencing a slackening of personal relationships, and are more free and more isolated at the same time (183). Thus, at the beginning of the millennium, we have two camps, the (late) Moderns who, despite the troubling if not nihilistic panorama, persist in reconciling the shattered pieces of a vaguely unitary, "iron-clad" [ferrea], identity, and the Post-Moderns who willy-nilly embrace mobile, recyclable, "plastic" identities (184).[8] Clearly Bodei is in the camp of the Late-Moderns, but in a different way than the J. Habermas of "Modernity as an Incomplete Project." In a subsequent collection of studies that appeared a few years later, *Destini personali* (2002), Bodei delves into how our self-consciousness has become alienated and colonized (259), and how *malgré tout* there is need to bring the "I" back (zurück!) to some semblance of re-cognizable sense of self.[9] The nature and possible range of options available to the "I," to the acting conscious individual, are limited and confusing and generate a specter of its former self, becoming impersonal (89–90), while the "us" has changed radically as well.

But that doesn't mean we have to give up the fight! After a series of close readings of authors who dealt precisely with the construction of the self, of the "I,"[10] Bodei proposes a theoretical model based on three elements: (1) "condensation," or "metaphor" (inspired by Freud); (2) the creation of a necessarily mobile barycenter (90; inspired by Nietzsche) that allows the diminished "I" to still maintain, at given time/place, a modicum of balance or measure; and (3) extend the range of the concepts of "heterotopia" and "heterocronia" (281–82; indirectly referencing both Michel Foucault and Gilles Deleuze)—"Only by taking advantage of the intermediate space provided by the back-and-forth between the Me and the Us, can we exit both the solitude of the purely self-referential consciousness and the assimilation into an Us that cannibalizes it; only this way can it find its proper way" (288). We can see how the philosopher is conjoining the need for a critical consciousness that, by focusing on what is yet available to it, can take advantage of its own sense of self, and this beyond what neuroscientists tell us is possible.[11] The question revolves around rediscovering the inputs from the body, from perception, and from an awareness of that perception. There "I" may be a construction, but it is spontaneous, instinctive, and we are often not aware of it. It would correspond to Sartre's *cogito pré-réflexive* (284), to Bertrand

Russell's notion that we always feel we have "an acquaintance" with/in us, or even an "obscure vital sentiment" according to Théodule-Armand Ribot. It's reconnecting with the *tactus intimus* (Cicero translating Aristippus) (284). The possibilities here would allow this diminished I or self of late-Modernity to cohabit, dwell with the *post*Moderns, explore how "things" can touch, feel, speak. To those who are willing to touch, feel, speak.

I think there are a number of points that relate meaningfully to the question of the status and spaces available for the migrant. Aside from the more material, pragmatic concerns that anyone shifting through often untranslatable semiotic systems, reorganizing their very existence as they navigate policies and ideologies that make sure the outsiders, the strangers, remain and are recognized publicly as "the foreigners," "the others," "them," there are means both to capture what they are saying, as well as means for us to get to see, hear, feel them, when they stop becoming objects and become living things, driving us to consider philosophy itself as grounded—in the age of the absence of foundations—on a moving interpersonal, intersubjective relation. In order to facilitate that, bring the relation to the existence of the being(s)-in-the-world, the things we are, the things we bear, and the things that stand outside of us all but which nevertheless determine where our itineraries may lead, the idea of reserving time and care to the voice and suggestions and breathing of other's own "things," may reveal that life is much more than what the neuroscientists tell us it is. It actually expands our sphere of perception, and therefore of possible signification. One need only think of the literature (and cinema) on migration issues. Writers and painters are proverbially endowed with a capacity (understood, in some more than others) to capture the pulse of the existence-within-the world, existence enriched, expanded and made malleable in the very moment of the exchange with the other/s. The migrant is particularly sensitive to this, ever on high alert, pre-prepared to see, hear, feel not just the others (those beings which are never merely "objects" of our perception but "subjects" with a mind, a past, and feelings and desires). Examples of individuals who, beyond the paradigmatic model of leaving-journeying-arriving, and the very real, painful, confusing stages of culture shock, may enlighten us on how they lived the constant dialectic between object and thing, to resolving perhaps to take care of objects but to love and cherish (certain) things, especially when the latter allow the migrant (or anyone for that matter) to find meaningful, life-affirming, oases of sense and compassion. The *letteratura dell'emigrazione*, of any country I explored, is replete with these cases where the life of things turns into a love for them, because what exists physically outside of us but psychologically, symbolically, politically inside us constitutes a very large part of who we are, humans amid other humans in a perennially declining universe.

Yet the ethical entreat here is that if we "pay attention," listen to the language, the murmurs, the allusions, the memories, the triggers offered by things, perhaps we can regain a bit of what philosophy has traditionally fought for, as its main "*cosa*": Contemporary philosophy has tried to recover the richness of quality and of meanings that things can absorb or emanate, giving back to them (at a theoretical level) the depth (*spessore*) that has been already attributed to them by literature, art or historiography (85). But a further development of this awareness, combined with the analysis of how the social agent changes things into objects and back, paradoxically can reveal, through a self-conscious, phenomenological assessment, how even *those* things (false, digitalized, alienated, capitalized) impact on our perceptions and interpretations of our reality, now preferably put in the plural: realities. Therefore, they need to be paid attention to. But what can we listen to, beyond a whisper, white noise, clicking keystrokes?

In the last pages Bodei touches lyrical levels as he takes us through the disclosing of cultural icons and values by way of painting, then Plotinus, Baruch Spinoza, Thomas Merton, pursuing the images of *life as lived*, and as it slips by, gifts us with images and ciphers that through poetry and philosophy, can also be captured and understood as seed, germ of what is to come. I believe Bodei's thought can be relevant to ecocriticism as well, for the way he engages authors on their relation to nature—to flowers and animals and mountains. In the end we are bodies, half object and half thing, forever on the move.

Notes

1. Two studies in particular deserve mention in the context of my reading, one by the already mentioned Gregory Feldman, author of *We Are All Migrants* (2015), which juxtaposes the condition of the migrant as prior to the question and legitimacy of citizenship. In fact, the alien, the stranger, the immigrant is such also if not primarily because she or he is not a citizen of a given modern nation-state. Feldman also points out that there have been cases where the state of migrant-hood does not always require travel between constituencies, or crossing any borders: just think of the Baltic Republics, which one day found themselves foreigners to the USSR sovereignty, or Palestine, or the scores of Amerindian nations, or Poland, or the Southern Italian citizens of the Kingdom of Naples, who after March 1861

found themselves foreigners of a non-pre-existing Italian state, albeit of the Savoy persuasion. On a more theoretical plane, among the few who actually rethink the whole migration question is Thomas Nail's *The Figure of the Migrant* (2015), which proposes a methodology based on forces and flows, and the stabilizing provided by cities and states contingent on contrived stops along the way. That would mean that cities and civilizations are mere bivouacs in the unfolding of lived time. Being migrant is the ontological condition of being homo humanus. His position also strengthens my view in "Migration, History, Existence" (2004).

2. I am quoting from the 2009 edition of *La vita delle cose*, 12. All translations are my own. On the polysemic complexity of the expression/concept "the thing itself" discussed on this page, see especially Giorgio Agamben, *Potentialities*, 1991, 17–38.

3. I am saying different kinds or types of migrants because in this context I cannot take a detour and delve into how Bodei's analyses of the self-other dialectic play out, for instance, with exiles, expatriates, explorers, spies, missionaries, and so on.

4. Bodei cites a passage from Lucrece, which notes that "within many cycles of the sun / the ring on the finger will wear down, / . . . / the falling of the rain will wear the stone / . . . / bronze statues / show how the hands were worn by touch" (*De Rerum Natura*, I, 311–21; quoted in 57). This suggest that change, wearing down, the decline of things, is part of our existence—for good or ill. A modern version, though with reference to character traits or virtues deemed to be "eternal," is echoed in Vittorio De Sica's voice-over at the beginning of *Ladri di bicicletta* (1948), which is the epigraph to this chapter.

5. To consider certain cultural objects as specifically and exclusively "aesthetic" (whether painting, sculpture, music, or theater) has had its own sociological impact, beginning with Benedetto Croce's 1902 *Estetica*, which entirely detached the immediate sensible experience of art from any further development, relationship, or cognitive content. See the trenchant critique of more than half a century of what amounts to aesthetic alienation and mystification, in Galvano Della Volpe's *Critica del Gusto* (1960), a classic waiting to be rediscovered.

6. One can here recall the multitude of publications on the "end" of metaphysics, of rationality, of the democratic vistas, of the self, that came out in the 1980s.

7. Hegel's fragment "Ever growing contradiction" (Der immer sich vergrössernde Widerspruch), written between 1799 and 1802, stated that "the feeling [Gefühl] of the contradicton between nature and its underlying life is the need to remove the contradiction . . . when it becomes a pure negative" (Das Gefühl des Widerspruchs der Natur mit dem bestehenden Leben ist das Bedürfnis, dass er gehoben werde . . . wenn es reines negatives geworden ist." Quoted in *Scomposizioni*, 1987:8).

8. On the variety of postmodern discourse and implications for philosophy and social theory, see my *Del Postmoderno* (2009), and a synthesis in English, "After All" (2017).

9. Without disagreeing with what some of his peers at the time were theorizing, such as Gianni Vattimo and his idea of a being without foundation, a weakened subject that would dismiss the strong, potentially totalitarian pretenses of a trans-historical ego, and accept and adapt to a more regional, necessarily interpersonal and humble ontology of being, one without certitudes yet still able to decide for oneself.

10. Among the authors, particularly in syntony with what we are exploring, we find the ever-present Hegel, and Bergson, Freud, Gentile, Locke, Jünger, Le Bon, Nietzsche, Pirandello, Sartre, Simmel, and Spengler. See, in particular, chapter 9, "Gerarchia e sacrificio: Mussolini e Gentile" (220–48).

11. Think of the recent uptick of publications on free will, or rather, on the fact that there is no such a thing at all! Among many, representative of the current is Sam Harris, *There Is no Free Will* (2015). I discuss this in detail in my *The Humanist Project* (2024).

Bibliography

Agamben, Giorgio. *Potentialities: Collected Essays in Philosophy*. Stanford University Press, 1999.

Bodei, Remo. "Il dado truccato. Senso probabilità e storia in Weber." *Annali della Scuola Normale Superiore di Pisa* VIII, no. 4 (1978): 1415–33.

Bodei, Remo. "Le malattie della tradizione: Dimensioni e paradossi del tempo in Walter Benjamin." *AUT AUT* 189–90 (May–August1982): 165–84.

Bodei, Remo. *Scomposizioni. Forme dell'individuo moderno.* (Einaudi, 1987).

Bodei, Remo. "The Broken Mirror: Dissolution of the Subject and Multiple Personality." *DIFFERENTIA: Review of Italian Thought* 2 (Spring 1989): 43–69.

Bodei, Remo. *La filosofia del Novecento*. Donzelli, 1997. https://commons.library. stonybrook.edu/differentia/vol2/iss1/5/.

Bodei, Remo. *Destini personali: L'età della colonizzazione delle coscienze*. Feltrinelli, 2002.

Bodei, Remo. *La vita delle cose*. Laterza, 2009.

Brettell, Caroline B., and James F. Hollifield, eds. *Migration Theory: Talking Across Disciplines*. Routledge, 2015.

Carravetta, Peter. *The Humanist Project: Will, Judgment, Society from Dante to Vico*. Lexington, 2024.

Carravetta, Peter. *After Identity: Migration, Critique, Italian American Culture*. Bordighera, 2017.

Carravetta, Peter. *Sulle tracce di Hermes: Migrare, narrare, riorientarsi*. Introduction by Remo Bodei. Morellini, 2012.

Carravetta, Peter. *Del postmoderno: Critica e cultura in America all'alba del duemila*. Bompiani, 2009.

Carravetta, Peter. "After All: Critical Theory and the Geography of Culture at the End of the Postmodern Age." *Agorapoetics. Poetics After Postmodernism*. Edited by Rolando Pérez. Davies Group Publishers, 2016, 29–70. [Expanded English version of Introduction to my *Del Postmoderno*, 2009.]

Carravetta, Peter. "Migration, History and Existence." *Migrants and Refugees*. 2004, 19–50. [Revised and expanded version is now the Introduction to *After Identity*, and in Italian appears as the first chapter of *Sulle tracce di Hermes*.}

Feldman, Gregory. *We Are All Migrants. Political Action and the Ubiquitous Condition of Migrant-hood*. Stanford University Press, 2015.

Nail, Thomas. *The Figure of the Migrant*. Stanford University Press, 2015.

Tilly, Charles. "Migration in Modern European History." In *The Migration Reader*. Edited by Anthony M. Messina and Gallya Lahav, 126–46. Lynne Rienner, 2006.

Waldenfels, Bernhard. *Topographie de l'étrange: Études pour une phénoménologie de l'étranger*. Translated by F. Gregorio et al. Van Dieren Éditeur, (1997) 2009.

6

When *Sōma* Is no Longer *Sēma*
(When the Body Is no Longer a Grave)

The Evolution of the Western Construction of the Body from Plato to Remo Bodei and Michel Foucault

Olimpia Pelosi

Epistemic Prolegomena: A Note

When I started this *enquête* I realized that, while abundant materials existed on the history of the Platonic dualism of body/soul, no critical points of reference could be found on the parallel Bodei's/Foucault's vision of corporeality, and that therefore I was stepping onto uncharted ground. To give the reader some basic information about the long-lasting philosophical/religious debate of which Bodei and Foucault are the epigones, I have chosen to adopt a thematic-panoramic approach. This overview will outline the ideological construction of the dichotomy body/soul (starting from its Platonic foundations) and will subsequently examine, in broad terms, its manifold ramifications that traversed Christianized Europe (for example, the Pauline image of the body as a temple, the Thomistic reevaluation of the *sōma* in function of the soul; the Cartesian mechanistic vision of the body-machine; Nietzschean corporeal "vitalism").[1] After sketching this diachronic frame, I shall proceed to demonstrate how Bodei's and Foucault's corporeal visions, even stemming from a different epistemological background, fully converge

75

in the rejection of the Platonic divide between flesh and "spirit," and consider the two entities as an intertwined biopsychic unity. For the sake of thematic coherence and in the interest of necessary brevity, I have opted not to extend my scrutiny to studies on corporeality and to gender theory that, in Foucault's and Bodei's epoch, either through crossed or parallel paths, elaborated its tenets, richly and foundationally, on the same topic.[2]

"Archeology" and "Genealogy" of the Conflict Body-Soul— The Body as a Tomb: Corporeal "Construction[s]" by Plato and Hellenistic Platonism

In the pages of one of his "most enigmatic dialogues," titled *Cratylus*, Plato writes the following:[3]

> *Some people* say that the body (*sōma*) is the tomb (*sēma*[4]) of the soul, on the grounds that it is *entombed* in its present life, while others say that it is correctly called "a sign" (*sēma*) because the soul signifies whatever it wants to signify by means of the body. I think it is most likely the followers of Orpheus who gave the body its name, with the idea that the soul is being punished for something, and that the body is an *enclosure* or *prison* in which the soul is securely kept [. . .]—as the name "*sōma*" itself suggests—until the penalty is paid (400c).[5]

The above-mentioned words—that Plato puts in the mouth of his own master, Socrates, in this dialogue—have resounded like a persistent echo in the imagery of the Western mind for longer than two millennia, and have been instrumental in the constructing of the rigid dualistic axiom that has shaped the creed and the cultural and sociopolitical destiny of Western civilization.[6] In fact, the Platonic idea of a superior, diaphanous, and everlasting soul, condemned to be trapped in a fragile and limited *simulacrum* of flesh, became indelibly rooted in the speculative vision of Christianized Europe.[7] Indeed, the dualism *sōma/pneuma* that sees the body as a perishable and dark prison of the soul (along with the idea of the *vertical descent* of the soul from a higher, immortal reality into a lower and degraded one) unfolded in a long series of Plato's epigones: the Stoic Epictetus in his *Dissertations* I, 20, 7, who, "refuting Epicurus' thought," depicted the human body as a shell containing a snail (the soul).[8] Plotinus, Plato's major interpreter, laid the seminal foundations of the "so-called ancient Platonic tradition" which operated in the Mediterranean area between the fourth century BC and the sixth century AD" (Rossi Monti, 2016, 181).[9] In his most notable work, the *Enneads*, Plotinus summarizes Plato's idea of the corporeal entrapment of the soul by stating that "the soul is in bondage and has buried itself within [the body]," and therefore it "is in prison" (IV, 8. 1, 30–32).[10] Plotinus's antinomy *sōma/pneuma* was further intensified in the writings of one of his most fervent acolytes, Porphyry, whose stern rejection of corporeality and draconian "ascetic disparagement" of the body as an abject "obstacle" to the attainment of spiritual perfection (Sipe, 2006, 6, 5) significantly contributed to exacerbating the already unbridgeable dichotomy between flesh and spirit and to demonizing the human body as an "animal body which by its corruption weighs down the soul" (Sipe, 10).[11]

Christian Implications of the Body-Soul Conflict— The Body as a Temple: The Pauline *sōma pnemautikón* and the Christian Patristic Construction of the Body According to Paul, Tertullian, Augustine, and Thomas Aquinas

In Corinthians 6:19–20, Paul vehemently says: "Do you not know that your body is a shrine [temple] of the indwelling Holy Spirit, and the Spirit is God's gift to you? You do not belong to yourselves; you were bought at a price. Then, honour God in your body."[12] This perspective clearly shows that the corporeal paradigm has shifted from the Platonic rigid divergence body/soul/low/high to the horizontal idea of the body as a receptacle of the divine that can also be found in Judaic mysticism.[13] The "empathically horizontal" and "historical" Pauline eschatological construction of the body as a temple, although it still considers the *sōma* as subordinate to the soul, indeed contemplates a second chance for human corporeality. By elevating the body to the rank of *soma pneumatikón* (a spiritual body), Paul transforms it into the dignified host of the divine and eventually constructs the image of the collective body of the community, the *"ecclesia."*[14] That means—to borrow Pauline language—that bodily flesh, *"sarka,"* can evolve to the higher perception and fruition of reality and become spirit (*pneuma*).[15] It is evident that such a concept, even though not overtly and drastically negative toward the physical body, subtly and profoundly undermines its relevance and autonomy per se. Paul's view of the body will be the beacon for all the Patristic writings after him, which extend from the Hellenistic Era to the European Late Middle Ages.[16] As links in a long chain, we see a large group of Early Christian commentators who—in their contribution to the "maturing corpus of Christian thought"—follow in Paul's footsteps and offer a re-interpretation of the dichotomy body-soul in which they assert the preeminence of the "spiritual" body over the physical body.[17] Tertullian, in one of his treatises, perfectly aligns with "Paul's hermeneutical category of flesh and spirit" when he states: "*Caro salutis cardo*," [the] flesh is the hinge of salvation"[18]; he, along with Irenaeus of Lyon, is one of the influential *auctores* who shapes the corporeal perceptions of Augustine of Hippo and Thomas Aquinas, two of the founding fathers of Christian thought in the West.[19] Augustine retains the Pauline vision that portrays a "disembodied transcendental" body in opposition to the physical one.[20] Moreover, he blends Paul's anthropology with Plotinus's vision and mixes the combination with traces of Porphyry's inclination toward corporeal contempt. Centuries later, on the verge of the Early modern era, Thomas Aquinas—although broadly following Augustine's path—will further elaborate on the idea of the connection body/soul and will "remove" its drastic "dichotomy" by replacing it "with the notion of the dependency of the body upon the soul, the soul being the body's ultimate goal."[21]

Corporeal Perceptions of the Modern Era: From the Body—"Tomb" and "Temple" to the Body— "Machine" According to Descartes, Spinoza, and Beyond

For the sake of brevity this inquiry will delineate via a Pindaric flight, the evolution that the Platonic idea of the body as a tomb or temple undertook during the centuries that followed Aquinas. In the Renaissance era, the body was restored to its beauty and dignity, inspired by the Greek philosophical principle of *kalokagathia* and perceived through the pantheistic perspective of Giordano Bruno and Tommaso Campanella.[22] Then came the Cartesian dualistic theory of *res extensa* (material body) and *res cogitans* (immaterial mind) and Descartes's idea of the body as a "natural" (in the sense of *physical*) "machine." His dualistic divide would prosper and ultimately craft the historical and socioeconomic construction of Western corporeality during the first industrial revolution that engendered a new relationship between means of production and the body.[23] In the Romantic era, Hegel, who was more inclined toward Spinoza's than toward Descartes's epistemology, wrote about the "mysterious" and "incomprehensible" yet clearly interdependent organic unity of body and soul.[24] Less than one century later, Nietzsche would stretch to the extreme Schopenhauer's vision of body and soul, conceived as a unitarian entity, and would utter his cry of defiant triumph against the Platonic "worshippers" of the body as a tomb of the soul:[25] "To the despisers of the body will I speak my word. I wish them neither to learn afresh, nor teach anew, but only to bid farewell to their own bodies—and thus be dumb. '*Body am I, and soul*'—so saith the child. And why should one not speak like children? But the awakened one, the knowing one, saith: '*Body am I entirely, and nothing more*; and *soul is only the name of something in the body*'" (*Thus Spake Zarathustra* IV, 76).[26] Nietzsche's bold statement would resound through the magmatic territories of the Western perception of corporeality of his time, and its echo would reach two of the giants of the speculative thought of the postmodern era, Remo Bodei and Michel Foucault.[27]

On the Shores of Postmodernity: The Evolution of Corporeal Perceptions in Remo Bodei (1938–2019) and Michel Foucault (1926–1984)

When I started the present *enquête*, I noticed that, apparently, there are no comparative studies on Bodei and Foucault. Furthermore, as far as I could ascertain, the lives of Bodei and Foucault proceeded on two parallel routes and never converged for what could have been a fruitful collaboration or an exchange of ideas. Although they never met, the Italian philosopher was an assiduous frequenter of Foucault's production and—hypothetically—Foucault might have been acquainted with some of Bodei's works antecedent to 1984.[28] Nevertheless, a net of multiform threads links their speculative *parcours*: "No one thinks or writes alone"; and in the "increasingly permeable" postmodern "boundaries" of *fin de siècle*, Bodei and Foucault stand as two kindred philosophical minds.[29] Only twelve years separate their birthdates; both were born in cities and regions characterized by a rich historical past, and an ordinary present.[30] From the fertile and competitive cultural *humus* of their peripheral spaces, in my opinion, both thinkers drew on their profound intellectual curiosity, which led them to elude the barriers of fenced specialization and to cross the still existing boundaries between philosophy and social and historical sciences.[31] Another common trait that Bodei and Foucault share is the furbished writing style, that in Bodei flows through a crystal-clear, composed, impersonal and quasi-poetic *cursus*, while in Foucault it unfolds as "[un] [. . .] grand style [. . .] baroque [. . .], fort beau, parfois juqu'à l'excès [. . .] par sa splendeur et sa précision."[32] An additional remarkable affinity that the two thinkers share resides in their initial literary formation: in both their love for philosophy stems—in their formative years—from their passion for literature and literary criticism.[33] In Bodei "l'uso della letteratura in chiave filosofica" is overtly shown in *Piramidi di tempo* (2006), one of his most intriguing books.[34] In it the thinker deals with the "history and theories of the *"déjà vu"* and explains the phenomenon from the psychological and philosophical viewpoint, quoting several literary voices that encompass Shakespeare, Verlaine, Rossetti, Ungaretti, and Borges. Concomitantly, as remarked by Panella and Spena, "since his beginning as a thinker Foucault's interest for literature and for literary writing is anything but occasional and is directly connected with his future speculative production."[35] An avid reader of writers such as Bataille, Roussel, Klossowsky, and profoundly fascinated by Blanchot's literary criticism, Foucault would later blend such components with Nietzschean vitalism and create his notion of corporeality.[36] An additional resemblance that aligns Bodei's and Foucault's vision is—as contradictory as it might appear—their common Platonic root, which is not related to the opposition body/soul, that they both reject, but is connected to the Platonic political vision as expressed in his *Seventh letter*.[37] In this work Plato exalts the courage of the ideal philosopher who—even if facing persecution or death like Socrates—must find the courage of utter *parrhesia*, that is the strenuous courage to tell the truth.[38] Also both Bodei and Foucault openly declare their laicity and embrace the *parrhesia* as a secular religion, a virtue that confers dignity on its followers and debunks the stereotyped *locus* that labels philosophers as useless "loafers" and makes them, instead, potential "martyrs of the truth."[39] After this necessary digression let us focus now on Bodei's and Foucault's perceptions of corporeality. The point of departure of both thinkers is to find a way to mend the dualism of the Platonic axiom that opposed body and soul and confined in a Procrustean bed the problem of their supposed antinomy. Bodei, a constant and thorough commentator of Foucauldian thought, is mainly interested in the "diagram" that Foucault drew in the "last five years [. . .] of [his] life (1979–1984)," that is the analysis of the "genealogy of the Western subject."[40] Paraphrasing Foucault, and sharing his views, Bodei writes: "Finora l'uomo occidentale ha dovuto conquistare la propria identità solo contrapponendosi all'altro da sé, al rimosso, al negativo di se stesso."[41] To heal this dualistic fracture and better conform to the Delphic maxim "Know thyself," says Bodei (2008, 129), Foucault predicates a new idea of immanent ethics, obtained through the Greek practice of *askesis*, that is, an array of "techniques of the construction of the self."[42] Such exercises allow the individual to reach the frame of mind that Foucault defines as *epimeleia autou* or *"souci de soi"* (care of the self).[43] This novel balance between body and mind (that reminds us so closely of *philautia*, a concept admired and studied by Bodei in his monumental *Geometry of the Passions*, 2018) is for both thinkers inextricably linked to philosophical practice.[44] For Bodei as well as for Foucault, philosophy and not theology is the portal to access an immanent truth, without severing body and mind in an artificial and distorted perception of reality. With the support of a self-scrutinizing hermeneutics, Western subjects will be able to free themselves from a millenary bias typical of their historical and speculative tradition and embedded in both classic and Christian roots.[45] A devout commentator of Baruch Spinoza and of his conception of a *Deus sive natura*, Bodei combines the Aristotelian and Spinozan vision of reality with the profound ethical dimension of the "last Foucault." This is a "space of freedom," born in the territories of Greek thought, that is pivotal for the construction of the subject.[46] The somber Platonic prison of the soul, the Pauline temple of the spirit, the Cartesian body-machine are no longer for Bodei, nor for Foucault, the appropriate keys to convey a postmodern idea of corporeality. The body has become, in the eyes of the two theorists, a self-sufficient biological entity detached from any ontology. It is captivating to remark the different nuances through which the two philosophers decline their novel idea of corporeality. The French *maître à penser*, in the second half of the last century, radically and pugnaciously reverses the Platonic duality by stating in one of his most famous books, *Surveiller et punir* (1975), that the soul has been a socio/ideological construct assembled by the political (and religious) power in order to exert its control on the single body and on the collective "corps social" with the aim of turning individuals into "corps dociles," passive and enslaved instruments to its will[47]: "L'âme, effet et instrument d'une anatomie politique; *l'âme, prison du corps.*"[48] Almost four decades later, having passed the threshold of the third millennium, Bodei—with the detached poise that is infused in all his writings—that I am inclined to compare to the *ataraxia* of the ancient Stoics, declares the following:[49]

> Tendiamo spesso a dimenticare che siamo ospiti della vita. Nasciamo senza volerlo e saperlo, in un determinato tempo e luogo, il corpo che abbiamo ricevuto in eredità biologica dispiega spontaneamente i suoi mirabili e, talvolta, terribili processi: il

sangue circola, le ghiandole secernono ormoni [. . .]; tutto questo avviene in maniera indipendente dalla nostra volontà, dalla nostra coscienza e dalla nostra memoria, così come involontaria, inconscia e immemore è stata la nostra nascita [. . .]. Siamo appunto ospiti della vita perché inseriti in processi naturali, "*autopoietici*," che ci fanno sentire la nostra dipendenza dal corpo e dai suoi mirabili automatismi che la cultura occidentale ha trascurato. *Noi non abbiamo semplicemente un corpo: siamo anche un corpo.* La cosiddetta anima vegetativa di cui parla Aristotele non è infatti mai stata indagata ed educata.[50] (Italics mine)

We often tend to forget that we are the guests of life. We were born unwittingly and unknowingly, our body, that we got as a biological heredity, spontaneously unfolds its admirable and sometimes terrible processes; our blood circulates, our glands secrete hormones [. . .]. All that happens in a way that is independent from our will, in the same way just as our birth, has been involuntary, unconscious, and unmindful [. . .]. We are indeed the guests of life, since we are part of some natural "autopoietic" [self-made] processes that make us feel our dependence on our body and on its admirable automatic mechanisms that have been neglected by Western culture. *We do not simply have a body: we are also a body.* The so-called vegetative soul that Aristotle describes, in fact, has never been investigated or trained. (Translation and italics mine)

By this statement—which summarizes the key concept of Helmuth Plessner, one of the founding fathers of philosophical anthropology—Bodei shows his agreement with Foucault's theory and conveys it through the lens of a less emotional, more scientific (and only apparently) mild, ideological scrutiny.[51] In the footsteps of Aristotle, Bodei regards the nexus body/soul as the essence of the corporeal, and therefore sees it as strictly intertwined with bodily functions and operations. He considers the soul as substance of the body and not as an immaterial *ens* fallen from the Platonic *hyperuranion* and confined—as a foreign host—in the body.[52] No longer somber Platonic tomb of the soul, neither Pauline temple of the spirit, nor Cartesian mechanical machine, the Bodeian idea of corporeality illustrates the idea of *sōma* within the terms of the Aristotelian *entelecheia*,[53] and gives preeminence to the physical self-generative nature of corporeality. Furthermore, through a veiled but precise indication (expressed through the adjective "autopoietico") Bodei also refers to the concept of *natura naturans* contained in Spinoza's *magnum opus*.[54] Finally, with the assertion "we are a body," Bodei synthesizes the Epicurean tradition that has been the subtext of modern materialist hermeneutics and that—via Nietzsche—has influenced, among others, the vision of Michel Foucault.[55] At the beginning of the present century Bodei's critical inquiry progressively acquires a marked shift toward Foucauldian themes. *Destini Personali: L'età della colonizzazione delle coscienze* (2002) focuses in fact on the evolution of modern "personal individuality."[56] Bodei's investigation presents—through a thematic and panoramic overview—the arduous dynamic process of emancipation and re-appropriation of the body that spans the centuries of the medieval era to the age of modern totalitarianisms. In the following quote from *Destini* the philosopher traces, in a superb and impersonal synthesis, the progressive evolution of the ancient conflict body/soul.

> Una volta [. . .] si credeva all'anima come si credeva alla grammatica o al soggetto grammaticale [. . .]. Quando la fede nell'anima immortale e nel soccorso divino diventa incerta e implausibile, questi sostegni della coscienza e della società vengono faticosamente sostituiti con altre nozioni importanti, quali identità personale e storia fatta dagli uomini [. . .]. L'identità personale si rivela erede e surrogato dell'anima, risultato della segreta elaborazione del lutto per lo scadere della garanzia cristiana che assicurava all'individuo una durata senza fine. Una volta oscurata o negata—sul piano teorico—la sostanzialità dell'anima, sembra infatti venir meno il fondamento stabile dell'io, l'unità dei suoi flussi di coscienza, che avrebbero dovuto prolungarsi oltre le barriere della morte. Allontanata la prospettiva dell'eterno, il singolo si trova progressivamente immerso nel tempo irredimibile della caducità. La riduzione della vita cosciente ai granelli di attimi dello shakespeariano "banco di sabbia del tempo," con la conseguente contrazione delle aspettative alla sola esistenza fisica, gli rivela la propria intrinseca fragilità, il suo essere esposto al pericolo sempre incombente della disgregazione e dell'oblio di sé. Per trapiantare le radici dell'io dal solido e immutabile terreno dell'aldilà nel *friabile e transeunte suolo del proprio corpo*, della propria biografia, delle istituzioni politiche e della storia, è stato necessario approntare una mole imponente di inedite

strategie teoriche [. . .]. È oggi difficile rendersi conto di quanto intimamente radicate fossero le concezioni e le passioni religiose riguardanti l'anima e la sua destinazione futura e quanti sforzi siano stati necessari per resistere alle vigorose controffensive delle chiese, che si riorganizzarono [. . .] e [. . .] non esitarono ad agitare contro i reprobi i lugubri vessilli della morte e della dannazione perpetua [. . .]. Né il senso della fine, né le promesse di vita eterna riuscirono tuttavia, a fermare—dal Settecento in poi—lo slancio verso *la riconsacrazione* del mondo e *del corpo* e il conseguente abbandono, da parte di molti, della condizione di "anfibi," di esseri capaci di vivere in due mondi: nell'al di qua dell'esperienza e nell'al di là dell'attesa." (85, 8–10; italics mine)

When faith in the immortal soul and in divine intervention becomes uncertain and implausible, [the] supports of conscience and of society are painstakingly replaced by different important notions, such as personal identity and history made by human beings [. . .]. Personal identity becomes the successor and surrogate of the soul; it is a result of that secret grieving process that unravels after the expiration of the Christian assurance promising individuals an eternal duration [life]. Once the substantiality of the soul is obscured or denied on the theoretical level, even the stable foundations of the self and its streams of consciousness (that were supposed to be prolonged beyond death) seem come to an end. Once the option of eternity has vanished, individuals find themselves immersed within the irredeemable caducity of time. The reduction of conscious life to the grains of moments of the Shakespearean "sandbank of time"—along with the resulting contraction of expectations to mere physical existence—shows individuals their own innate fragility, the fact that they have been exposed to the constant and impending danger of disintegration and the oblivion of the self. Individuals have [therefore] to transplant the roots of their selves from the solid and immutable terrain of the afterlife to the friable and transient soil of their own bodies, of their own biographical events, of their political institution and of history. To make it possible, it has been necessary to prepare an impressive amount of novel theoretical strategies [. . .]. It is nowadays hard to realize how deeply the religious and ideal passions were rooted [in the minds of the individuals] and to fathom how many strong efforts were made to resist the harsh counteroffensives of the ecclesiastic establishments that reorganized themselves [with the Counter-Reformation] and did not hesitate to wave against the reprobates [rebels] the grim banners of death and perpetual damnation [. . .]. Neither the sense of an end, nor the promises of eternal life were able however to halt—from the eighteenth century on, the impulse toward a reconsecration of the world and of the body and the resulting abandonment, on the part of many, of an "amphibian" condition: that means being able to live in two worlds at once: in the immanent world of experience and in the afterlife of the waiting [for eternal life]. (Translation mine)

Bodei's objective and serene exposition, that blends in a harmonious fusion sociology, history of ideas and philosophical concepts, appears so close in essence to (and so distant in style) to the direct and paratactic structure of Foucault's invective, blatantly conveyed through the use of the first person.

Le mot grec qui veut dire corps n'apparaît chez Homère que pour désigner le cadavre [. . .]. Peut-être la plus obstinée, la plus puissante de ces utopies par lesquelles nous effaçons la triste topologie du corps, c'est le grand mythe de l'âme qui nous la fournit depuis le fond de l'histoire occidentale. L'âme fonctionne dans mon corps d'une façon bien merveilleuse. Elle y loge, bien sûr, mais elle sait bien s'en échapper [. . .]. Elle est belle, mon âme, elle est pure, elle est blanche; et si mon corps boueux [. . .] vient à la salir, il y aura bien une vertu, il y aura bien une puis-sance, il y aura bien mille gestes sacrés qui la rétabliront dans sa pureté première. Elle durera longtemps, mon âme, et plus que longtemps, quand mon vieux corps ira pourrir. Vive mon âme! C'est mon corps lumineux, purifié, vertueux, agile, mobile, tiède, frais; c'est mon corps lisse, châtré, arrondi comme une bulle de savon. (*Le corps utopique*, 2009, 18, 11, 12)

The body just appears in Homer [*Iliad*] to designate the corpse. Perhaps, the most obstinate, the most powerful among the utopias by which we cancel the sad topology of the body is the great myth of the soul, as provided to us, since its inception, by Western civilization. The soul functions in my body in an

> admirable way. It resides there but it knows quite well how to
> escape from it [. . .]. It is so beautiful my soul, pure, white;
> and if my muddy body makes it dirty, there is always a virtue,
> a power, a thousand sacred gestures that will reestablish it in
> its pristine purity. My soul will last for a long time, and more
> than a long time [even] when my old body will rot. Long life
> to my soul! It is my luminous body, purified, virtuous, agile,
> mobile, warm, cool. It is my smooth, castrated body, rounded
> like a soap bubble. (Translation mine)

A hiatus of almost two decades separates *Destini personali* from Bodei's last work, *Dominio e sottomissione* (2019)—released only two months prior to his death. This book that has been defined by many as Bodei's spiritual will, serves superbly the onerous task of collecting Foucault's legacy on the *microphysique du pouvoir* and of the *biopouvoir*.[57] Bodei's reflection on the ultimate corporeal commodification, slavery, encompasses, in fact in an articulate and captivating architecture, the Foucauldian discourse on "le partage" [et] l'assujetissement [. . .] [de]s [. . .] corps dociles."[58] While Foucault had focused in a general theoretical fashion on the dynamics connecting enslaved bodies to total lack of freedom and therefore, to absolute lack of power, Bodei's investigation primarily dwells—with meticulous chrono-historical references—on the development of slavery in the early modern age (where "il fenomeno della schiavitù subisce un brusco salto di scala, raggiungendo una dimensione planetaria, che coinvolge nella "tratta atlantica" la vita e il destino degli abitanti di tre continenti: America, Europa e Africa").[59] Subject to exploitation and degradation, stripped of its own identity, the enslaved human body is for its master a mere aggregate of cells, an object, that after being used and abused in life, is turned, after death, "in una sorta di livrea che il servo riconsegna a conclusione del periodo di lavoro trascorso con il padrone[60]: [per] millenni innumerevoli uomini sono stati trattati non come persone, ma come oggetti [. . .] ambiguamente definiti attraverso categorie opposte, quasi fossero [. . .] anelli di congiunzione tra animale e uomo, corpo e anima, oggetto e persona" (11).[61]

In the last section of the investigation, Bodei faces a topic that Foucault—had he inhabited the new millennium—would have certainly been eager to fathom: the birth of artificial intelligence, more dehumanizing than the assembly line of the industrial era, that is progressively invading the inner mechanisms of the "entire social body" on a global scale.[62]

Mentre le macchine che abbiamo conosciuto fino a qualche decennio fa non richiedevano molta intelligenza da parte del lavoratore e ne "espropriavano" solo il corpo, quelle nuove, autonome, sono capaci di assorbirne l'intelligenza e la volontà. Per effetto delle tecnologie informatiche, della robotica e dell'insieme dei dispositivi dotati di Intelligenza Artificiale si sta infatti passando rapidamente e irresistiblilmente dalla macchina "ausiliatrice" alla macchina "sostitutrice." ("I sommersi e i salvati," 350–51, 356)[63]

While the machines that we have been acquainted with up until some decades ago did not demand a lot of intelligence on the workers' part and would "expropriate" only their bodies, the new ones, self-operating, are able to absorb human intelligence and will. As a result of computer science technologies, of robotics, and of the array of devices equipped with artificial intelligence we are shifting quickly and ineluctably from the "helping" machine to the "substitute" machine. ("The Drowned and the Saved"; translation mine)

"Non ci sono vie di fuga," writes Bodei at the end of his inquiry, describing the increasingly intrusive presence of artificial intelligence in human lives. With the courage and the ponderation of ancient Stoics, however, he suggests that his readers can find a balance between the "fear" of a possibly dehumanized future ruled by the machines and the "hope" in a novel unitarian evolution of body and mind, through which humans will be able to construct the dignified and democratic social body of the future.[64]

Concluding Remarks

Bodei and Foucault: two of the finest minds of postmodern thought, internationally acclaimed, paladins of the dignity and the freedom of the human *sōma*, stern opposers of any faceless power that subjugates and humiliates corporeality, courageous detractors of the ideologies claiming that the *sōma* is "a tomb, temple or machine," portrayers of the body as a "self."[65] What else connects their corporeal perceptions? After thorough consideration, I am inclined to say that *the idea of the sōma as a limit* is a logic-mathematic concept that—if applied to a body—refers directly to its finitude and perishable nature. Here is Bodei, three years before his death: "I limiti ci circondano e ci condizionano da ogni lato e sotto ogni aspetto a iniziare dall'involucro stesso della nostra pelle [. . .], per poi finire con il termine ultimo della morte" (*Limite*, 2018, 7).[66] The balanced *concinnitas* of Bodei's reflection reveals his humble awareness of human fragility and exhorts whoever reads it to live life fully and to celebrate the uniqueness and the beauty of the body, with the certitude that—as Bodei repeats several times through his reflections: *thanatos athanatos* (only death is immortal). Even refusing to be confined within the safe boundaries of the Kantian island of knowledge "dagli immutabili confini," and choosing to be an indefatigable and relentless searcher of truth, Bodei embraces the limit of his own human finiteness with a graceful, patient, and composed acceptance.[67] Foucault's voice, on the other hand, rings more harshly than Bodei's. From his tormented epoch of profound ideological as well as social rupture, Foucault's cry resounds more wretched, "tragic and dynamic at once," in an utterance that, along with its denial of the utopic corporeality, still aims to break in the limits of the material body, and sees it as an *atopia* or, in his own words, as an *eterotopia*, a "*lieu* [. . .] *sans lieux, hors de tous les lieux, toujours ailleurs.*"[68]

> Mais peut—être faudrait—il descender encore au-dessous du vêtement, peut—être faudrait—il atteindre la chair elle-même, et alors on verrait que dans certain cas, à la *limite, c'est le corps lui-même* qui retourne contre soi son pouvoir utopique et fait entrer tout l'espace [. . .] de l'autre monde, tout l'espace du contre-monde, à l'intérieur même de l'espace qui lui est réservé. Alors, le corps, dans sa matérialité, dans sa chair, serait comme le produit de ses propres fantasmes. Après tout, est-ce que le corps du danseur n'est pas justement un corps dilaté selon tous un espace qui lui est intérieur et extérieur à la fois? Et les drogués aussi, et les possédés, dont le corps devient enfer; le stigmatisés, dont le corps devient souffrance, rachat et salut, sanglant paradis. (*Le corps utopique*, 17)

> However, it would be necessary to go beyond the clothes, per-haps it would be necessary to reach the flesh itself, and then one will see that in certain cases, at the limit, it is the body itself that uses the utopian power against itself and lets enter all the space of the other world, and all the space of the counterworld, within the space that is reserved for it [for the body]. At that

time, within its materiality, and its flesh, it [the body] will be like the product of its own ghosts [demons]. After all, isn't the body of dancers just a dilated body in relation to all that is an interior and exterior space for them? And what about the drug addicts, what about the possessed, whose body turns into hell; what about the mystics, whose body turns in to pain, redemption, and salvation, [and] bloody paradise? (Translation mine)

If Bodei, solid and lucid Hegelian of materialistic formation, absorbs the serene teaching of the Greeks and acknowledges the corporeal caducity with an Apollonian imperturbability, Foucault harbors, till the end, the restless, Dionysian spirit that—as a common thread has been passed to him from Hölderlin via Nietzsche and Blanchot.[69] Totally fascinated by the outside, *le dehors*, Foucault throws himself *à corps perdu* into the unlimited *aorgic* abyss of the inorganic, the "tempestuous ocean" [. . .] that surrounds the wandering sailor in search of new discoveries[70]: Être attiré [. . .] c'est éprouver, dans le vide [. . .], la présence du dehors [. . .]. Le dehors est là, ouvert, sans intimité, sans protection ni retenue [. . .], le vide qui s'ouvre indéfiniment sous le pas de qui est attiré [. . .]. Les barrières sont rompues, tout déborde (2015, II, *La pensée du dehors*, 1222, 1227).[71]

The corporeality that Foucault sees as an extreme Dionysian dance (Bodei, 2008, 8) projected toward a void, luring abyss, is in the end perceived by Bodei as a sign, a *sēma that is* no longer a tomb, but—in the Homeric sense—stands, as a memorial trace and within the spirit of the Delphic precept that he dearly cherished and that says: "il Signore che sta a Delfi non dice e non nasconde, *ma fa segno [oute leghei, oute kryptei, alla semainei].*"[72]

All'orizzonte si profilano indubbiamente nuovi esperimenti, di umanità e di post-umanità in cui individui geneticamente modificati, pluritrapiantati [. . .] romperanno le barriere che separano la materia vivente dalle macchine, diventeranno un amalgama di organico e inorganico e supereranno le frontiere mentali (e persino fisiche) che dividono i sessi o gli uomini dagli altri animali [. . .]. Bisognerà attendere ancora per assistere al consolidarsi di altre forme di umanità [. . .] che esistono in germe, in quanto ogni nuovo mondo è preceduto da *messaggeri*, ma ha bisogno dell'agire degli uomini per diventare reale. (Bodei 2019, 291–92; italics mine)[73]

> On the horizon are looming new experiments of humanity and posthumanity, where individuals who [have been] genetically modified and multitransplanted will be able to break the barriers that separate organic matter from machines. They will evolve into a combination of organic and inorganic [substance] and will overcome the mental and even the physical frontiers that separate sexes or humans from other animals [. . .]. We will have to wait for a while to see the consolidation of other forms of humanity [. . .] that exist now in an unexpanded form; since every new world is preceded by messengers and needs the human action, in order to become a reality. (Translation and italics mine)

I think that in these words resides Bodei's last legacy of his ethical mission as a philosopher and as a human being: to be the objective messenger of the ongoing, unavoidable changes, to signal to us and to posterity a feasible way to "dance" with and positively adapt to change; and to open—through his exemplary *corpus* of writings—the portal for a possible way of immanent human redemption.

Acknowledgments

All my gratitude goes to Professor Paolo Cherchi for his generous and invaluable advice.

Notes

1. The expression is found in Harrison, 2008, 428.
2. See for instance the performative gender discourse of Butler, 1993.
3. The quotation derives from the "Introduction" of Barney, 2001, 1. For the *Cratylus*'s "playful and even ironic context," see Ferwerda, 1985, 269.
4. As Ford, 1994, remarks, the multifaceted nature of the word *sēma* adopted by Plato had already been present in Homeric poetry. In fact in the *Iliad* it is used not only with the meaning of a "marked grave with a tumulus and perhaps a stone stele above it" (143, 141) that "early served to mark a place as sacred," but it also indicates the "sign of the place of burial" of a hero (*Iliad* 7, 84–91) (143). It can also refer to a "clear sign" or a landmark's pivotal point, for example, the "racing goal" that "old Nestor [*Iliad* 23, 326–334] [. . .] describes to his son as he points

out to him the best turning point on a racecourse" (144). Ford's inquiry on the ambivalence of the term *sēma* in Homer was preceded by the study of Ferwerda, 1985, 271, which deals with the Homeric concept of *sēma* as "original[ly]" conveying the meaning of "memorial sign" (271). De Vogel (1986, 234), attributes to the Homeric use of word *sēma* the "connotation of a "fence" or "firm enclosure."

5. In Cooper, 1997, 118–19. The italics are mine. It has been hypothesized in late antiquity that the *"some"* to whom Plato refers to, were the followers of Pythagoreanism, an initiatory religious and philosophical school whose founder, the philosopher and mathematician Pythagoras of Samos (570–495 BCE) preached the doctrine of *metempsychosis* or transmigrations of souls. According to Pythagoras's beliefs, souls are immortal; and once the body that they occupy dies, they transmigrate in a newborn's body, and would repeat such a transmigration over and over, in an endless cycle. As Ferwerda, 268, reports: "According to Clement of Alexandria (*Strom.* 3, 3, 17) [. . .] the Pythagorean Philolaos maintained that the ancient theologians and soothsayers believed that, in order to pay penalties, the soul was yoked to the body and was buried therein as in a grave." A few pages later, Ferwerda specifies: "The line I quoted from Clement of Alexandria apparently supports this assumption, because he says that he found it in a book written by the Pythagorean Philolaus. However, we are not sure that the 'theologians' of Philolaus are the Pythagoreans and, in addition to that, there are grave doubts whether this line is a literal quotation from Philolaus' book" (270). A common source that could relate both to the Orphic mysteries and to the Pythagorean mysteries is undoubtedly the Egyptian cult of Osiris expressed through the *Papyrus of Ani*, chapter 92, in the Egyptian *Book of the Dead*, XCII, 474, chapter titled "Opening the Tomb to the Ba-Soul and Shadow": "The place which is closed is opened, the place which is shut is sealed. That which lieth down in the closed place is opened by the Ba-soul which is in it." (For ancient Egyptians, the *Ba* was one of the sections of the soul, a mobile and ethereal energy.) *Cratylus* is not the sole Platonic *locus* where the body is defined as a grave or an enclosure: see, for instance, *Gorgias*, 493a, in Cooper, 836: "Once I even heard one of the *wise men* say that we are now dead and that our bodies are our tombs." Also, for the images of imprisonment in the bodily "tomb" see, among others, *Phaedrus*, 250c, in Cooper, 528, where the dualism body-soul is conveyed through the images of the oyster and the pearl: "[We are] buried in this thing we are carrying around now; which we call a body, *locked in it* like an oyster in its shell." See also *Phaedo*, 62b (in Cooper, 54), where it is said: "There is the explanation that is put in the language of the mysteries, that we men are in a kind of *prison*, and that one must not free oneself and run away."

6. For Platonism defined by "Dewey a brood and nest of dualisms" that "dominate[d] the history of Western philosophy," see Rorty, 1999, xii, also quoted in Peters, 2004, 14. On the idea that "the [. . .] general characterization of the European philosophical tradition [. . .] consists of a series of footnotes to Plato," see Whitehead, 1979, 39.

7. On the Platonic difference between *simulacrum* and *eikon*, whereas the first is considered lesser than the second, see Smith, 2005, 89: "Simulacra" are "phantasmata" [semblances, shades], while *eicones* (icons or "copies") better represent the "ideal" Platonic "reality." The quotations are from Smith, 2006, 89. Caprotti, 2009, 99, elaborates on the concept of the body as tomb and "prison of the soul," that has been rooted across more than twenty centuries in "Western philosophy."

8. Epictetus (ca. CE 50–ca. 135) *Pneuma*, in ancient Greek was a term indicating "breath" and or "soul." Caprotti, 100, remarks how Marcus Aurelius Antoninus (AD 121–80), a Roman emperor and a Stoic philosopher, wrote in his *Meditations*, 4, 41, in Hard, 2011, 31: "You are a little soul carrying a corpse around, as Epictetus used to say." The reference to the body as a corpse, prison, and tomb of the soul is also contained in the *Hermetica* (or *Corpus Hermeticum*), VII, 2–3, in Copenhaver, 1992, 24: "You must rip off the tunic [the body] that you wear, the garment of ignorance, the foundation of vice, the bonds of corruption, the *dark cage*, the living death, the sentient *corpse*, the portable *tomb* [. . .]. Such is the odious tunic [the body] you have put on. It strangles you and drags you down with it so that [. . .] you [don't] look up and see the fair vision of truth [. . .], so that you do not hear what you must hear nor observe what you must observe" (italics mine).

9. Plotinus (CE 204/205; CE, 270).

10. The quotations are taken from Gerson, 2018, 513.

11. Porphyry, (AD 234–305), was the instrumental editor and divulgator of the *Enneads*. In his letter *Ad Marcellam* (*To Marcella*) he suggests to his wife, Marcella, that, just as "people amputate some limbs to save their lives," she "should be prepared to amputate the whole body to save [her] soul" (1987, 75). It is said that Porphyry pursued so zealously and *ad litteram* the Plotinian principles of the inferiority of the body and the disgust for it that he would (unsuccessfully) attempt to take his own life with the purpose of "liberating" his soul from its bodily prison. Sipe, 18 and passim, shows that "this dualistic understanding of the mind and the body [. . .] penetrated deeply into the core of the Western paradigm [. . .] and "because women have throughout Western culture traditionally been associated with the bodily—this sort of hierarchical dualism put forth by Porphyry and [later] by Augustine has lent a hand to patriarchy in that it justifies subjugating women as we all must struggle to control the body."

12. *The New English Bible*, 1970, 286.

13. On the image of the body as a temple in the Jewish mystical tradition, see Costa, 2010 and Garuti, 2011. On the Jewish mystical idea of the corporeal attributes of God, see Costa, 284.

14. The quotations are taken from Fredriksen, 1991, 80, 82. On the verticality of the "Hellenistic" idea of "redemption" and on the "vector of Jewish restoration theology" as "empathically horizontal [and] historical," see the same author, 80. On the Pauline construction of the collective ("communal") spiritual body see Gupta, 2010, 520–21.

15. Fredriksen, 81. I am quoting the Greek expression from Pamment, 1985, 375. On the *sōma pneumatikon,* see Corinthians 15:45–49. On the translation of the Pauline word *pneuma* not only as "spirit" but also as "mind," see Pamment, 373. On the "horizontality" of the Jewish mystic *Weltanschauung,* solidly anchored to its historical context, versus the Hellenistic vision, widely imbued with a hypostatic agenda, see Fredriksen, 80. On the threefold anthropologic components of Paul's writings that are the Jewish, the Hellenistic, and the Proto-Christian, see still Fredriksen, 80.

16. In Corinthians, 15:50, Paul clarifies the concept that only a spiritualized body can be participant of the divine.

17. The expression in quotation marks is taken from Stroumsa, 1990, 27.

18. Tertullian (CE 155–ca. 230). The first quotation is taken from Otten, 2013. The second is from Stroumsa, 25. Although he was never officially recognized as Father of the Church, Tertullian was the first theologian to adopt the word "trinity" to define the threefold essence of the divine.

19. Augustine of Hippo (CE 354–430); Thomas Aquinas (1225–1274). Irenaeus of Smyrna (CE 130/140–202) aka Irenaeus of Lyon, mirrors in his construction the Pauline "trichotomic anthropology" (Almario, 2013, 1) made of *pneuma* (spirit), *psyché* (soul), and *sōma* (body) that Paul stated in his First Epistle to the Thessalonians 5:23. On this topic see also Pamment, 53.

20. The quotation is taken from Harrison, 429.

21. The quotations are taken from Bertagni, 6: "Tommaso [nella *Summa Theologiae*] rimuove la dicotomia tra corpo e anima, ma la sostituisce con un rapporto che—partendo dalla dipendenza del corpo dall'anima—approda alla nozione dell'anima come finalità del corpo." (Thomas in his *Summa Theologiae* eliminates the dichotomy body-soul; however, he replaces it with a connection that—taking as a starting point the dependency of the body from the soul—reaches in the end the conclusion that the soul is the body's ultimate goal") (translation mine). On the same topic see Ghisalberti, 2005 and Klima, 1997.

22. Giordano Bruno (1548–1600); Tommaso Campanella (1568–1639). *Kalokagathia* is a term already used by the Greek historian Herodotus (ca. 484–425 BCE) and designates, in Aristotelian terms (*Eudemian Ethics,* VIII, 3, 1248b), an ideal perfection, both physical and moral. On the *kakokagathia* as "unity of all the virtues" in the "*Eudemian Ethics*" see Bonasio, 2020. On the founding father of modern Neoplatonism, Marsilio Ficino, and on his complex and multifaceted treatment of corporeality, which is immanent and transcendent at once, see Crawford, 2004. On Bruno's corporeality, see Jorn, 2002; on Bruno's pantheism see Wang, 2018. On Campanella, see De Lucca, 2015.

23. René Descartes (1596–1650). On "Cartesian bifurcation of reality," see Peters, 2004, 14. On the same subject, see also Schmaltz, 1992. Baruch Spinoza (1632 1677) who had the merit of integrating in his theorization philosophical rationalism and "Galilean science," rejected the Cartesian dualistic vision and introduced the concept *Deus sive natura* (God or nature, that is, the interchangeability between

God and creation). The quotations are taken from Cacioppo, 2007, 35 (translation mine). John Locke (1632–1704) further denied the "mind-body distinction" by asserting that it is only "nominal," that is, it is a problem "created by us" and it is related to our perception of reality (Kim, 2008, 440).

24. The expression is taken from Hegel, 1991, 291, paragraph 216. On the same topic see Achella, 2012, 10–15.

25. Arthur Schopenhauer (1788–1860). On Schopenhauer's vision of the body as a "unitarian phenomenon" see Giaculli, 2019, 93.

26. Italics mine.

27. It is important to remark that while Foucault was profoundly influenced by Nietzschean thought, Bodei, in his role of historian of ideas, impartially examined it as a significant contribution to the modern speculative epistemology.

28. My heartfelt thanks go to Remo Bodei's spouse, Professor Gabriella Giglioni Bodei, who graciously informed me that—although the two philosophers might never have met or exchanged correspondence—Bodei harbored a sincere admiration for the French philosopher, particularly for his idea of *parrhesia* (that is, the philosophers' moral obligation to tell the truth, at any cost).

29. The quotations are from Mitrano, 2015, 95.

30. Remo Bodei was born in Cagliari, the capital city of Sardinia. In the interview released to Benso, 2017, 19, he said: "I have never intellectually claimed [. . .] to belong to a specific philosophical national tradition. Once Richard Rorty [prominent American philosopher, 1931–2007] defined me as "the least peninsular of the Italian philosophers." By that, he meant that I had a more international formation. I answered only partly as a joke: "Yes, because I am the most insular." Actually, once I left Sardinia, which is geographically closer to Africa than to Italy, the trauma of separation was overcome. I have moved a lot, with a desire to understand the diversity of cultures but not to be influenced more than some" (translation mine). Michel Foucault was born in Poitiers, Western France. He writes about his city in a postcard dated August 13, 1981: "Such is the city where I was born: decapitated saints, book in hand, watch to assure that justice is just and chateaux strong [. . .]; that is where I inherited my wisdom." (The citations are taken from Eribon, 1991, 4).

31. In Benso, 17, Bodei defines himself as "a philosopher and an historian of ideas." Before becoming a celebrated academic Foucault held the position of director of the local French Cultural Institute in Sweden (Uppsala), Poland (Warsaw), and West Germany (Hamburg).

32. The quotation is taken from Blanchot, 1986, 11: ("A lavish baroque style beautiful to a fault, so splendid and detailed it was" (translation mine).

33. In Benso, 19, Bodei states: "In the years of my formation [. . .] I have been concerned with the aesthetics of the tragic, the ugly, and the sublime and with authors such as Hölderlin, Goethe, and Thomas Mann, who, like rough diamonds, contain ideas that philosophy can cut out, and make clearer to its own advantage."

34. "The use of literature in a philosophical key" (translation mine). The quotation is from Panella and Spena, 2006, 28. The two critics, 31, further elaborate on the Foucauldian "notion" of authoriality (for example, the author disappearing within the "unfathomable abyss of his own language") (translation mine).

35. Panella and Spena, 27, write about Foucault: "Fin dai suoi esordi come 'pensatore' [. . .] l'interesse dimostrato dallo studioso francese per la letteratura e per la scrittura letteraria è tutt'altro che occasionale e privo di rapporti con la sua produzione successiva." (Since his beginnings as a 'thinker' the interest shown by Foucault for literature and literary criticism is anything but occasional and it is strictly connected with his later production) (translation mine). As Bodei himself writes in his foreword to Panella's and Spena's volume, 9: "Per Foucault la letteratura [. . .] metamorfizza e reduplica la realtà. Sfugge contemporaneamente al principio di realtà e al principio di piacere, occupa una sorta di terzo regno tra il piatto rispecchiamento del mondo e la fantasia banalmente sfrenata. Fa morire il mondo per ricrearlo" (For Foucault literature metamorphoses and reduplicates reality. It escapes at once the principle of reality and the principle of pleasure; it occupies a kind of third realm [located] between the flat mirroring of reality and trivially unleashed creativity. It makes the world die, in order to recreate it) (translation mine). Fortier, 1993, 129, writes about "le statut interdiscursif du travail foucauldien, qui efface les frontières entre la littérature, la philosophie et l'historiographie" (the interdiscursive charter of the Foucauldian production that eliminates the boundaries between literature and historiography) (translation mine).

36. Saghafi, 1996, 79, gives a larger list of authors on whom Foucault wrote literary essays. Besides the ones mentioned above, he lists "Hölderlin, Robbe-Grillet, Sollers, Laporte, Artaud, Sade, Flaubert, Nerval." Foucault showed a profound admiration for Blanchot during his *apprentissages*. As reported in Eribon, 58: "Thus began the period of Foucault's fascination with literature, which would last until the end of the 1960s when it gave way to a more political perspective. Foucault once described the 1950s to [the historian] Paul Veyne: "At that time, I dreamt of being Blanchot," and said that he had been a passionate reader of Blanchot's columns, published regularly in the *Nouvelle Revue Française* (NRF)."

37. In *Una scintilla di fuoco*, a manual of philosophy assembled for Italian high school students, 2005, 6, and dedicated to all "his students scattered around the world," Remo Bodei explained the inner essence of philosophy by quoting Plato's *Seventh Letter*, 341 C–D: "La filosofia non è una disciplina che sia lecito insegnare come le altre; solo dopo una lunga frequentazione e convivenza col suo contenuto essa si manifesta nell'anima, come una luce che subitamente si accende da una scintilla di fuoco, per nutrirsi poi di se stessa" (Platone, Settima Lettera 341 C–D)" (Philosophy is not a discipline that we are allowed to teach as any other [subject]; only after a long acquaintance and coexistence it manifests itself in our soul as a light that suddenly originates from a spark of fire and then consumes itself [Plato, *Seventh Letter*, 341 C–D]) (translation mine).

38. This is Foucault's own definition of *parrhesia*, 2001, 19: "Parrhesia is a kind of verbal activity where the speaker has a specific relation to truth through frankness, a certain relationship to his own life through danger, a certain type of relation to himself or other people through criticism (self-criticism or criticism of other people), and a specific relation to moral law through freedom and duty." Bodei, on the courage required by philosophers, also wrote the following in *Una scintilla di fuoco*, 20, quoting Foucault in the paragraph titled "Il coraggio del filosofo" (the philosopher's courage): "Sulla scia di questo esempio [Socrate] il filosofo comincia a configurarsi come un uomo capace di pronunciare e argomentare verità sgradevoli a chi non vuole intenderle e di non recedere davanti ai pericoli e alle minacce che esse suscitano" (In the wake of Socrates's example philosophers start to appear as men able to utter and debate a disagreeable truth and to utter it to whoever does not want to [hear and] understand it. [The philosopher] is [also able] not to back down in face of the dangers and the threats that such a truth can raise against him) (translation mine). As well remarked by Miller, 2018, 4, Foucault's apparent "withdrawal from the political arena" during "his final years of life and his 'return' to the philosophers of the ancient world, and specifically to Socrates and Plato" was not a "renunciation of commitment" as some critical commentators have inferred. Miller, 5, also stresses that indeed, "in Foucault's turn to Plato what we see is not a capitulation to a fundamentally conservative nostalgia but a radical re-envisioning of what it means to be an intellectual, of what it means to speak truth to power, of what Plato saw as the essence of philosophy." Candiotto, 2020, 298, further elaborates on Miller's theses and shows "how much" the French philosopher learned from a very Socratic Plato in his development of "an account of transformative philosophy as a mode of life embedded in the power dynamics." On Foucaldian *parrhesia*, see also Dyrberg, 2016.

39. On the interpretation of the Platonic notion of *parrhesia* see Foucault, 2010 and 2011. See Bodei, 2005, 21, on the topic: "Nell'intento di conservare la propria coerenza, di testimoniare con la vita la validità delle proprie teorie, di mostrare che non è un semplice perdigiorno dedito a mettere in imbarazzo gli altri o un sognatore desideroso di sovvertire le tradizioni e le credenze di un popolo per creare un ordine sociale impossibile, il filosofo diventa colui che si assume la responsabilità delle proprie convinzioni ed è per questo talvolta condannato e ucciso" (With the aim to keep their own coherence and to witness with their own life the validity of their theories, and to show that they are not mere loafers devoted to embarrassing others, or [that they are not] some dreamers who wish to subvert the traditions and the beliefs of a people in order to create an impossible social order, philosophers become the ones who take upon themselves the responsibility of their own convictions and it is for this reason that sometimes they are condemned and killed) (translation mine). A persistent reader of Foucault, Bodei, 2008, 126–27, ideally placed the French *philosophe* next to Plato in his love for truth:

Il desiderio di produrre soggettività in "giochi di verità" aperti caratterizza—secondo Foucault—la nostra civiltà. Rappresenta, anzi, il contrassegno [. . .] degli uomini occidentali. Ma dire la verità significa soprattutto accettare una verità rischiosa, contrapporsi rischiosamente ai detentori del potere. Implica una sfida frontale nei confronti dell'autorità della tradizione e il reciso rifiuto delle menzogne ufficiali, il testimoniare la verità con le proprie scelte e la propria vita, come quando lo stesso Foucault esce dal Pcf nel momento in cui la morte di Stalin viene attribuita a una congiura di medici ebrei. La *parrhesia* ha un costo, esige *coraggio*. È il coraggio mostrato da Socrate dinanzi ai suoi accusatori o quello di Platone quando si imbarca per Siracusa con la prospettiva di convertire dapprima il tiranno Dionigi I, poi Dionigi II, alle sue idee, in modo da radicarle nello stato e da far loro assumere corpo e realtà. "Se fossi riuscito a persuadere un solo uomo, avrei assicurato il compimento di tutto il bene possibile. Con questo pensiero e con questa ardita speranza salpai, non per la ragione che alcuni credevano, ma perché mi vergognavo molto di apparire di fronte a me stesso *un uomo capace solo di parole*" [Platone, 7° lettera, 328c]. Anzi per l'esattezza nella *Settima lettera* si dice: "di non apparire solo parola di fronte a me stesso." Così, arditamente, a sessant'anni, Platone mette in gioco tutto: la vita, la fama, la sicurezza. È, del resto, tipico della saggezza antica, mantenere la coerenza tra i propri insegnamenti e la propria condotta. Né Platone, né Foucault, avrebbero accettato di scambiare la verità con l'opinione della maggioranza.

The desire to produce subjectivity in open "games of truth," characterizes—according to Foucault—the civilization of Western human beings. But telling the truth means above all to accept a risky truth, to perilously counteract those who are in power. It involves a frontal challenge of authority and tradition, as well as it implies the drastic rebuttal of official lies, [it requires one] to be the witness of truth through one's own choices and one's own life, as when [for instance] Foucault himself quit the French Communist Party when Stalin's death was ascribed to an [alleged] conspiracy of Jewish physicians. Parrhesia has a price, requires courage. It is the same courage shown by Socrates before his accusers, or Plato's courage when he sails to Syracuse with the intent to convert to his ideas first the tyrant Dionysius I, then Dionysius II, so that his [Plato's] ideas could be rooted within the state and could become a reality. [Plato writes]: "If I had been able to convince even only one man, I would have ensured the accomplishment of every possible good. With this thought and this intrepid hope [says Plato], I sailed, and not for any other reason that was guessed by others, but because I was ashamed to appear to myself as a man only able to utter words" [Plato, 7th Letter 328c]. Indeed, to be precise [Plato] in the Seventh letter says [verbatim]: "Not to appear only as a word to myself." In so doing Plato, at sixty years of age, courageously puts everything at stake: life, fame, safety. Keeping consistency between one's teachings and one's conduct is, after all, [an attitude] typical of ancient wisdom. Neither Plato, nor Foucault would have accepted to swap the truth with the views of the majority) (translation mine).

As remarked by Caramore in her preface to Bodei, 2001, 7, the Italian philosopher has faced the problem of atheism with "l'onestà di approccio di un filosofo che non suppone di aver trovato la chiave di comprensione che apra tutte le porte della realtà, ma si dichiara esplicitamente 'nel mezzo' del cammino della ricerca, pronto ad aprirsi su nuovi squarci d'orizzonte, ad arricchire l'inventario del paesaggio, a mutare sentiero qualora se ne presenti uno ancora insondato" (The honesty of approach of a philosopher who does not assume to have found the key to open all the doors of reality, but who overtly declares to be in the middle of the path of his quest, being ready to open [his mind] on new glimpses of the horizon, and to enrich the inventory of his landscape, [ready even] to switch path if another path still unfathomed, appears) (translation mine). Opposite Bodei's flexibility, stands Foucault's more pronounced adherence to atheism and his interest in "some religions" (above all, the Christian one), only because "of their salience in the genealogy of contemporary forms of power" (Jordan, 2015, 10).

40. The quotations belong to Bodei, 2008, 124 (translation mine).

41. Bodei, 1997, 146. (Up until now Western human beings had to conquer their own identity only counteracting *the other than himself* [the alterity] their suppressed [emotions], their negative [side]of themselves) (translation mine).

42. The Foucauldian notion of "*askesis,*" 2015, II, 763, is based on the original meaning of the Greek word *exercise.* As McWhorter, 1992, 243, writes: "In the Introduction to the *The Use of Pleasure* Foucault calls his work an *askēsis,* "an exercise of oneself in the activity of thought."

43. Foucault, 2015, II, 1008, defines the concept of *epimeleia autou* and dwells on the multiformity of its roots that include also Platonism: "*L'epimeleia autou, la cura sui,* est une injonction qu'on retrouve dans beaucoup de doctrines philosophiques. On la recontre chez les Platoniciens." (The *epimeleia autou,* the *cura sui,* is an injunction that can be found in many philosophical doctrines. It can be found among Plato's followers) (translation mine). On the topic, see also Gros, 2005; and Iftode, 2013.

44. In his monumental *Geometry of the Passions,* 303, Bodei defines *philautia* [*amour-propre,* love and respect of self] in both Aristotelian and Spinozan terms, as *utilitas* and assimilates it to the Stoic concept of *oikeiosis,* that is "the act of

appropriating oneself, feeling in some way at home in the world" and therefore as "the inclination in which every living being tries to reconcile itself with itself."

45. As Bodei, 2008, 125, writes: "Tipico della tradizione occidentale, nelle sue radici classiche e cristiane, sembra proprio essere l'impegno costante ad approfondire, in misura maggiore, rispetto alle altre civiltà del pianeta, le forme di scissione e di presa di distanza da sé, le procedure e le tecniche dello sdoppiarsi, del guardarsi come un altro da sé" (An attitude typical of Western tradition in [both] its classical and Christian roots seems to be indeed the constant commitment to examine in depth—and to a greater extent than other world's civilizations—the forms of separation and of distancing from the self, the procedures and the techniques of the doubling, [that is] of looking at oneself as to an other than himself) (translation mine).

46. The interest on ethics and morality as in ancient Greece's and Rome's epistemology, although already present in all his works, culminates in the elucidations of Foucault, 2005. The words in quotation marks are taken from Candiotto, 299.

47. Foucault, 2015, 720, 399 ("social body"; "docile bodies"), translation from Foucault, 1995, 90, 135.

48. The quotations are taken from Foucault, 2015, 291. (The soul in fact in the tool of a political anatomy: the soul, the prison of the body) (translation and italics mine).

49. *Ataraxia* (ataraxy) is a term that is used in the Epicurean and Stoic schools of thought that indicated a lucid, detached, and imperturbable state of mind.

50. The first part of the quotation is taken from Bodei, 2013, 9, the second part belongs to a booklet by Bodei titled: *Ospiti della vita*, published in a limited edition (only 49 copies) by Numa, a cultural laboratory located in Lumezzane (Brescia), 2006. (The sentence in italics can be found verbatim also in Bodei, 2002, 84.)

51. Helmuth Plessner (1892–1985) stated that humans identify themselves either with having a body (*Körperhaben*) or with being a body (*Leibsein*). Plessners's theories influenced, among others, Maurice Merleau-Ponty (1908–1961) and Jean-Paul Sartre (1905–1980). Foucault, 2009, 14, expresses the same concept: "Pour être utopique, il suffit que je sois un corps" (In order to be utopian, it is sufficient for me to be a body) (translation mine). In Bodei's production the ideological discourse is never frontal but proceeds *per cenni* (by glimpses) following Socrates's method of the *maieutikē tēchne*, or maeutics (art of midwives) according to which disciples must find the answers by themselves and teachers must only function as helpers/facilitators who ask questions.

52. A term literally meaning higher than heaven, by which Plato designated the immaterial locus (higher than the Greek Pantheon), where all perfect forms (ideas) engendering material reality, reside.

53. *Entelecheia* (entelechy): a term used by Aristotle to indicate something that potentially harbors life through a dynamic (energetic) process (*De anima*, II, 412).

54. The reference is to Spinoza's *Ethics* (1677). In *Geometry of the Passions*, 272, Bodei writes about the Spinozan concept of "energy of the body that [. . .] progressively" accompanies "growth in the functions of the soul."

55. Epicurus (341–270 BCE), stated that the soul is material, made of atoms lighter than the corporeal ones. For the influence of Epicurean philosophy on Nietzsche, see Knight, 1933.

56. Bodei, 2002, 81 (translation mine).

57. The Foucauldian microphysics of power and biopower indicate, respectively, the capillary diffusion of social control that power exerts on body and mind, and the management and control implemented by power on both individual bodies and entire populations. Bodei, 2008, 131, writes: "Il lavoro di Foucault—costitutiva-mente interminabile, perché non potrà mai giungere all' 'ombelico' del soggetto—è tuttavia filosoficamente inaggirabile *e meriterebbe di essere proseguito*" (Foucault's work—structurally endless, because it will never be able to reach the "navel" [the center] of the subject, is however philosophically unavoidable and would be worth continuing) (translation and italics mine).

58. (The separation and the subjugation [. . .] [of] bodies). The quotations are taken from Foucault, 2015, I, 429, and II, 483. On the Foucauldian concept of *partage*, see Bodei, 1986, 899:

> Il s'agit essentiellement d'utilizer des dispositifs d'exclusion, qui ne consistent seulement en négations, en interdictions [. . .], mais en opérations de subdivision e de distribution, dans le *partage*—et ceci vaut aussi dans le cas du "pouvoir." Le terme "partage" reproduit le mot allemand *Urteil*, Jugement, dans le sens étymologique de *Ur-teilung* (division ou partition originaire) que lui donnent Hölderlin, Hegel et Heidegger. Le partage est donc l'opération qui sépare, isole, divise—par des mécanismes de pouvoir—le sens du non-sens. Le régime de vérité qui se produit par le biais d'un tel partage est un régime de pouvoir.

> It is about utilizing exclusion devices that are not only made of denials and interdictions [. . .] but also of operations of subdivision and distribution, within the *partage*—and this is also valid in the case of "power." The term "partage" reproduces the German word *Urteil*, Judgement, in its etymological sense of *Ur-teilung* (original division or separation) that is given by Hölderlin, Hegel and Heidegger. Partage is therefore the operation that separates, isolates—divides, through power mechanisms—sense from nonsense. The regime of truth that is produced by the bias of such partage is a power regime. (translation mine)

59. Foucault 1982, 221: "Slavery is not a power where a man is in chains. In this case it is a question of a physical relationship of constraint," Bodei, 2019, 14. (The phenomenon of slavery undertakes a sudden change of scale reaching a planetary dimension that involves in the "Transatlantic slave trade" the life and destiny of the inhabitants of three continents: America, Europe, and Africa) (translation mine).

60. Bodei, 2010, 58, talking about euthanasia in an interview released to Daniela Monti, stated: "Ci sono molte funzioni della vita organica che non dipendono dalla nostra volontà e dalle nostre intenzioni [. . .]. Su questi automatismi, estranei alla nostra volontà e alla nostra coscienza [. . .] la Chiesa fonda la concezione che la vita non ci appartiene, arrivando fino a sostenere, secondo la metafora biblica, che il corpo sia una sorta di livrea che il servo riconsegna, a conclusione del periodo di lavoro trascorso col padrone." (There are many functions of organic life that are independent from our will and our intentions [. . .]. On such automatisms, that are alien to our will and our consciousness, the Church founded the conviction that life does not belong to us, going as far as stating, along with the pertinent biblical metaphor, that the body is a kind of livery which the servant gives back at the end of the stint spent at the service of his master) (translation mine).

61. (For millennia countless human beings have been treated not as humans, but as objects [. . .], ambiguously defined through opposite categories, as if they were connecting rings between animals and humans, body and soul, object and person) (translation mine).

62. The words in quotations are from Foucault, 1995, 89.

63. While the machines that we have been acquainted with up until some decades ago did not demand a lot of intelligence on the workers' part and would "expropriate" only their bodies, the new ones, self-operating, are able to absorb human intelligence and will. As a result of computer science technologies, of robotics, and of the array of devices equipped with artificial intelligence we are shifting quickly and ineluctably from the "helping" machine to the "substitute" machine ("The Drowned and the Saved") (translation mine).

64. Bodei, 2019, 380. ("There are no escape routes") (translation mine). The quoted words are taken from the subtitle of Bodei's *Geometry of the Passions*.

65. The quotations are from Synnott's title.

66. (The limits surround us and affect us on all sides, and in all aspects starting from the very shell of our skin [. . .] to end then with the last limit: death) (translation mine).

67. In his book of 1987 titled *Scomposizioni*, 61, Bodei writes about Immanuel Kant and about a nautical metaphor contained in his *Critique of Pure Reason* (1781) by which the German philosopher defines knowledge. For Kant "the territory of pure intellect is an island" with "immutable boundaries," surrounded by a "vast and tempestuous ocean" (Translation mine).

68. Formaggio, 1997, 173, writing on George Bataille (1897–1962), an author who was foundational in Foucault's formation, says that Bataille constructed in his works a "materialismo tragico e dinamico insieme" (materialistic vision that is tragic and dynamic at once) (translation mine). The words in quotations are from Foucault, 1995, 89.

Atopy, a philosophical term designating a "place without place." Foucault, 2009, 12, 10, 17 ("A place without a place [. . .], outside of any place [. . .], always elsewhere") (translation mine). On the notion of heterotopia, see Foucault, 1986.

69. The antinomy between Apollonian and Dionysian aesthetics was first illustrated by the archeologist Johann Joachim Winckelmann (1717–1768). With the first term, Winckelmann referred to the serene, harmonious, and balanced sculpture and architecture of ancient Greece inspired by Apollon; with the second term, he would indicate the chaotic, emotional, and primeval tone of lyrical Greek poetry, inspired by Dionysus. The two concepts exerted a profound fascination on Nietzsche who, in his *Birth of Tragedy* (1872), expressed his profound attraction toward the Dionysian *Weltanschauung*. In Panella and Spena, 9, Bodei writes: "Al pari di Nietzsche, Bataille, Blanchot, anche Foucault cerca [. . .], così dice, di giungere tramite l'esperienza a quel punto della vita che è il più vicino possibile all'impossibilità di vivere: al suo punto limite per coglierne il massimo di intensità" (Like Nietzsche, Bataille, and Blanchot, even Foucault—so he says—tries to reach, via his own experience, that point of life that is as close as possible to the impossibility of living; [he attempts] to reach the limits of life, the tipping point of it, to seize the fullest potential of its intensity") (translation mine).

70. Waibel, 2021, 99, writes: "Aorgic [. . .] seems to be a neologism that [Friedrich] Hölderlin [1770–1843] coined in [is unfinished play titled] *The Death of Empedocles* [1797–1800], and [is a term] that he opposed to the organic." Bodei, 1980, 27, writes about how Hölderlin gives the term *aorgic* the meaning of "incomprehensible, not perceivable, limitless."

71. (To be attracted is to feel in the void the presence of the outside. The outside is there, open, devoid of any sort of intimacy, protection, restraint [. . .]. The void, that unravels indefinitely, below the steps of whom is attracted by it [. . .]. The boundaries are broken. Everything overflows) (translation mine).

72. The citation is taken from Heraclitus's Fragment 97DK, contained in Bodei, 2008, 127. (The Lord who is in Delphi, does not say and does not hide, he simply signals) (translation mine).

73. (On the horizon are looming new experiments of humanity and posthumanity, where individuals who [have been] genetically modified and multitransplanted will be able to break the barriers that separate organic matter from machines. They will evolve into a combination of organic and inorganic [substances] and will overcome the mental and even the physical frontiers that separate sexes or humans from other animals [. . .]. We will have to wait for a while to see the consolidation of other forms of humanity [. . .] that exist now in an unexpanded form; since every new world is preceded by messengers and needs the human action, in order to become a reality) (translation and italics mine).

Bibliography

Achella, Stefania. "Un 'mistero incomprensibile': Il problema mente-corpo nella filosofia dello spirito di Hegel." *Etica & politica* XIV, no. 2 (2012): 8–27.

Almario, Guillermo. "Antropologia tricotomica di Paolo in 1 Tes 5, 23." https://guillermo almario.wordpress.com/2013/06/06/antropologia-tricotomica-di-paolo-in-1tes-523.

Barney, Rachel. *Names and Nature in Plato's "Cratylus."* Routledge, 2001.

Benso, Silvia. "Logics of Delusion, Passions, and Time: A Conversation with Remo Bodei." In *Viva Voce: Conversations with Italian Philosophers*, 17–26. State University of New York Press, 2017.

Bertagni, Gianfranco. *Percorso tematico: Il corpo e la dimensione della corporeità*, 1–30. Accessed December 15, 2024. http://www.gianfrancobertagni.it/materiali/corpo/grussu.pdf.

Blanchot, Maurice. *Michel Foucault tel que je l'imagine.* Fata Morgana, 1986.

Boccadoro, Brenno. "Marsilio Ficino: The Soul and the Body of Counterpoint." In *Number to Sound: The Musical Way to the Scientific Revolution*. Edited by Paolo Gozza, 99–134. Kluwer Academic, 2000.

Bodei, Remo. *Dominio e sottomissione: Schiavi, animali, macchine, Intelligenza Artificiale.* Il Mulino, 2019.

Bodei, Remo. *Geometry of the Passions: Fear, Hope, Happiness: Philosophy and Political Use.* Translated by Gianpiero W. Doebler. University of Toronto Press, 2018.

Bodei, Remo. *Limite.* Il Mulino, 2018.

Bodei, Remo. *Immaginare altre vite. Realtà, progetti, desideri.* Feltrinelli, 2013.

Bodei, Remo. "L'epoca dell'antidestino." In *Che cosa vuol dire morire.* Edited by Daniela Monti, 53–78. Einaudi, 2010.

Bodei, Remo. "Il dire la verità nella genealogia del soggetto occidentale." In *Foucault, oggi.* Edited by Mario Galzigna, 124–33. Feltrinelli, 2008.

Bodei, Remo. *Piramidi di tempo: Storie e teorie del* déjà vu. Il Mulino, 2006.

Bodei, Remo. *Ospiti della vita:* Numa di Lumezzane, 2006.

Bodei, Remo. *Una scintilla di fuoco.* Zanichelli, 2005.

Bodei, Remo. *Destini personali: L'età della colonizzazione delle coscienze.* Feltrinelli, 2002.

Bodei, Remo. *I senza Dio. Figure e momenti dell'ateismo.* Edited by Gabriella Caramore. Morcelliana, 2001.

Bodei, Remo. *Le logiche del delirio. Ragione, affetti, follia.* Laterza, 2000.

Bodei, Remo. *La filosofia nel Novecento.* Donzelli, 1997.

Bodei, Remo. *Scomposizioni. Forme dell'individuo moderno.* Einaudi, 1987.

Bodei, Remo. "Foucault: pouvoir, politique et maîtrise de soi." *Critique* XLII, no. 471–72 (1986): 898–917.

Bonasio, Giulia. "*Kalokagathia* and the Unity of the Virtues in the *Eudemian Ethics.*" *Apeiron* 53, no. 1 (2020): 27–57.

Butler, Judith. *Bodies that Matter: On the Discursive Limits of "Sex."* Routledge, 1993.

Cacioppo, Maria Angela. "L'etica ontologica: Cartesio e Spinoza a confronto." *Spiragli* XIX, no. 1 (2007): 35–37.

Candiotto, Laura. "Care of the Self and Politics: Michel Foucault Heir of a Forgotten Plato?" In *Platonism: Ficino to Foucault*. Edited by Valery Rees, Anna Corrias, Francesca M. Crasta, Laura Follesa, and Guido Giglioni. Brill, 2020.

Caprotti, Erminio. "La metafora dell'ostrica e la condizione umana." *Bollettino Malacologico* 45 (2009): 99–104.

Costa, José. "Le corps de Dieu dans le Judaïsme rabbinique ancien: Problèmes d'interprétation." *Revue de l'histoire des religions* 3 (2010): 283–316.

Crawford, Katherine. "Marsilio Ficino, Neoplatonism, and the Problem of Sex." *Renaissance and Reformation* 28, no. 2 (2004): 3–35.

De Lucca, Jean-Paul. *Corpo, spirito e anima-mente: l'antropologia della libertà in Campanella*. Olschki, 2015.

De Vogel, Cornelia J. "The *Sōma-Sēma* Formula: Its Function in Plato and Plotinus Compared to Its Use by Christian Writers." In *Rethinking Plato and Platonism*, 233–48. Brill, 1986.

Dyrberg, Torben B. "Foucault on 'Parrhesia': The Autonomy of Politics and Democracy." *Political Theory* 44, no. 2 (2016): 265–88.

The Egyptian Book of the Dead: The Hieroglyphic Transcript of the Papyrus of Ani, the Translation into English and an Introduction by E. A. Wallis Budge, Late Keeper of the Egyptian and Assyrian Antiquities in the British Museum. University Books, 1960.

Eribon, Didier. *Michel Foucault*. Translated by Betsy Wing. Harvard University Press, 1991.

Falk, Pasi. "Corporeality and Its Fates in History." *Acta Sociologica* 28, no. 2 (1985): 115–36.

Ferwerda, Rein. "The Meaning of the Word *Sōma* in Plato's *Cratylus* 400 C." *Hermes* 113, no. 3 (1985): 266–79.

Ford, Andrew. "The Text: Signs of Writing in Homer." In *Homer: The Poetry of the Past*, Cornell University Press, 1994, 131–71.

Formaggio, Dino. "L'esplosione della filosofia nello Hegel di Bataille." *Belfagor* 52, no. 2 (1997): 171–78.

Fortier, Frances. "Michel Foucault: L'espace textuel d'un double langage." *Etudes littéraires* 25, no. 3 (1993): 129–44.

Foucault, Michel. *Surveiller et punir: Naissance de la prison*. In *Oeuvres*, II. Edition publiée sous la direction de Frédéric Gros. Avec, pour ce volume, la collaboration de Jean-François Bert, Daniel Defert, François Delaporte et Philippe Sabot, 263–612. Gallimard, 2015.

Foucault, Michel. *La pensée du dehors*. In *Oeuvres*, II. Edition publiée sous la direction de Frédéric Gros. Avec, pour ce volume, la collaboration de Jean-François Bert, Daniel Defert, François Delaporte et Philippe Sabot, 1214–37.

Foucault, Michel. *The Courage of Truth: Lectures at the Collège de France*, 1983–1984. Translated by Graham Burchell. Palgrave Macmillan, 2011.

Foucault, Michel. *The Government of Self and Others: Lectures at the Collège de France 1982–83*. Translated by Graham Burchell. Palgrave Macmillan, 2010.

Foucault, Michel. *Le corps utopique, Les hétérotopies.* Edited by Daniel Defert. Nouvelles Editions Lignes, 2009.

Foucault, Michel. *The Hermeneutics of the Subject: Lectures at the Collège de France 1981–1982.* Translated from French by Graham Burchell. Palgrave Macmillan, 2005.

Foucault, Michel. *Naissance de la biopolitique.* (Cours au Collège de France 1978–79). Edited by Michel Sellenart. Seuil, 2004.

Foucault, Michel. *Fearless Speech.* Edited by Joseph Pearson. Semiotext(e), 2001.

Foucault, Michel. *Discipline and Punish: The Birth of the Prison.* Translated from French by Alan Sheridan. Vintage Books, 1995.

Foucault, Michel. "Of Other Spaces." Translated from French by J. Miskowiec. *Diacritics* 16, no. 1 (1986): 22–27.

Foucault, Michel. "The Subject and Power:" *Michel Foucault: Beyond Structuralism and Ermeneutics.* 2nd ed. Edited by Hubert L. Dreyfus and Paul Rabinow. University of Chicago Press, 1982.

Fredriksen, Paula. "Vile Bodies: Paul and Augustine on the Resurrection of the Flesh." In *Biblical Hermeneutics in Historical Perspective.* Edited by Mark S. Burrows and Paul Rorem, 75–87. William B. Eerdmans, 1991.

Garuti, Paolo. "Il Tempio e il Corpo, antica concezione del sacro e Nuovo Testamento." *Angelicum* 88, no. 3 (2011): 813–28.

Genest, Olivette. "L'autre du corps dans la Bible." *Théologiques* (on the theme: *Le Corps: du Dualisme à l'altérité*) 5, no. 2 (1997): 51–70.

Ghisalberti, Alessandro. "Anima e corpo in Tommaso d'Aquino." *Rivista di filosofia neo-scolastica* 97, no. 2 (2005): 281–96.

Giaculli, Fiorella. Tra metafisica e fisiologia: Il corpo quale fenomeno unitario in Schopenhauer, Cabanis e Bichat." *Voluntas: Revista internacional de filosofía* 10, no. 1 (2019): 93–109.

Gros, Frédéric. "Le souci de soi chez Michel Foucault: A Review of the Hermeneutics of the Subject: Lectures at the Collège de France, 1981–1982." *Philosophy and Social Criticism* 31, no. 5–6 (2005): 697–708.

Gupta, Nijay, K. "Which Body Is a Temple (1 Corinthians 6:19)? Paul Beyond the Individual/Communal Divide." *Catholic Biblical Quarterly* 72, no. 3 (2010): 518–36.

Harrison, Paul. "Corporeal Remains: Vulnerability, Proximity, and Living on after the End of the World." *Environment and Planning* 40 (2008): 423–45.

Hegel, Georg Wilhelm Friedrich. *The Enciclopaedia Logic (with the Zusätze).* A new translation with Introduction and notes by T. F. Geraets, W. A. Suchting, and H. S. Harris. Hackett, 1991.

Hermetica. The Greek *Corpus Hermeticum* and the Latin *Asclepius* in a new English translation, with notes and introduction by Brian P. Copenhaver. Cambridge University Press, 1992.

Hölderlin, Friedrich. *Sul tragico.* Edited by Remo Bodei, 5–48. Feltrinelli, 1980.

Iftode, Cristian. "Foucault's Idea of Philosophy as "Care of the Self": Critical Assessment and Conflicting Metaphilosophical Views." *Procedia: Social and Behavioral Sciences* 71 (2013): 76–85.

Jordan, Mark D. *Convulsing Bodies: Religion and Resistance in Foucault.* Stanford University Press, 2015.

Jorn, Ole. "Corporeità in Bruno: Senso e figura." *Bruniana & Campanelliana* 8, no. 1 (2002): 159–80.

Kim, Han-Kyul. "Locke and the Mind-Body Problem: An Interpretation of His Agnosticism." *Philosophy* 83, no. 326 (2008), 439–58.

Klima, Gyula. "Man = Body + Soul: Aquinas's Arithmetic of Human Nature." Lecture. 3nd International Congress on Medieval Studies, Western Michigan University. May 11, 1997. Accessed December 10, 2024. https://faculty.fordham.edu/klima/bodysoul.htm.

Knight, A. H. J. "Nietzsche and Epicurean Philosophy." *Philosophy* 8, no. 32 (1933): 431–45.

Lee, Lisa Y. *Dialectics of the Body: Corporeality in the Philosophy of T. W. Adorno.* Routledge, 2014.

Letteratura e psicoanalisi. Edited by Remo Bodei. Zanichelli, 1974.

Marcus Aurelius. *Meditations.* Translated by Robin Hard. Oxford University Press, 2011.

McWhorter, Ladelle. "Asceticism/Askēsis: Foucault's Thinking Historical Subjectivity." In *Ethics and Danger: Essays on Heidegger and Continental Thought.* Edited by Arleen B. Dallery, Charles E. Scott, and P. Holley-Roberts, 243–54. State University of New York Press, 1992.

Miller, Paul A. "Queering Plato: Foucault on Philosophy as Self-fashioning and Resistance in Plato's 7th Letter." *TRANS-Revue de littérature générale et comparée: Littérature comparée et Gender* 23 (2018): 1–13. DOI: https://doi.org/10.4000/trans.1807.

Mitrano, Mena. "Field or Movement?" Introduction to *Forum: American Studies and Italian Theory: RSA Journal. Rivista di Studi Americani* 26 (2015): 95–105.

The New English Bible. The New Testament. 2nd ed. Cambridge University Press, 1970.

Nietzsche, Friedrich W. *Thus Spake Zarathustra: A Book for All and None.* Floating Press, 2009.

Otten, Willemien. "Tertullian's Rhetoric of Redemption. Flesh and Embodiment in *De carne Christi* and *De resurrectione mortuorum.*" In *Studia Patristica*, vol. LXV. Edited by Markus Vinzent, 331–48. Peeters, 2013.

Pamment, Margaret. "Raised a Spiritual Body: Bodily Resurrection According to Paul." *New Blackfriars* 66, no. 783 (1985): 372–88.

Panella, Giuseppe, and Giovanni Spena. *Il lascito Foucault.* Clinamen, 2006.

Peters, Michael. "Education and the Philosophy of the Body: Bodies of Knowledge and Knowledges of the Body." In *Knowing Bodies, Moving Minds: Towards Embodied Teaching and Learning.* Edited by Liora Bresler, 13–27. Kluwer Academic Publishers, 2004.

Plato. *Complete Works*. Edited, with Introduction and Notes, by John M. Cooper. Associate Editor D. S. Hutchinson. Hackett, 1997.

Plotinus. *Enneads*. Edited by Lloyd P. Gerson. Translated by George Boys-Stones, John M. Dillon, Lloyd P. Gerson, R. A. H. King, Andrew Smith, and James Wilberding. Cambridge University Press, 2018.

Porphyry. *To Marcella*. Edition, translation and notes by Kathleen O'Brien Wicker. Scholar Press, 1987.

Porphyry. "On the Life of Plotinus and the Order of His Books." *In Plotinus: Porphyry on Plotinus, Ennead I*. Edited and translated by A. H. Armstrong. Harvard University Press, 1966.

Porter, James. I. *Constructions of the Classical Body*. University of Michigan Press, 1999.

Rorty, Richard. *Philosophy and Social Hope*. Penguin Books, 1999.

Rossi Monti, Martino. "Il carcere, la tomba, il fango. Sulla fortuna di alcune immagini da Platone all'età di Plotino." *Atque. Materiali tra filosofia e psicoterapia* 18 (2016): 181–202.

Saghafi, Kas. "The "Passion for the Outside:" Foucault, Blanchot, and Exteriority." *International Studies in Philosophy* XXVIII, no. 4 (1996): 79–92.

Schmaltz, Tad M. "Descartes and Malebranche on Mind and Mind-Body Union." *Philosophical Review* 101, no. 2 (1992): 281–325.

Sipe, Dera. "Struggling with Flesh: Soul/Body Dualism in Porphyry and Augustine." *Concept* 29 (2006): 1–38. https://concept.journals.villanova.edu/article/view/266/229.

Smith, Daniel, W. "The Concept of the Simulacrum: Deleuze and the Overturning of Platonism." *Continental Philosophy Review* 38 (2005): 89–123.

Stroumsa, Gedaliahu G. "*Caro salutis cardo*: Shaping the Person in Early Christian Thought." *History of Religions: The Body*, 30, no. 1 (1990): 25–50.

Synnott, Anthony. "Tomb, Temple, Machine and Self: The Social Construction of the Body." *The British Journal of Sociology* 43, no. 1 (1992): 79–110.

Vercellone, Federico, and Emilio Carlo Corriero, eds. *Cristalli di storicità. Saggi in onore di Remo Bodei*. Rosenberg & Sellier, 2019.

Waibel, Violetta, L. "Hölderlin's Idea of "Bildungstrieb": A Model from Yesteryear?" in *Bildung and Paideia*. Edited by Marie-Élise Zovko and John M. Dillon, 92–103. Routledge, 2021.

Wang, Zheng. "Bruno's Organic Universe and the Natural Magic." *International Journal of Theology, Philosophy, and Science* 2, no. 2 (2018): 105–16.

Whitehead, Alfred N. *Process and Reality: An Essay in Cosmology*. Eds. David R. Griffin and Donald W. Sherburne. The Free Press, 1979.

7

Hölderlin

A Tortured Soul Tragically Trapped Between a "Destitute Time" and Utopia

Christoph Wulf

March 19th, 2020 marked the 250th anniversary of the birth of Friedrich Hölderlin, one of the greatest poets in the German language. This occasion was celebrated by many discussions of his work. Quite rightly it was pointed out that people have constantly tried to use Hölderlin for their own political or philosophical ends. More than 100,000 copies of Hölderlin's poems were handed out to soldiers in the Second World War to encourage them to be prepared to be killed for the fatherland. Because of his love of nature and the "Heimat," the National Socialists reinvented Hölderlin as a nationalist prepared to sacrifice himself for the nation. They concealed his democratic and republican philosophy of life and his desire for freedom. In the student movement of the 1960s and '70s Hölderlin was looked up to as a political revolutionary,[1] a "Jacobin," a "crypto-Marxist," and a pioneer of socialism. People saw in him a champion of a new, better world—a world that the student movement also aspired to create.

However, in this anniversary year, it was different—people refrained from categorizing him, seeing his importance as lying in the very fact that his poetry cannot be reduced to one perspective. Remo Bodei drew attention to this in his perceptive study of Hölderlin.[2] He shows that the high aesthetic quality of this poetry lies in the very fact that it is contradictory and ambiguous, which means that we experience and view it in different ways. For Hölderlin it was not Christianity but the world of the Greek gods that was the utopia of a better life. It was toward such a 'no place' (*ou-topos*) that his powerful religious longing aspired. This is where he hoped to experience everything that was impossible in the time in which he lived—perfect love, merging with nature, an end to the division of labor and alienation. Guided by poetry, Hölderlin was striving for a life in a utopian world governed not by utility and rationality but beauty and rapture. The result is the "high tone" that is characteristic of Hölderlin's poetry. Since his longing for a perfect life is directed toward a nonexistent mythical place (*ou-topos*), it has no alternative but to go into the void and is disappointed. The tragic experience is inevitable. There is no place for humor and irony in this poetry.

With great sensitivity Remo Bodei shows how Hölderlin suffered from living in the time into which he was born and with how much yearning he designed another world in which he might lead a successful life, with the help of poetry.[3] It was to Ancient Greece that he turned in order to be able to fulfil his longing. Poetic dreams and myths became a lifeline for him.[4] The goal of these dreams was a world free of contradictions and obstacles, of isolation and loneliness, a world of openness toward other people and the divine, a world in which everything is in harmonic movement, flowing and converging. Poetry creates the dream that crosses boundaries and supports humanity in their attempt to design themselves and continue their development. As a poet, how can one live in a "destitute time" if one's longing for a better world cannot be fulfilled? Hölderlin responded to this by becoming more and more inward looking, which led to a blurring of the boundaries between his inner and outer worlds. He entered a condition that is commonly known as madness.[5] He spent thirty-five years in this state in Tübingen, in a tower on the River Neckar, where he was looked after until his death by master joiner Zimmer and his family.

If we are to understand the uniqueness, complexity, and exceptional quality of Hölderlin's poetry it is important to know something of his life and also something about the time of the turn of the eighteenth and nineteenth century. This was a time of immense political and cultural upheaval of which he was fully aware, and which also found expression in his writing.

Hölderlin's Childhood and Youth and the
Formative Influences of This Time

Friedrich Hölderlin was born in 1770. In 1773 Goethe's *Götz von Berlichingen* appeared, and in 1774 his *Die Leiden des jungen Werthers* (*The Sorrows of Young Werther*). In 1773 Johann Gottfried Herder had published five essays under the heading *Von deutscher Art und Kunst* (Of German Character and Art), which described the fundamental changes in the way art was understood at that time. In the year of Hölderlin's birth, Immanuel Kant was appointed professor of logics and metaphysics at the University of Königsberg. In 1781 he published his *Critique of Pure Reason*, in 1789 his *Critique of Practical Reason*, and in 1790 his *Critique of the Power of Judgement*. It was the time of the French Revolution and the United States Declaration of Independence, and the 1776 Declaration of the Rights of Man and of the Citizen, which had a long-lasting influence on Hölderlin, supporting his longing for freedom and self-determination.

Hölderlin's mother, who was trapped in Swabian Pietism, had to take charge of the family after the death of his father and then even more so after the early death of her second husband, and she was adamant that her son should enter the ministry. At a very early age Hölderlin had piano and flute lessons and developed a lasting love of music that was to have a profound influence on his life and works. After attending the Monastery School of Denkendorf and the Higher Monastery of Maulbronn, Hölderlin began his studies in theology and philosophy at the University of Tübingen and obtained his degree. It was only with great effort that he was later able to avoid entering the ministry, something he had a real horror of, right through his life. During this period, he met Hegel with whom he developed a lasting friendship. He also became friends with Schelling, and it was at this time that *Das älteste Systemprogramm des deutschen Idealismus* (The Oldest Systematic Program of German Idealism) appeared. This has been available since the 1980s in a critical edition by Schneider and Jamme.[6] Ever since it appeared, this document has always been seen as connected with Friedrich Schlegel's project of a "new mythology." There is also a link with Kant's transcendental philosophy of Practical Reason. It develops in a programmatic way the ideas of *a future idealism as an ethics*, containing a complete system of all the ideas of idealism. Although this document was in Hegel's handwriting, its authorship is still debated. What is certain, however, is that it refers to thoughts and discussions that Hegel, Schelling, and Hölderlin developed jointly and that characterized the works of all three authors in different ways. At the basis of the "Systematic Program" is the idea of the self as a creative, self-conscious being, that approaches nature as a creative spirit. Together with the idea of humanity, the idea of "God," "freedom," and "immortality" are at the center of our free spirit. Finally, the idea of beauty or the aesthetic, with particular regard to poetry, is added. All these ideas come together in the myth of a *belief in reason that is fundamentally aesthetic.*[7]

Already at that time it was possible to see several elements that caused the oscillation between the *utopian* and the *tragic* that characterizes Hölderlin's work. One was the death of his stepfather, something that Hölderlin held responsible for the *sadness* running right through his life and work. Then there was *religion*, without which his utopian poetic conceptions would have been unthinkable. There was also his intensive experience of *music* from his own piano playing, which had a clear influence on the "musicality" of Hölderlin poems. And finally there was his *love* of nature and philosophy, which resulted in Hölderlin's philosophy of life and creativity, the "One and All" or *Hen kai Pan.*

During the period he lived in Waltershausen and Jena in 1794 and 1795, Hölderlin met many well-known figures of the time who played an important role in helping him to *find himself as a poet.* Although Hölderlin only had a distant relationship with Goethe, Schiller became a kind of father figure to the young poet. He was a role model for him and helped him get his work published. Schiller inspired many of his ideas. As well as his *Odes* there were also Schiller's insights into the fundamental importance of the *aesthetic* and *play*, which resulted in Hölderlin turning his back on Kant's transcendental philosophy, or at least in him expanding his own personal understanding of philosophy. Fichte's ideas of the *self, or I, that is constantly repositing itself* also found their way into Hölderlin's understanding of himself and the world. The first volume of *Hyperion*, published in 1795 by Klett Cotta with the help of Schiller, bears witness to these numerous influences, which Hölderlin processed in his own individual way. Hölderlin developed more and more his philosophy of "Hen kai Pan," or of *a unity in which the individuality of those who are united is maintained.* Hand in hand with this was also his insight into the limits of the philosophy of reason, which Hölderlin believed could only be surpassed by the *aesthetic*, and by poetry in particular. The *beautiful* in a work of art has the task of mediating between differences, thus connecting what we have grasped philosophically with the experience of the life that we live in the community. Art is a game that does not directly intervene in what we do in our lives. On this subject, Hölderlin goes on to say.

> In the philosophical letters I want to find the principle that will explain to me the divisions in which we think and exist, but which is also capable of dispelling the conflict between subject and object, between our self and the world, indeed also between reason and revelation—theoretically, in intellectual intuition, without which our practical reason would have to come to our aid. For this we need an aesthetic sense, and I will call my philosophical letters "New Letters on the Aesthetic Education of Man."[8]

The aim is to overcome the division between art and life, thus achieving freedom in a practical sense, in a way that is only possible in the realm of dreams.

Remo Bodei demonstrated very vividly that what constitutes the tragic in Hölderlin's life and work is the fact that *unity of being* is only attainable in the imagination, in utopia, in poetry, and is not possible in life.[9] This is why life contains *loneliness and suffering from the fact that the longing for the unity of being cannot be fulfilled.* To use Hölderlin's words,

> We all follow an eccentric course, and no other path is possible from childhood to the end. Spiritual unity, being, in the true sense of the word, is lost for us and we have had to lose it if we are to strive and fight to achieve it. We tear ourselves from the peaceful *Hen kai Pan* of the world in order to create it through our selves. We are at odds with nature, and what was once one, so we believe, is in conflict with itself, and rulers and servants change places. It often seems to us as though the world is everything and that we are nothing. *Hyperion* was also split by these two extremes. To end that eternal conflict between ourselves and the world, to restore the peace of all peace that is higher than all reason, to unite ourselves with nature to become one eternal whole, that is the goal of all our striving, whether we understand it or not.[10]

The Productive Years

Early in 1796 Hölderlin took a position as tutor at the Gontards' house in Frankfurt. It was not long before he and Susette Gontard fell in love. In *Hyperion* the character of Diotima was based on Susette. In the fall of 1796, the final version of the first volume of this epistolary novel in two volumes appeared. In 1797, together with his poems "An den Äther" and "Der Wanderer," Hölderlin sent this novel to Schiller, who published the "Wanderer" in his *Horen*. During this period Hölderlin translated Antigone into German, a work that influenced his own poetic writing. The result was a Sophocles/Hölderlin interpretation of the tragedy. There was no way out of the dilemma: *pity* and *fear, eleos* and *phobos* are unavoidable.[11] In *catharsis* there occurs first of all the purification of superfluous feelings and thus the *intensification of the passions*, second purification *by means of the passions*, and third *a purification of the passions*, that is, reducing them to a healthy level that results in our protecting ourselves and freeing ourselves from them.

In 1798 a conflict arose with Susette Gondard's husband, and Hölderlin left Frankfurt. The two lovers saw each other for the last time in May 1800. In the elegy titled "Abschied" (Parting) Hölderlin gives poetic expression to the pain of parting: *We wanted to part, thought it good and wise: But when we did so why did the deed pain us, like murder? Oh! How little we know ourselves, for a God prevails within us.*[12]

In 1797 Hölderlin wrote the first version of his play *Der Tod des Empedokles* (The Death of Empedocles); in 1799 the second volume of *Hyperion* was published and the second and third versions of Empedocles, which, like the first version, were never finished.[13] The first version contains reflections on the dialectic of nature and art, the second reflections on the new historical situation produced by the French Revolution and the fear of the new that had resulted from this. In the spring of 1800, Hölderlin finally gave up on his work on Empedocles, where we find a sentence that is characteristic of Hölderlin's republican outlook: "This is no longer the time of kings" (V. 1418). It became clear to Hölderlin that there can be no unifying or reconciling of science with life, of art and taste with genius, or of the educated man with nature. He expressed this in the fragment "The death of Empedocles," which depicts Empedocles plunging into the volcano, an act of self-sacrifice. The plunge into the volcano is Hölderlin's plunge into the state of madness.

It was not until the beginning of the twentieth century that it was discovered how important Hölderlin was for German literature. This was based first and foremost on a new assessment of the poetic value of his poems and a new assessment of the literary importance of his epistolary novel *Hyperion*. Compared with the rather more conventional style of his Tübingen hymns (1790–1793), his odes, written in Frankfurt in 1795 and 1796, achieve an "original, rhythmic tension and diversity of language."[14] Using numerous Greek verse meters, these odes in the German language open up new possibilities of poetic expression. Among Hölderlin's great odes are "Der Rhein," "Friedensfeier," and "Patmos." Their mythological motifs and their metrical pattern give these poems an artificial quality which makes them fundamentally different from the poems of Goethe. "Their aesthetic charm is also to be found in the combination of this quality of artificiality and subjective expression; it both distances and makes them more distinct at the same time."[15]

We cannot fail to see how Hölderlin was inspired by Pindar. We see this in the free rhythms and the construction of the stanzas. In these odes Hölderlin aspired to create the Epiphany of God and to comprehend the relation of the divine to the real and to poetry. How does the divine express itself in earthly things? This concern with religion is quite foreign to the time of the French Revolution. During the "holy night" (Brot & Wein, V. 123) it is one of the tasks of poetry to remind people of a higher form of life. Hölderlin saw himself as a poet in a time of revolution, whose task it was to capture and interpret history by means of poetry. A poem for Hölderlin is a way of combining processes of nature and historical and cultural processes to create something of a higher aesthetic quality. Writing poetry is understood as the act of an individual poet and as the expression of natural and historical processes. Accordingly, Hölderlin saw himself as a singer, educator, and prophet.

Hyperion

I would now like to focus on the presentation and interpretation of *Hyperion*, which is considered to be Hölderlin's main work. Remo Bodei has given us some very important insights into the tragic nature of this work. After Rousseau's *La nouvelle Héloise* and Goethe's *Die Leiden des jungen Werthers*, this was the last epistolary novel of the eighteenth century, and it must be said it was not very successful with contemporary readers. *Hyperion* has elements of the Bildungsroman or Entwicklungsroman (a novel dealing with the development of a person from early years to maturity),[16] in which, after losing the perfection of childhood, after enduring pain and suffering, the protagonist has the opportunity to find himself anew. As a child Hyperion had a harmonious life. As he became self-aware this harmony was lost, leading to isolation and loneliness. It is only after experiencing these things that it becomes possible for him to regain that original harmony on a higher plane. In 1770 Hyperion takes part in the Greek uprising against the Turks. After growing up on a small Greek island, Hyperion goes out into the world to get to know foreign lands. In Smyrna he becomes friends with Alabanda. Together they design images of a society that is free and beautiful. Whereas Alabanda actively prepares for revolution, Hyperion resignedly retreats to his own island where he meets Diotima who inspires him to become the "teacher of his own people." At the beginning of the second volume, Hyperion takes part in the uprising against the Turks and renews his friendship with Alabanda. Diotima and Alabanda represent the two sides of Hyperion. Alabanda is the revolutionary and he embodies Hyperion's revolutionary striving; Diotima is the embodiment of beauty, the expression of harmony with nature, of self-sufficiency and of peace. After the death of these two friends Hyperion goes to Germany. Here he gives his "speech of rebuke" to the Germans: "Masters and servants, youths and adults, but no human beings—is that not like a battlefield where hands and arms and limbs all lie broken and scattered, while the life blood that has been shed seeps away into the sand?"[17] He proceeds to accuse the Germans of barbarism, a slave mentality, a failure to understand genius and a higher form of life.

The first volume of his epistolary novel *Hyperion* was published by Cotta in Stuttgart in 1797; the second volume in 1798. Hölderlin also found inspiration in Schiller's letters "On the Aesthetic Education of Man," although his own plan to write "New Letters on the Aesthetic Education" never came to fruition. Unlike in Goethe's *Werther*, apart from those to Diotima, the letters look back in time. The novel has two narrative levels—one level is where the events take place that are then recounted on the second narrative level. "This inversion of two different periods, the earlier of which is captured in the later one in memories, was not invented by Hölderlin but lifted from the Odyssey. In books 9 to 12, Homer has Odysseus report back on his earlier adventures from between the Trojan War and coming to Calypso. This only happens after Odysseus had reached the Phaeacians after leaving Calypso."[18] Hölderlin's work also has elements of a coming-of-age novel. It begins with his childhood in Tina and the encounter with Adamas; then follows Hyperion's journey to Smyrna and his encounter with Alabanda, the "man of action," their quarrel and then Hyperion's return to Tina. In the following April there is the journey to Kalaurea and the encounter with Diotima and then in winter a second encounter with Alabanda. The third year sees the siege of Koreon, the storming of the castle Ministra, and the farewell letter to Diotima and then her death in Kalaurea. Once more Hyperion takes leave of Alabanda and sets off for Germany. The following year he journeys to Corinth, writes his first letter to Bellarmin, arrives in Salamis, and writes more letters to Bellarmin and Diotima.

In the novel, feelings and memories become interwoven. In 1794, in a *Hyperion* fragment, Hölderlin sketches out his conception of human life, which forms the basis of this work as follows: "The eccentric path that man, both in the universal and the individual sense, follows, from one point (of more or less pure simplicity) to another (of more or less perfect completion), seems, *in its essential directions*, to be always the same."[19] For Hölderlin a harmonious life is not a homogeneous one. Rather more, it consists of contrasts; it is a "*Hen kai Pan*," unity succeeding in the multiplicity of differences and dissonances. "In order to recognize himself, man must tear himself away from pure identity with the world and the loss of himself in objective life, in order to gain his real identity through recognition of the harmony in the discrepancies of the world and his own self."[20] In *Hyperion*, Hölderlin constructs the image of a harmonious, fulfilled old age, juxtaposed by the wretchedness of the actual world. This image is our goal in both our cultural and personal development. We can clearly see the tension between our futile striving for perfection and the violence and imperfection, which is our actual experience, in these words of Hyperion: "What do I care about the shipwreck of the world, I know nothing other than my blissful island." The irreconcilability of the two metaphors "shipwreck" and "blissful island" describes the insurmountable basic condition of our human life that Remo Bodei called "the tragic."

This dualism is wonderfully expressed in Hyperion's famous "Schicksalslied" (song of fate). The first two stanzas describe the realm of divine life, the "blissful island." The harsh reality of human life ("the shipwreck") in the third stanza is a sharp contrast with this. Here we find a portrayal of human turmoil, loss, and transience, from which there is no escape, but which we can learn to live with. Thus, in his reply to Bellarmin's question we find: "Dear friend! I am calm, because I can wish for no better thing than the gods. Must everything not suffer? And the more fitting it is, the deeper! Does not sacred nature suffer?"[21]

Schicksalslied

You move up there in the light
On easeful ground, blessed Geniuses!
Bright divine airs
Touch you lightly,
As the player's fingers
Her holy strings.
Outside of Fate, like the sleeping
Babe, the Heavenly Ones breathe;
Chastely guarded
In modest bud,
Ever for them
The spirit blooms,
And their blessed eyes
Gaze in still,
Eternal light.
But to us it is given
Nowhere to rest,
Suffering men
Falter and fall
Blindly from one
Hour to the next,
Like water flung down
From cliff to cliff,
Yearlong into uncertainty.

Outlook

In this famous poem we see once more that Hölderlin believes that it is the task of poetry to make people aware of what it is to have an ideal life, which is, however, the preserve of the gods. Poetry can give people the strength to perceive and endure the tension between a life they cannot possibly have and a life full of pain and suffering. Poetry, imagination, and dream show people the way to a better life. However, it is also clear that they cannot live this life in a "destitute time." This situation in which Hölderlin, Kleist, and Nietzsche find themselves is later fittingly described in these words of Nietzsche: *"I love those who do not know how to live, except by going under, for they are those who cross over."*[22]

Notes

1. Adolf Beck, *Hölderlin als Republikaner*, 1967/78.
2. Remo Bodei, *Hölderlin: La filosofía y lo trágico*, 1990.
3. Bodei, *Hölderlin*.
4. Manfred Frank, "Hölderlin über den Mythos," 1990/91.
5. Pierre Bertaux, *Friedrich Hölderlin*, 1981.
6. Christoph, Jamme, and Helmut Schneider, eds., *Mythologie der Vernunft. Hegels ältestes Systemprogramm des deutschen Idealismus.* (English translation by Diana I. Behler in *Philosophy of German Idealism: Fichte, Jacobi, and Schelling*, edited by Ernst Behler.)
7. Dieter Henrich, *Der Grund im Bewusstsein: Untersuchungen zu Hölderlins Denken (1794–1795)*, 1992.
8. Hölderlin, *Sämtliche Werke und Briefe*, vol. 2 (2019), 614 f. (translation mine).
9. Bodei, *Hölderlin*.
10. Hölderlin, *Sämtliche Werke und Briefe*, vol. 2 (2019), 598 f. (my translation).
11. Aristotle, *Poetics*, chapter 6, 1449b ff.
12. Hölderlin, *Sämtliche Werke und Briefe*, vol. 1 (2019), 321 (my translation).
13. Peter-André Alt, "Subjektivierung, Ritual, Implizite Theatralität: Hölderlins 'Empedokles'—Projekt und die Diskussion des antiken Opferbegriffs im 18 Jahrhundert," 2010/11.
14. Gerhard Kurz, "Postscript to: Friedrich Hölderlin," 228 (my translation).
15. Kurz, *Postscript*, 229 (my translation).
16. Gerhard Mayer, "Hölderlins Hyperion: ein frühromantischer Bildungsroman," 1975/77.
17. Hölderlin, *Hyperion oder Der Eremit in Griechenland*, 261 (my translation).
18. Michael Knaupp, "Postscript to Friedrich Hölderlin: *Hyperion*" (1958), 184 (my translation).
19. Hölderlin, *Erläuterungen und Dokumente* (1997), 83 (my translation).
20. Hölderlin, *Sämtliche Werke und Briefe*, vol. 1 (2019), 184 (own translation).
21. Hölderlin, *Hyperion*, 258 (own translation).
22. Nietzsche, *Thus Spoke Zarathustra*, Zarathustra's Prologue, section 4.

Bibliography

Alt, Peter-André. "Hölderlins "Empedokles"-Projekt und die Diskussion des antiken Opferbegriffs im 18. Jahrhundert." *Hölderlin-Jahrbuch* 37 (2010/11).

Aristotle. *Poetics*. Introduction, Commentary, and Appendixes by D. W. Lucas. Clarendon Press, 1968.

Behler, Ernst, ed. *Philosophy of German Idealism: Fichte, Jacobi, and Schelling*. Bloomsbury Academic: 1997. (Including the anonymous text "The Oldest Systematic Program of German Idealism" variously attributed to Hegel or Schelling.)

Beck, Adolf. "Hölderlin als Republikaner." *Hölderlin-Jahrbuch* 15 (1967/68).

Bertaux, Pierre. *Friedrich Hölderlin*. Suhrkamp, 1981.

Bodei, Remo. *Hölderlin: La filosofía y lo trágico*. La balsa de la Medusa, vol. 33. Machado Grupo de Distribución, 1990.

Frank, Manfred. "Hölderlin über den Mythos." *Hölderlin-Jahrbuch* 27 (1990/91).

Gadamer, Hans-Georg. "Die Gegenwärtigkeit Hölderlin." *Hölderlin-Jahrbuch* 15 (1982/83).

Henrich, Dieter. *Der Grund im Bewusstsein: Untersuchungen zu Hölderlins Denken (1794–1795)*. Klett-Cotta, 1992.

Hölderlin, Friedrich. *Sämtliche Werke und Briefe in drei Bänden*. Edited by Michael Knaupp. Hanser, 2019.

Hölderlin, Friedrich. *Hyperion oder Der Eremit in Griechenland: Sämtliche Werke und Briefe*, Vol. 2. Edited by Günter Mieth. Aufbau-Verlag, 1995.

Hölderlin, Friedrich. *Hyperion or The Hermit in Greece*. Translated by Benjamin Ross. Archipelago, 2008.

Hölderlin, Friedrich. *Hyperion: Erläuterungen und Dokumente*. Reclam, 1997.

Jamme, Christoph, and Schneider, Helmut, eds. *Mythologie der Vernunft: Hegels ältestes Systemprogramm des deutschen Idealismus*. Suhrkamp, 1984 (with a critical edition of the text).

Knaupp, Michael. "Postscript to Friedrich Hölderlin: *Hyperion*." Reclam, 1958.

Kurz, Gerhard. "Postscript to Friedrich Hölderlin: *Gedichte*." Reclam, 2003.

Mayer, Gerhard. "Hölderlins Hyperion: ein frühromantischer Bildungsroman." *Hölderlin-Jahrbuch* 19/20 (1975/1977).

Nietzsche, Friedrich. *Thus Spoke Zarathustra*. Translated by Walter Kaufmann. Random House, 1954.

Safranski, Rüdiger. *Hölderlin: Komm! ins Offene, Freund!* Hanser, 2019.

8

Torquato Tasso and His "Virtù Eroica" as a Passion of the Will

Paolo Cherchi

The recent flourishing of the studies on emotions and virtues has brought about a most refreshing renewal in this area in the late medieval period, when the subject was intensely researched producing highly diversified results. This renewal may be a bit surprising considering that the medieval thinkers dealt with the passions (*turbationes animi*, as they prefer to call them) from a Christian vantage point, which implied the notions of sin and its consequences. Medieval moral philosophers were engaged in a vigorous quest for the origins and control of the passions, given that only a virtuous managing of them could lead to eternal salvation. This neglect was due, at least in part, to the way "modern" philosophers study our inner soul. In recent decades the interest in medieval psychology and ethics has overcome this neglect and numerous studies have reconstructed a rather vivacious panorama of the debates on nature and the role that passions play in people's moral life. Several books[1] give excellent overviews and guide dilettantes like me through the maze of *summae* and *quodlibeta* produced in the centuries before Descartes's *Les passions de l'âme* (1649). I consulted many of them while researching the history of *honestum*, and in particular that of the *virtus heroica* for a section of my book.[2] I found very little, in fact almost nothing. I remember consulting with Remo Bodei, whose *Geometria delle passioni* had made the strongest impression on me. He was helpful and suggested some readings drawn from his immense bibliographic archive. Today, on the

121

occasion of honoring his memory, I go back to that question and offer the little I have learned about a special virtue/passion that encountered serious difficulties in finding a stable place in the geometry of any moral system. Hence the reason for the present paper.

Aristotle in his *Nichomachean Ethics* (VII, 1 1145a15–20) talks about "a superhuman excellence, a kind of heroic and divine virtue," but describes it in such essential terms that caused endless speculations on its nature. He says that is the opposite of bestiality and illustrates this point by quoting Homer's line—"He did not seem to be the son of a man but rather to be of the same nature of a god" (*Iliad*, 24, 258)—in which Priam, the king of Troy, deems godly his son's prowess, implying that Hector's virtue had some divine quality. There have been two ways of reconstructing the history of the discussions on the "heroic virtue": one proceeds by analyzing single themes (Lambertini in the eighteenth century), and another follows the historical development of the interpretations; the first was done by a Pope who was interested in establishing on *ne varietur* terms what must be understood for "virtus heroica" because it as an indispensable element in the process of beatification of the saints, and the other way is the one followed by historians of philosophy. We use the first one for collecting data, and the second one for providing a historical context in which to view Tasso and other vernacular authors who spoke of this virtue. This double purpose makes it already clear that there are two notions and two users of "heroic virtue," one for the saints and one for the secular heroes. Two different histories but bound to stimulate and interfere with each other to stress both their similarities and their differences—each one of them searching for their specific identity, both praising heroes who served different Lords. Seeing these similar/different histories in a parallel survey helps to understand better what they had in common and what distinguished them.

Antiquity had plenty of heroes whose virtues were highly celebrated, but it never felt necessary to give any special name to them since it was clear that they were special if they elevated a normal person to the level of the hero. Christianity had to have its special persons and to distinguish them, called "heroic" their action as the virtue that generated them. St. Augustine (*De civitate Dei*, X, 21) did not doubt in identifying these new heroes with the "martyrs" who sacrificed their lives for the Christian God; but if the idea of a Christian hero was already alive in Augustine's day, the notion of *heroica virtus* began to be used once Aristotle's *Nicomachean Ethics* was integrally translated into Latin by Robert Grosseteste in the early thirteenth century, and then the existence of a "virtus heroica" automatically became the hallmark of a saint.[3]

All very simple. But when it comes to defining the nature of this quasi-divine virtue, things prove to be difficult if not utterly impossible. Proceeding *magnis itineribus* not to abuse the space allotted to us, we can start with Albertus Magnus and his hitherto unpublished commentary on *Nicomachean Ethics*.[4] Here the *virtus heroica* is considered to be a sort of *continentia* in the highest degree, which has total control of the *passiones* that agitate the soul. Albert accepts the Plotinians gradation of virtues, and in this scale, the *virtus heroica* stands in the highest level of control. But a virtue that suppresses all passions departs from Aristotle who conceives virtues not as tamers of passions but as a rational habit that directs the passions to the right end. A soul and a mind free from all perturbations must have appeared to provide the perfect status for a saint, dominated exclusively by the love of God. This position, close to Augustine and opened to mystical outcomes was influential for many generations to come, yet it lacked theological or philosophical support and did not produce a definition of the *virtus heroica*.

This merit goes to Thomas Aquinas, who dealt with the problem on two occasions. In his commentary on Aristotle's *Nicomachean Ethics*, he calls this virtue *divina*. He assigns it to the purest rational part of the soul, the part that communicates with the divine substances, and for this reason, can be called *divina*: "Ita enim rationalis pars, quando in homine perficitur et formatur ultra communem modum humanae perfectionis, et haec nominatur virtus divina supra humanam et commune" (So, indeed the "rational part" is when in man is given and created a perfection that surpasses the common human perfection, and this is called "divine virtue" which is superior to the human and common virtue).[5] It remains all in the realm of the rational soul. But in his *Summa*, Thomas offers a different explanation: this exceptional virtue is different from all the others because it is enriched by the infusion of a *donum* of the Holy Spirit. It is not acquired by the beholder but is a gift he has obtained from God.[6] This solution respects in a way Aristotle's allusion to its godlike quality, and at the same time, it departs from the philosopher's basic idea that moral virtues are habits attained through human's effort. Yet, despite this ambiguity or perhaps because of it, Thomas's definition of heroic virtue was an enduring one and survived with slight variations for centuries. It explained that "heroic" actions remain human but at the same time they exceed all norms; on the other end, the infusion of a *donum* coming from the Holy Ghost gave heroic virtue a legitimate place in the theological frame, potentially changing its nature from political and moral into a theological one.

Within the theological framework, attempts were made to explain how heroic virtue is attained and how it preserves both the requirements of being a "habit of controlling passions" and the same time a divine infusion. Henry of Ghent envisages a sort of "growing" by which the normal virtue would ascend through the following phases: *initium, progressus, perfectio*, and *excessus*, and the latter would proceed from *perseverantia* to *continentia, to temperantia*, and finally to *virtus heroica*.[7]

John Buridanus offered another solution that kept heroic virtue in the class of moral or cardinal virtue but did not deny a possible divine origin that theologians recognized in the *dona* from the Holy Ghost and in the theological virtues. John Buridanus saw the *virtus heroica* as a form of perfect *prudentia*, a choice that made it possible to sustain the ambiguity just mentioned because *prudentia* is a cardinal virtue that also takes the name of *phronesis*, a preeminent intellectual virtue, the one that is placed at the borderline with the theological virtues. So, while *prudentia* may have control of the practical aspect of life, *sapientia* controls the spiritual part of moral life. Thus, heroic virtue would remain under man's power but would produce actions that would seem to surpass his human capacity. This virtue would reach an extraordinary capacity of operating memorable actions not only in the spiritual area but in the practical one as well. Only some people endowed with special qualities can perform deeds out of the normal range. Some of these qualities come with birth and upbringing in a noble milieu.[8] In Buridanus's attention to the social elements that predispose one to heroic virtue, it is possible to foresee that this special virtue will percolate into the lay society. This premonition will be confirmed.

Our cursory survey prevents us from bringing in more data to prove that slowly but firmly and steadily the notion of heroic virtue became more and more common in the language of the philosophers of the fifteenth and sixteenth centuries, and at a certain point, it became an official requisite, spelled in the precise terms of "virtus heroica," in the trials for beatification and sanctification of holy men and women. It was in the air since the notion of special virtue had long been associated with the idea of sanctity. It took an event to make it happen; in the meantime, the theologians of the so-called Seconda Scolastica (Francisco Suarez among others) had been refining the notion by perfecting some points of Thomas Aquinas's thesis. The event that made the *virtutes heroicae* enter as a legal formula in Canon Law took place in 1602. In that year some theologians from Salamanca sent to Pope Urban VIII a memorial recommending the beatification of Saint Teresa of Avila, and for the first time, the request presented the *virtutes heroicae* as one of the requisites for beatification. They were so successful that even today these special virtues are necessary elements in all processes of beatification and sanctification. They were presented as qualifications no less important than miracles and martyrdom. Proving their presence and the consequent perfection in the life of a saint was a difficult task, considering the lack of a univocal definition of these special virtues. For sure such awareness prompted a strenuous commitment to come up with a definition that had a valid juridical strength. The ongoing criticism raised by the Protestant world on the Catholic saints and the Catholic effort to clean the store and repel many saints acclaimed by popular superstition (the Bullandists were born for this purpose), did not allow this matter to be taken lightly. Catholics wanted to be more severe than the Protestants, who did not have saints but recognized that there were some special individuals gifted with some virtues superior to the known ones, a sort of *virtus heroica*, suited to persons that would-be leaders, like some great biblical characters such as Moses and Abraham. Protestants maintained that these great men had an infusion of divine grace, a "donum" as Aquinas had hinted; they stressed the "leading" or *fürstlich* power of these special virtues.[9] The Catholic world could not exist without the inspiring presence of its saints, but it was urgent to define once and for all those *virtutes heroicae* that were necessary to validate the sanctity of those special men, whose life was scrutinized at the judicial trials supervised by the Popes themselves, who, in times of Counter-Reformation, adopted the strictest guidelines of their code.

The demand yielded results. In 1668 the cardinal Lorenzo Brancati di Lauria published his *Commentaria in tertium librum sententiarum* [. . .] *Duns Scoti* (1682) in two folios, containing many disputations, one of which bears the title *De virtute heroica*. Here, to the question of how one must understand the heroic quality of virtue, he answers: "Heroicitas christiana dicitur ille virtutis gradus, perfectio, seu fulgor, et excellentia, quae facit ut homo circa materiam illius virtutis supra communem aliorum hominum operandi modum operetur, et in hoc Deo similis sit" (We call "Christian heroism" that degree of virtue, of perfection or of splendor and of excellency that causes a man to perform in a superior way, far above that modus operandi common in other men, and in this he is similar to God).[10] This definition considers the effects of heroic virtue; as to the origins of this special virtue, this is what Brancati says.

> Ut aliqua virtus christiana constituatur inesse heroica in actu primo, necesse est, ut habeat annexum aliquod donum Spiritus Sancti, et de habenti ex Dei instinctu operari expedite, prompte ac delectabiliter, supra communem naturae modum, ex fine supranaturali sine humano ratiocinio, cum abnegatione operantis et affectum subjectione.

> In order for a virtue to be called heroic in its primary act, it is necessary for it to have attached some gift of the Holy Spirit, and to have from God some instinct of functioning expeditiously, rapidly and cheerfully, in a measure above average, without the interference of reason, beyond the limits of reason, with abnegation and without any dependence on any feelings.[11]

It comes back to Thomas who in *virtus heroica* sees the presence of a *donum* from the Holy Spirit. It adds that this virtue must have the quality of spontaneity, confirming the notion that it is a habit even if it has some elements of divine infusion. Moreover, Brancati adds something new: whoever practices *virtus heroica* is de facto imitating Jesus in his superior qualities, in his abnegations, in his extraordinary actions. What could not be said with a definition is finally explained with an analogy, through the presence of a model: to practice this indefinable *virtus heroica* one must just imitate Christ.

The classic work on the subject is *De Servorum Dei Beatificatione et Beatorum Canonizatione* by Prospero Lambertini, Benedict XIV, already quoted as the major source of our bibliographical information, an added reason why it deserves the epithet of "classic." Indeed, it deals with all the matters concerning the process of proving sanctity. It clarifies, for example, that heroics can take different forms in men and women, and martyrdom does not necessarily mean the loss of life. To our unique virtues, he devotes several chapters in volume three: chapter XXI ("De virtute heroica," 1753, 213–16); chapter XXII (In quo proponuntur et explicantur nonnullae quaestiones ad heroicitatem virtutum pertinentes," 216–19); and chapter XXIII (De virtutibus theologalibus fide, spe et caritate, et heroicitate uniuscuiusque ex iisdem" 219–24), subdivided into four sections, one for each one of the first two virtues, and two more on *caritas*, first "in Deum" and then "in proximum." In his historical perspective, he asks himself whether the pagans had episodes of heroic virtue, and he does not deny it but asserts that historians should be the ones to judge this matter, not theologians for whom it is clear that the heroical nature of saints is a theological problem. Ancient heroes were endowed with the potentiality of this supervirtue, but they never had the possibility of proving it because they never sacrificed themselves for the love of God. If we look for a general criterion to go to the essence of *virtus heroica*, we can say that for Benedict XIV this is nothing else but perfection. This measurement or standard is extended to all and each virtue, cardinal and theological, and the grade or level or heroics must be present in every aspect and moment of a saint's life. Heroics is wholeness or plenitude of virtue sustained at the highest level and throughout the entire life. A Christian hero must preserve from baptism onward the *innocentia* granted to him by that sacrament, as it is expressly stated in chapter XXII, paragraph 11. In other words, heroic virtue is not found in single or sporadic acts, but it must be a *habitus*, a constant living in perfection, and it must manifest itself in every virtue. Whoever attains this ideal grade of virtue accedes to God and is a saint.[12]

Lambertini's notion of heroic virtue remains unchanged in today's processes of beatification and sanctification. If this special virtue established a parameter in conferring the status of sainthood, was there any such standard and scrutiny to elevate a man to the status of a hero? Antiquity did not have any, and yet it proclaimed many heroes without any trial. Their distinguishing virtues were *pietas* or *magnanimitas* or *fortitudo* or several others, and whichever it might have been, its degree was always the highest. The medieval heroes (the Rolands, the Lancelots, and the memorable leaders of so many *chansons de geste* and *sagas*) were already fighting for the Christian faith and were celebrated for their prowess, loyalty, or unselfishness, but in no recorded case the notion of *virtus heroica* came up. As we said, it was clear that the new religion had created new heroes who fought and even died for the celestial king, but recognition of the new heroes had no virtue that could distinguish them until the discovery of Aristotle's *Nicomachean Ethics* found it: it was *virtus heroica*, which, however, was difficult to define, as new concepts often are. And if holy people and saints possessed it, were the normal people precluded from attaining it? Problems were bound to arise because heroic was primarily an attribute of excellence, regardless of the ends pursued, be they pious or earthly, sublime or modest. Buridanus, as we saw, seemed to hint that practicing *virtus heroica* was not an exclusive prerogative of saintly persons. But it took a long time before a secular person was said to be gifted with heroic virtue. The thirteenth to the fifteenth centuries produced many great saints, but there were also a growing number of civil leaders and "condottieri" that exhibited virtues similar in quality to those of ancient heroes. The humanistic culture encouraged the imitation of ancient models, and for a long time, the way of extolling the greatness of a hero was to compare him favorably with an ancient forerunner. It is interesting to realize that it was the Protestants who used the notion of *virtus heroica* to explain why some individuals had a special moral gift for accomplishing great deeds. In this category, they put Moses, Abraham, and many other religious and political leaders, endowed with *heldenerischen Tügenden* and touched by the Grace of God, as they were divine *dona*. Protestants had no saints, and leaders were the only model to invoke to be guided in life. It was a deciding cultural innovation, and the contrast with the Catholic world was sharp.[13]

In Italy—the only area of interest here—the cultural changes caused in part by the religious clash with the Protestant Reformation, finally brought the term *virtù eroica* among people who up to that point left it to the saints. It appeared with the technical connotation accumulated over several centuries. It happened in 1564, imported from France by way of philosophical treatises.

The carrier was Giulio Landi's *Le attioni morali*, a collection of essays. Here in the first dialogue between Lorenzo Bartolini (pseudonym of Landi), Jacopo Fabro (Jacques Lefèvre), and Clitoveo (Josse Clichtoveus), Landi reproduces the scheme of the moral virtues found in Lefèvre's *Artificialis introductio per modus epitomatis in decem libros ethicorum Aristotelis*, which was published in 1497 with the commentary by Clichthoveus. In this table, "virtù eroica" appears in the highest place among the intellectual virtues, with its manifestations or "affetti" of continence, perseverance, shame, and just indignation, all of which sound very close to what we have seen in Henry of Ghent. Each virtue is presented in the middle of its opposite vices, but *virtù heroica* is one of the very few exceptions. Of this virtue, he says the following:

> Non ci è specificato il vitio suo contrario, non essendo un nome proprio; ma si può intendere che sì come la virtù heroica sovrastà a tutte le altre virtù d'eccellenza e di dignità, e si come ella tutte l'altre virtù in sè contiene, così il vizio heroico sovrastà a tutti gli altri vitij di brutezza, e d'ischiffità, quando che tutti i vitij in se contiene.

> There is no specific or any opposite vice since it does not have a proper name; yet it is possible to understand that just as heroic virtue stands above all virtues in excellence and dignity, and

since it contains in itself all other virtues, so too does heroic vice stand above all vices in ugliness and disgust since it contains in itself all vices.[14]

It would seem that "virtù heroica" is not a virtue in itself, but rather a degree of virtuousness, and it can be applied to any of the moral or political virtues; therefore, it can be considered as all virtues in one. We assume that being so perfect and without any risk of degenerating into its contrary, it brings happiness. Landi goes no further, and the little he says begs for a definition or at least for some more generous consideration. One thing, however, comes through: it is a virtue to be found in men who are capable of greatness, even if this is not sanctity.

The difficulties in encapsulating the essence of this special virtue persisted, indeed they increased once the problem of holiness was left out. The reproaches to Aristotle for not having been clearer became a staple in the discussions on the nature of this virtue. Just as an example we remember Antonio Scaino who wrote about the virtues of a prince, and was quite explicit on this subject.

> Quanto poi alla virtù heroica, con poche parole Aristotele se ne spedì, trattandone nel settimo libro dell'ethica, con dire ch'ella sia un genere di virtù ch'eccede la virtù morale [. . .] E se poi Aristotele non passò pù oltre in fare più distinta trattatione delle virtù heroica in quella maniera che haveva fatto prima delle virtù morali, non è da meravigliarsene, atteso che la materia non le dava campo, essendo molto ristretta la sua cognizione, come quella virtù che è poco praticata fra gli homini.

> As for heroic virtue, Aristotle got rid of it with just with few words, talking about it in the seventh book of his *Ethics*, by saying generally that it exceeds moral virtues. And it is not surprising that Aristotle did not go further in making a specific study of heroic virtue as he had previously done for the other virtues, because this particular virtue did not give to him enough materials to talk about it, since its knowledge is scanty, because it is a virtue rarely used by men.[15]

Scaino makes this observation after having stated that kings must possess heroic virtue to deserve their title, but it is hard to say what exactly this virtue is. Notice the contradiction: it was equally difficult to define and ignore the presence and the greatness of this virtue once it manifested itself. Scaino was not deranged, and his difficulties are signs of the times when Machiavelli loomed in the background and "la ragion di stato" was increasingly becoming the main reason for demanding greatness among rulers.

But traditional principles were not waning as of yet. Francesco Piccolomini, the "last representative of the Humanistic school,"[16] in 1583 published a voluminous *Universa philosophia de moribus*, of which twenty-three chapters—the whole "gradus sextus" or level in the scale-value of virtues—are devoted to *virtus heroica*,[17] the largest treatise ever. We would expect that such an effort would clarify once and for all the notion of *virtus heroica*, but in fact, rather the opposite occurred because the ambition of thoroughness leads to some dispersion. In those chapters, we find the history of the notion, several chapters on the vice of "bestiality" as the opposite of heroic virtue, and many historic examples. It is impossible to summarize here the complex and rich content of those twenty-three chapters, but a synthetic definition may do so: heroic virtue "oritur ex flagranti amore honesti."[18] The burning love for *honestum* generates heroic virtue, and *honestum* is the Ciceronian notion of the highest good that consists in the perfect integration or the *pulchrum* (the beautiful) with the *utile* (expediency). This is, for sure, an earthly *summum bonum*, for there is even a higher good that can be desired *flagranti amore*, equally strong if not more intense, but this belongs to another order of values religious in nature. Piccolomini distinguishes the two and deals mostly with the lower one, which is suited for secular heroes. The *honestum* they passionately pursue is not a virtue in itself but the combination of the four cardinal virtues, all of them practiced at the highest level. In celebrating *honestum* Piccolomini proved to be one last defender of that human "dignitas" theorized by Pico Della Mirandola, and he kept it in the sphere of the human realm. But since he saw the *virtus heroica* as a form of love, he had to find its appropriate place in the soul, using for this purpose the Platonic tripartition of the *anima*. In chapter 6, "In qua animae facultate collocata sit Virtus"[19] he establishes that it is not a contemplative or intellectual virtue—although some of its parts may justify such classification—but has its roots in the irascible part of the soul. It is a notion to keep in mind because it will occur in Tasso as well. It is also important to observe that these psychological limits do not exclude divine intervention. This was perhaps the major reason why Piccolomini's work was so well received by the Protestant theologians, engaged as they were in rejecting the presence of sainthood and promoting instead the figure of the charismatic leader.[20]

Piccolomini envisioned a man who had heroic virtue, but he was hardly a hero in any traditional sense. His hero was made up in a philosophical treatise, with all the virtues found in books. He was perhaps a righteous ruler, a brilliant thinker, a great civic leader, but essentially, he was a paper hero, even if Piccolomini quotes many examples of contemporary princes or dukes praised as heroes. Something had changed and the chivalric and Plutarchean heroes were not in demand anymore. The changes brought by some cultural earthquakes, such as those caused by Luther or Machiavelli, or Copernicus, demanded heroes different from the typical and fabled knights, who were on their way out or would survive only in the mind of Don Quixote. Piccolomini's *virtus heroica* documents such a demand well, but only a poet could satisfactorily meet it. This poet was Torquato Tasso, who in 1583, the same year Piccolomini published his work, composed a *Discorso sulla virtù eroica e sulla carità*. Written in vernacular, it was by far more contained than the treatise of his teacher and friend Piccolomini, and was composed in a convent of the Olivetani rather than in an academic environment (Piccolomini was a professor of philosophy at the University of Padua). It was a companion essay to the poem *Gerusalemme Liberata*, published in 1581, and its hero was of the new hoped-for breed.

Tasso was a great epic poet who meditated with remarkable originality and depth on the artistic problems posited by the nature of epics in a time that this notion was addressing new values and a new audience. He was, or better "wanted to be," an Aristotelian, convinced as he was that the principles presented in the *Poetics*, recently made available and intensely discussed, could give unity and order to a poem that was breaking loose because of all sorts of innovations that Tasso wanted to bring into the genre. This ambition was bound to create tension at multiple levels, in the creation itself and the theory. It was not easy, for example, to combine episodes of "meraviglioso" or diabolic magic with the notion of verisimilitude, or to maintain a strict unity of the poem when the action required a fragmentary composition; nor was it any easier to conform the figure of a Christian hero to the model of the ancient ones. The most important writings on the subject were his *Discorsi dell'arte poetica* (composed ca. 1565) later expanded in *Discorsi dell'arte poetica e del poema eroico* (1587). A major focus in these works is the "passions" deemed to be appropriate for an epic hero since the action and the readers' response depends on them. One short sample shows how the kind of passion is a distinctive feature in an epic poem.

> E oltre ciò, la ragione e l'autorità di Platone par che ci confermi quella d'Omero, perché tra le potenze dell'animo nostro, io dico la ragione e l'appetito irascibile e 'l concupiscibile, senza fallo nobilissima [è] la ragione quasi regina dell'altre; ma il concupiscibile appetito somiglia più tosto al rubella popolare, il qual, sollevandosi e facendo tumulti nell'animo, nega di prestare obedienza alla ragione, là dove l'irascibile è quasi guerriero e ministro della ragione in raffrenare l'altro che le fa contrasto. Dunque dell'ira più tosto che dall'amore dee prendere soggetto il poeta eroico. E ciò peraventura sarebbe vero se gli eroi fossin tutti e sempre soggetti alle passioni; ma se l'amore è non solo una passione e un movimento dell'appetito sensitivo, ma uno abito nobilissimo della volontà, come vuole san Tomaso, l'amore sarà più lodevole ne gli eroi, e per conseguente nel poema eroico.

> Moreover, it seems that Plato's reason and authority corroborates Homer's because, among the powers of our soul—that is reason, the irascible appetite, and the concupiscent appetite—reason reigns over the others; while the concupiscent appetite resembles a rebellious citizen, who, rebelling and protesting in his own soul, refuses to obey reason, whereas the irascible appetite acts like the warrior and the minister of reason in refraining the one which opposes it. Therefore, wrath rather than love must be the subject of the epic poet. And this would be true if all heroes were always subjected to passions. Yet if love is not just a passion and a movement of the sensitive appetite but rather a quite noble habit of the will, as S. Thomas maintains, then love would be more appreciated among heroes, and consequently in the heroic poems.[21]

And talking about the virtues, he writes the following:

> L'Epico all'incontra vuole nelle persone il sommo delle virtù, le quali eroiche dalla virtù eroica sono nominate. Si trova in Enea l'eccellenza della pietà, della Fortezza militare in Achille, della prudenza in Ulisse, e per venire ai nostri giorni, della lealtà in

Amadigi, della costanza in Bradamante; anzi pure in alcuni di questi il cumulo di tutte queste virtù.

On the contrary epics require characters at their highest degree of virtues, which are called heroic by the type of virtue they represent. Aeneas is found to be excellent in the virtue of piety, Achilles in military prowess, Ulysses in prudence, and coming to our times, Amadigi excelles in the virtue of loyalty, Bradamante in that of the costancy, and, in some of these characters we find a compilation of all these virtues.[22]

Given the stature of Tasso as a poet, it is understandable that many scholars have written on our theme. But let us ignore this criticism and instead examine an essay that Tasso himself wrote on "virtù eroica" that critics seem to have overlooked.[23]

After the conventional parts of the dedication, the *Discorso della virtù eroica e della carità* briefly surveys the main philosophical schools and sees how each one has dealt with and classified the moral virtues. Aristotle is the unrivaled master in this area. He relates some of them to the passionate or affective part of the soul and others to the intellective one; some of the latter are contemplative and some have their object in the realm of the affections or passions. Where does he locate the heroic virtue? He mentions it, of course, but says only that it surpasses or exceeds all human limits, and its opposite is bestiality. This leaves us with some problems. If it is an excess, can it be considered a vice? If it is a virtue, is it an active or a contemplative one? Aristotle says bestiality is the opposite of heroic virtue, but since he neither defines nor describes bestiality, this opposite provides no help in understanding the nature of its contrary. Moreover, he seems to place this special virtue above men but below the supreme goods, thus in no place. Being a virtue should be in the middle of two opposites, but being an intellectual virtue, the notion of "mean" or *mediocritas* does not apply. If we say that heroic virtue contains all the others, how can we have *prudentia* taming the *ira* or wrath if this must have all its force when it creates heroic acts? These and other objections fill the few pages Tasso devotes to Aristotelian supervirtue.

Tasso even comes to doubt the existence of such a virtue.

Crederò io più tosto ch'ella termine non abbia, nè subietto particolare; ma che suo soggetto sia tutto ciò che può cadere

> sotto l'altre virtù: e sì come la magnanimità in virtù contiene
> l'altre virtù; perciò che degno delle cose grandi non può essere,
> nè aver l'altre condizioni ch'al magnanimo s'attribuiscono, colui
> che di tutte le virtù non è fornito: così la virtù eroica comprende
> in sè ciascun'altra virtù. Ma in quella guisa, che nel cielo sono
> gli elementi, in lei sono l'altre virtù in un modo più nobile, o
> (come i filosofi dicono) eminente: sì che diremo a differenza della
> liberalità e della magnificenza civile o regia, ch'alcuno eroicamente
> sia liberale, ed alcun eroicamente magnifico.

> I would rather believe that it [the heroic virtue] has neither an
> end nor a particular subject, but that its subject is all that can
> be in the reality of all the other virtues; and as magnanimity is
> a virtue that contains all the other virtues, therefore he who has
> not all virtues cannot be considered worthy of great things, nor
> have any of the conditions which are attributed to magnanimous
> persons. Similarly, the heroic virtue contains in itself all other
> virtues. But in the same way that the elements are found in the
> heavens, in the heroic virtue all other virtues have a more noble
> or more eminent (to use the philosopher's language) quality: thus,
> we would say that in a way that is different from the liberality
> or of the civic and royal magnificence, we would say that some-
> one is heroically liberal and someone is heroically magnificent.[24]

These are some indications of the discomfort Tasso experienced for being
an orthodox Aristotelian. Essentially, he does not define the *virtus heroica*,
nor does he succeed better than anyone before him.

But Tasso could not dismiss this special virtue because, after all, he
was shaping a new kind of hero. He was able to seize its essence going not
through a philosophical demonstration, but through a rhetorical one, namely,
through the figure of analogy. The analog, indeed, the synonym of "heroic"
is written in the title of the "discorso," and bears the name of "*carità.*"

This theological virtue contains in itself the other two, and such
inclusiveness makes it similar to the heroic one. The similarities do not
stop here. Is charity a virtue that only Christians know? Tasso asks. A set
of examples demonstrate that ancient pagans knew it, although they did
so imperfectly because true charity has its object in God. But the *species*
of such virtue was the same because charity is excessive and overwhelming
love for a superior good.[25] Since Christians are the only ones to know

the Highest Good, they practice the real *caritas*. Yet there is an earthly highest good, one even higher than *honestum*, and this is glory, in which shines honor and the moral virtues at a superlative level. The intense and persistent love for glory is "virtù eroica," which pushes one to great deeds for no other return than mankind's well-being. There is no vanity in this pursuit of glory, and *virtus heroica* and charity are identical in their abnegation, in their drive for love that grows the more one possesses it and the more one shares with others. The vehement love for the highest ideal distinguishes the Christian hero from a tyrant who is also driven to attain the supreme grade of greatness, but the tyrant's aim is selfish while the Christian hero is never selfish. Rather, his aim is an intense drive to attain glory; it is never motivated by vanity, but by the noble design to spread Christian values all over the world. This comparison is made by Tasso in two celebrated dialogues, *Il Forno primo* and *Il Forno secondo*, and we bring it up here because it helps to refine the notion of heroic virtue. In observing the similarities between the hero and a tyrant, Tasso wants to underline the nature of irrepressible love that animates them both, but the nature of their respective aim marks the neat difference. Tyrants offer no model to be admired, nonetheless, they show how powerful the desire of excelling can be when supported by an unrestrained will. Tyrants' drives are so perverse and successful that they incarnate that bestiality that Aristotle mentions but does not analyze.[26]

This analogy of *virtus heroica* with *caritas* confirms that Tasso could not satisfactorily define the nature of that special virtue that eluded many theologians and philosophers. Tasso was looking for a formula that could not come from Aristotelian ethics. He would have fared better pursuing the Augustinian and the Franciscan line of a Duns Scotus, who would have considered *virtus heroica* as a passion of the will, a passion born in the irascible soul but guided by an undeflectable will, nurtured by a love that grows bigger as it succeeds. This solution, had he proposed it in philosophical rather than in rhetorical terms, would have settled the question of heroic virtue.

Some authors who wrestled with the problem found themselves imitating Tasso. A case in point is Gabriel Zinano, author of *L'Amata overo della virtù heroica* (Bartholi, 1591), a brief dialogue between Amata and Alfonso. Here the male character starts defending the use of *maschia*, "virile," as an attribute appropriate for a woman who exhibits manly virtues, and then the conversation leads to talk of *virtù eroica*, which gives occasion to repeat the criticisms Tasso made against Aristotle; ultimately it settles in a vague definition of a supervirtue, never mentioning *caritas*. In the end, Zinino lists many women who proved capable of practicing heroic virtues.

In the same year, 1591, Francesco India, a Veronese physician, took a stand against Tasso with his *L'heroe overo della virtù heroica*. This dialogue opens with the same question seen in Zanino, namely, whether women can attain heroic virtue, but the answer will come much later once the search for that special virtue has been exhausted. And it is a long search taking the reader through the back and forth of the dialogue between three friends, one being a philosopher, another a theologian, and a third having the role of moderator. The problems are not new to us: What are virtues, where do they originate, what is their function . . . and most of all, what is a heroic virtue? Aristotle, but now Tasso as well, are blamed for not having been more forthcoming in clarifying its nature. But finally, after pages and pages of debates we have a definition.

> Adunque per conclusione et per definition della virtù heroica, diremo che ella altro non sia che un habito nobilissimo, splendore, et eccellenza delle virtù morali, appartenente all'appetito dei sensi, nato da un sublime desiderio d'honore, che sopra la condizione humana va l'huomo innalzando.

> So, in concluding and formulating a definition of "heroic virtue," we shall say that it is nothing but a very noble habit, a splendor, and an excellency of moral virtues, belonging to the appetite of the senses, born from a sublime desire for honor, which elevates man above the human condition.[27]

The definition says that this special virtue is the wholeness of the moral virtues, with the added attribute of the splendor of that burning love for the highest good. When this combination occurs, we have heroic virtue. There is no mention of divine intervention, but later on, we are told that heroic virtue is one step below divine virtue.

> Noi veggiamo che cinque sono i gradi delle virtù, il primo de quali è la naturale, o vogliam dire di schiata, il secondo de costume, il terzo dell'intelletto, il quarto heroic, il quinto supremo divino; così habbiamo a sapere che per questi cinque gradi l'huomo si va innalzando; per mezzo del primo grado diviene bello, giocondo et sano; per favore del secondo si fa buono et da bene, e tale si dice essere il buon Cittadino, e l'ottimo principe; per favore

del terzo si fa sapiente; per l'eminenza del quarto fassi heroe, et
per la sublimità del quinto diviene divino.

We see that five are the degrees of virtues. The first of them is
the natural one, or the one found in our origin; the second is
that of habit; the third one is that of the intellect; the fourth
is the heroic one; the fifth and supreme is the divine one. And
we have to know that these are the degrees through which men
strive to perfection. Through the first step we become beautiful,
happy and healthy; through the second we become good and
urbane, and as such we become good citizens, and good princes;
through the third we become wise; through the eminence of the
fourth, we become heroes; and by the sublimity of the fifth we
become divine. (88–89)

Up to this point India coincides by and large with Tasso, even if he tends to
see heroic virtue more as a quality and a degree, and places it closer to the
realm of the moral virtues. But on one point he strongly disagrees—when
he comes to talk about "bestiality."

Una depravatione, et mutatione di natura, de gli appetite ragione-
voli, et humani, in ferigni, struggitrice dell'uso della ragione, nata
dal disprezzo del vero amore, per causa della quale l'huomo sotto
la conditione di se stesso si va deprimendo, e sotto questo nome
di ferità devremo intendere il tiranno, il crudele et il profano.

A depravity, a change in nature of the reasonable and human
appetites into bestial ones which destroys the use of reason, being
born out of dispising true love, causing in people a depression
of their own making, and under this name of bestiality we must
understand the cruel and profane tyrant. (73)

Hence, he rejects Tasso's idea that tyrants can have heroic characteristics,
energy, and ardent love for glory. In the last section of his treatise, India
extrapolates long passages from Tasso's dialogues *Il Forno*, and firmly argues
against him: heroic qualities are to be judged by their aim, and tyrants
never pursue laudable aims.

Much more could be said about India's work—the role of nobility
and education, the kind of historical examples of heroic virtue, the recognition that female virtues can be heroic—but what we said should suffice

to demonstrate that the need for explaining the nature of this special virtue was a burning and difficult question. And there was no way of finding a neat solution. We could quote many other authors who tackled this problem—Zuccolo,[28] Mascardi,[29] Gramigna,[30] and Tesauro,[31] among others—and we would not find a definitive answer. We would have reached the same results had we gone out of the Italian boundaries and looked at authors like Baltasar Gracián or John Milton.[32] It seems that *virtus heroica* would not fit in any *geometry of passions*, always standing part of a borderline rather than of any center. This situation in turn poses a question: Why did this problem become so relevant in the period running between the autumn of the Renaissance and the dawn of the Enlightenment?

There was no heroic virtue before some medieval commentator of Aristotle's *Nicomachean Ethics* brought it to life, and found that saints, the new heroes of the Christian age, would be the most deserving representatives of such a distinguished virtue. When the age of the "condottieri" had given rise to a good share of tyrants and absolute monarchies began to give a new order to the world that was so conflictual because of religious crises, a quest for a new hero began to emerge—a hero closer to a savior than to a Roland, and on this new hero was bestowed the power of acting with heroic virtue. Not a normal man, but not a saint either: just a superior man close to Good and with the responsibility of setting the world straight. When this kind of superman was not necessary anymore, *virtus heroica* vanished and the only ones to retain it were the saints because they were anointed by a supreme religious authority through a judicial trial and the outcome was permanent; the earthly heroes, instead, were elevated to a pedestal by human opinion, therefore their status had no guarantees of permanency. The eighteenth-century needed a new kind of hero whose greatest heroic feat was to win over themselves or sacrifice what they loved the most to the laws of reason. The heroes of Metastasio or Alfieri, just to name well-known models, had a different way of being heroic, and it was not any easier, because it is never easy to be a hero.

Notes

1. Simo Knuuttila, *Emotions in Ancient and Medieval*; Carla Casagrande and Silvana Vecchio, *Passioni dell'anima. Teorie e usi degli affetti nella cultura medievale*; Barbara H. Rosenwein, *Generation of Feelings: A History of Emotions, 600–1700*;

A. Corbin, J. J. Courtine, and G. Vigarello, *Histoire des émotions*, vol. I: *De l'antiquité aux Lumières*. On the method of studying passions in their historical context, see, Barbara H. Rosenwein, "Problems and Methods in the History of Emotions." Accessed December 3, 2020. https://www.passionsincontext.de/uploads/media/01_Rosenwein.pdf,

2. Paolo Cherchi, *Il tramonto dell'onestade*, 274–78.

3. Augustine (*De civitate Dei*, X, 21; in *PL*, 41, 298–99) is quoted in Prospero Lambertini (Pope Benedict XIV), *De Servorum Dei Beatificatione et Beatorum Canonizatione*, vol. I, 214. Book 3 of this work is entirely devoted to heroic virtue. Lambertini's documentation is quite rich and provides a treasure of bibliographical data organized by subject. A chronological history is provided by the essays quoted in the previous note, to which one should add the more recent and most comprehensive A. Royo Mejía, *Apuntes sobre la evolución histórica del concepto de heroicidad de las virtudes aplicado a las causas de los santos*, in REDC 52 (1995), 19–561. We will not mention these works every time, which is quite often, we have used them.

4. We know enough of it thanks to August Pelzer, "Un cours inédit d'Albert Ie Grand sur Ie Morale à Nicomaque. Recueilli et rédigé par S. Thomas d'Aquin," *Revue philosophique de Louvain* 95 (1922): 333–61.

5. *Ethica Nicomachean*, in *Opera Omnia*, lib. 7, lect. 1, 224.

6. See Jacopo Costa, "Heroic Virtue in the Commentary Tradition on the Nicomachean Ethics, of the Second Half the Thirteenth Century," in Istvàn Bejczy, Ed., *Virtue Ethics in the Middle Ages: Commentaries on Aristotle's Nicohomachean Ethics, 1200–1500*, 151–72, in particular, 156–60.

7. *Quodlibet* 5, q. 16: "Utrum habitus acquisitus per quemlibet actum pertinentem ad ipsum generetur et deinde per quemlibet sequentem augmentetur," quoted by A. Royo Mejía, 530.

8. A fundamental text on Buridanus is Risto Saarinen, "Virtus heroica: 'Held' und 'Genie' als Begriffe des christlichen Aristotelismus," *Archiv für Begriffsgeschichte* 33 (1990): 96–114; and *Die heroische Tugend*, als Grundlage der individualistischen Ethik im 14.Jahrhundert," in *Individuum und Individualität im Mittelalter*, edited by Jan A. Aertsen and Andreas Speer, De Gruyter (1996, 454–63). It must be said that "special persons" gifted with heroic virtue were present in late medieval political culture: they were most often the kings, whose virtues had to be superhuman (see Biörn Tjällén, *Aristotle's Heroic Virtue and Medieval Theory of Monarchy*, in *Shaping Heroic Virtue*, 55–68).

9. The problem is studied by Risto Saarinen in his *Die heroische Tügend*, cit., with interesting considerations on the political and ideological consequences. On this point, see the succinct but incisive observation by Hellerstedt and Fogelberg Rota in their introduction to *Shaping Heroic Virtue*, 7–11.

10. L. Brancati de Lauria, *Commentaria in III et IV Librum Sententiarum Ioannis Duns Scoti*, 2, Roma 1653–1682, disp. 32: "De virtute" 709–826.

11. L. Brancati di Lauria, *Commentaria in III et IV*, article 6, no. 77.

12. On the subject see at least A. Rossi, "Il concetto di virtù eroica in Benedetto XIV," *Rivista di Ascetica e Mistica* 4 (1961): 608–14.

13. The problem is studied by Risto Saarinen in his *Die heroische Tügend*, with interesting considerations on the political and ideological consequences. On this point, see also the succinct but incisive observation by Hellerstedt and Fogelberg Rota in their introduction to *Shaping Heroic Virtue*, 7–11.

14. Giulio Landi, *Le attioni morali*, 39.

15. Antonio Scaino, *Sei discorsi sopra diverse materie civili*. The quotation is from "Secondo discorso circa l'utilità che si può prendere da i libri politici d'Aristotele," carta. 18r.

16. See Antonio Poppi, *L'etica del Rinascimento tra Platone e Aristotele*, 59–78.

17. Francesco Piccolomini, *Universa philosophia de moribus*. The "gradus sextus," out of the ten forming the work, with its twenty-three chapters are at 328–55.

18. Piccolomini, *Universa philosophia*, VI, 8, 337.

19. Piccolomini, *Universa philosophia*, 335–36.

20. On this point see Risto Saarinen, *Virtus heroica*, 108–11; and the introduction to *Shaping Heroic Virtue*, 10.

21. From *Discorsi dell'arte poetica e del poema eroico*, ed. Luigi Poma, 106. Poma reconstructs the textual tradition of this works up to its first edition (1587).

22. *Discorsi dell'arte poetica e del poema eroico*, ed. Luigi Poma, 12.

23. One exception is Guido Laurenti: "'Poter filosofando aprir la prigione e scuoter il giogo della servitù': filosofia morale e retorica encomiastica nel discorso "Della virtù eroica e della carità" di Torquato Tasso," In *Studi Tassiani* 59–61 (2011–2013): 133–58.

24. The quotation is taken from *Delle opere di Torquato Tasso*, in twelve volumes published between 1735 and 1742, vol. VIII, 212–13.

25. Piccolomini defines *charitas* as "fervens amor" of the highest good that generates all virtues. And even more to our point: "Charitas ex principiis Aristotelis nil aliud est, nisi Amor honesti cuius radix est dilectio Dei et proximi," Gradus quartus, chapter XXXVI, 214.

26. On the hero/tyrant similarities has written with sharp insights and erudition Maiko Favaro, "The virtues of the tyrant and the passion of the hero," *Germanisch-Romanische Monatsschrift* 67 (2017): 3–20.

27. Francesco India, *L'heroe overo della virtù heroica*, 53.

28. Ludovico Zuccolo, *De honesto gloriae studio sive de vera virtute heroica*. As the title shows, a way of understanding heroic virtue is to see it as a perfect form of the *honestum*.

29. Agostino Mascardi, speaks of virginity as *virtus heroica* in oration "Alla Signora Magherita Doria quando si monacò nel monistero della Santissima Annunciata in Genova, in his *Prose Vulgari*, part II, 75–76.

30. Vincenzo Gramigna, "Della virtù Eroica" is the first essay of his *Opuscoli*, 1–12.

31. Emanuele Tesauro, *Della filosofia morale derivata dal grande Aristotele Stagirita*. The entirety of book XIX, "Della virtù heroica," 571–78, is devoted to heroic virtue. Here is the definition: "Altro non è la Virtù Heroica se non un così perfetto regolamento del Giuditio, et un dominio tanto assoluto sopra le passioni, che niun oggetto ha forza di smuover l'heroe dal ragionevole, onde pare che egli habbia più del divino che dell'humano, come del suo Hettore disse Homero" [Virtue is nothing else but a perfect regulation of the judgment, and an absolute control of the passions to the point that nothing has the power to move a hero from what is reasonable, so that it may seem that is more divine than human, as Homer said of his Hector]. In the most orthodox Aristotelian terms, heroic virtue is considered a purely intellectual virtue. On Tesauro see Kristine Kolrud, *The Gem and the Mirror of Heroic Virtue: Emanuele Tesauro and the Heroic in the Court of Savoy*, in *Shaping Heroic Virtue*, 69–94.

32. On Milton, see John M. Steadman, "Heroic Virtue and the Divine Image in *Paradise Lost*," in *Journal of the Warburg and Courtauld Institutes* 22 (1959): 88–105.

Bibliography

Brancati di Lauria, Lorenzo. *Commentaria Fr. Laurentii Brancati de Lauraea in III et IV Librum Sententiarum Ioannis Duns Scoti*, vol. 2. Corbelletus, 1653–1682.

Cherchi, Paolo. *Il tramonto dell'onestade*. Edizioni di Storia e Letteratura, 2016.

Casagrande, Carla, and Silvana Vecchio. *Passioni dell'anima. Teorie e usi degli affetti nella cultura medievale*. SISMEL—Edizioni del Galluzzo, 2015.

Corbin, Alain, Jean-Jacques Courtine, and Georges Vigarello. *Histoire des émotions*, vol. I: *De l'antiquité aux Lumières*. Seuil, 2016.

Costa, Jacopo. "Heroic Virtue in the Commentary Tradition on the *Nicomachean Ethics*, of the Second Half of the Thirteenth Century." In Istvàn Bejczy, Ed., *Virtue Ethics in the Middle Ages: Commentaries on Aristotle's Nicohomachean Ethics, 1200–1500*. Brill, 2006.

Favaro, Maiko. "The virtues of the tyrant and the passion of the hero" *Germanisch-Romanische Monatsschrift* 67 (2017): 3–20.

Gramigna, Vincenzo. *Opuscoli del signor Vincenzo Gramigna segretario*. Cecconcelli, 1620.

India, Francesco. *L'heroe overo della virtù heroica*. Girolamo Discepolo, 1591.

Knuuttila, Simo. *Emotions in Ancient and Medieval Philosophy*. Claredon Press, 2004.

Lambertini, Prospero (Pope Benedict XIV). *De Servorum Dei Beatificatione et Beatorum Canonizatione*, vol. 1. Salomone, 1753.

Landi, Giulio. *Le attioni morali*. Gabriel Giolito de' Ferrari, 1564.

Laurenti, Guido. "'Poter filosofando aprir la prigione e scuoter il giogo della servitù': Filosofia morale e retorica encomiastica nel discorso 'Della virtù eroica e della carità' di Torquato Tasso." *Studi Tassiani* 59–61 (2011é2013): 133–58.

Mascardi, Agostino. *Prose Vulgari*. Bartolomeo Fontana, 1635.

Pelzer, August. "Un cours inédit d'Albert Ie Grand sur Ie Morale à Nicomaque: Recueilli et rédigé par S. Thomas d'Aquin." *Revue philosophique de Louvain* 95 (1922): 333–61.

Piccolomini, Francesco. *Universa philosophia de moribus*. De Francisci, 1583.

Poppi, Antonio. *L'etica del Rinascimento tra Platone e Aristotele*. Città del Sole, 1970.

Rosenwein, Barbara H. *Generation of Feelings: A History of Emotions, 600–1700*. Cambridge University Press, 2015.

Rosenwein, Barbara H. "Problems and Methods in the History of Emotions." Accessed December 3, 2020.https://www.passionsincontext.de/uploads/media/01_Rosenwein.pdf.

Rossi, A. "Il concetto di virtù eroica in Benedetto XIV." *Rivista di Ascetica e Mistica* 4 (1961): 608–14.

Royo Mejía, Alberto. "Apuntes sobre la evolución histórica del concepto de heroicidad de las virtudes aplicado a las causas de los santos." *Revista Española de Derecho Canónico* 52, no. 139 (1995): 519–61.

Saarinen, Risto. "Die heroische Tugund als Grundlage der individualistischen Ethik im 14.Jahrhundert." In *Individuum und Individualität im Mittelalter*, edited by Jan A. Aertsen and Andreas Speer: 450–63. De Gruyter, 1996.

Saarinen, Risto. "Virtus heroica: 'Held' und 'Genie' als Begriffe des christlichen Aristotelismus." *Archiv für Begriffsgeschichte* 33 (1990): 96–114.

Scaino, Antonio. *Sei discorsi sopra diverse materie civili*. Case del popolo romano, 1578.

Steadman, John M. "Heroic Virtue and the Divine Image in *Paradise Lost*." *Journal of the Warburg and Courtauld Institutes* 22 (1959): 88–105.

Tasso, Torquato. *Delle opere di Torquato Tasso*. Stefano Monti, 1738.

Tasso, Torquato. *Discorsi dell'arte poetica e del poema eroico*. Edited by Luigi Poma. Laterza, 1964.

Tesauro, Emanuele. *Della filosofia morale derivata dal grande Aristotele Stagirita*. Pezzana, 1671.

Tjällén, Biörn. "Aristotle's Heroic Virtue and Medieval Theory of Monarchy." In *Shaping Heroic Virtue: Studies in the Art and Politics of Supereminence in Europe and Scandinavia*, edited by Stefano Fogelberg Rota and Andreas Hellerstedt, 55–66. Brill Academic Publishers, 2015.

Zuccolo, Ludovico. *De honesto gloriae studio sive de vera virtute heroica*. Dei, 1615.

9

Personal Destinies

On Genealogy and Crisis of Individuality

Andrea Borsari

Triptych

Destini personali (Personal destinies) by the philosopher Remo Bodei is a book one cannot discuss as a single unity only; it is part of a "triptych," which also consists of *Geometria delle passioni* (Geometry of the Passions) and *Scomposizioni* (Decompositions).[1] *Destini personali* entails a long series of chapters dedicated to the genesis and development of phenomena, conceptions, and theories of individuality, connected originally to two points of view, Locke's and Schopenhauer's. These chapters concern the birth of cytology as study of cells, the origin of the notion of "multiple self," and the French *medécins-philosophes* (Ribot, Janet, Binet), Nietzsche and his center of gravity, philosophers and writers like Bergson, Proust, Pirandello, and Simmel, as well as psychologists and thinkers who influenced the political action through their work, such as Gustave Le Bon's crowd psychology and Georges Sorel's myth of the general strike, and Mussolini's and Giovanni Gentile's conceptions of politics. A book, finally, that focuses on the current—at the time it was written and published, in 2002—horizons of the I/self, of the individual and individuality. For this reason, to better understand the book's meaning, we have to consider the essential lines of the two other books that compose the triptych and keep in mind—or at least in perspective—the future developments that Bodei afforded the same themes.

In order to outline and reconstruct the complex of individuation in Bodei's thought, first of all it will be necessary to point out the modern genesis of the attention to *res singulares*, which debunks the prejudice of the ineffability of the individual in the name of the cognitive passion, the *amor intellectualis* that enhances the singularity of the things and people it sets as its object; and to retrace its opposite counterpoint in the conformative drive to shape individuals with politics and virtue through the paradoxical despotism of freedom (section 2). Then, it will be useful to define the antinomic thrust that between the eighteenth and nineteenth centuries generates, on the one hand, the development and safeguarding of individuality and, on the other hand, its dissolution into appearance and nihilistic emptiness. Up to the oscillation between the "I" and the "We" in twentieth-century developments and the possible return to an individualism of differences (section 3). In a further deepening, it will be appropriate to go back to the origins of the research project to redefine the strategies of individuation, starting from the dialectic as a tool and a procedure for the building, enrichment, and socialization of individuality, and to then describe its crisis and the questioning of its capability to build a superior form of dealing with reality through exposure to the negative and the return to a heightened self, the very idea of development through contradictions (section 4). For the purpose of exploring the next step of Bodei's research, it will be convenient to retrace the pyramidal model of construction of the individual from its formulation in the age of Goethe to its reduction in surface in the multiple self of the late twentieth-century. A process that passes through the statement that the transformation of substance into subject has now become impossible and that the contrast between life and forms produces a deposit of knowledge external and independent from the subjective and individual consciousness in structural and continuous delay on it (section 5). On the basis of this survey of the entire process, it will be possible to return to the problematic core of *Destini* and identify some fundamental theoretical keys or patterns of analogy that constitute the tools for understanding the current consequences of these transformations. In this way, the following schemes will be examined: the condensation or approximation by juxtaposition of different selves; the self-consciousness as a barycenter or place of restatement and reformulation of the many experiences and thoughts of the self; the heterochronic and heterotopic dimension of lives that involves both the coexistence of real and imagined spaces and times and the coexistence of singular experience (through the body and the intimate sense) and shared social and cultural experience of thoughts, memories, affections, and perceptions (section 6). The conclusion of the essay will finally attempt to define some developments of the same themes in parallel or subsequent works by Bodei himself and to propose some open questions about the research he has transmitted as a legacy to those who remain (section 7).

If, to introduce his reflection, we start from the discursive exposition that Bodei has provided of the way to understand the problem of the ontogenesis of personal identity, that is, to figure out how individuality, subject, and personality are built, we could note that he sees it as related to the task of understanding how certain forms of irrationality, such as passions, delusions, and ideologies enter that process. Bodei often refers to a phrase by Friedrich Schelling: Madness does not come from outside, but it is reason that subdues psychic turmoil. Reason seems to be a reactive formation against madness and chaos, as has been shown by psychiatry and post-Freudian psychology, especially by childhood researchers. Already in Anna Freud's work, it is possible to trace the idea that the child grows in the first six months into a current of psychotic turbulence. Simplifying, one can say that there is the chaos before, and then reason comes as an attempt to organize something, but it fails completely. As Nietzsche claimed, underlining the logic of dreams, in the dream surfaces the most archaic part of us, aspects of our existence that could not be rationalized. It starts, thus, from a situation in which the logic of the dream was twenty-four hours a day, even for the whole time of the vigil. Then the logic of reason slowly colonized the day, and the archaic logic, that is phantasmagoric, remained in the night.[2]

Two Focuses of the Ellipsis: The Geometry of the Passions

Following his *Geometry of the Passions*, subtitled *Fear, Hope, Happiness: Philosophy and Political Use* (1991), the underlying conviction that has moved Bodei's whole quest in this direction is that a world of passions always belongs to our personality, passions that are not simply something that disturbs reason, but they are that resistance—like the notorious Kantian dove—without which reason does not move, and which must also be under control, though knowing that passions are vital forces. Moreover, Descartes, who wrote the *Passions of the Soul*, was not the rationalist philosopher that he seemed; he argued in fact that without the pathos, tension and energy that passions entail, reason could not work. The fuel of reason, in other words, are the passions themselves. And then the great lesson for Bodei came from Spinoza. This was not the Spinoza of the savage anomaly, nor even that of the French school, who put it as an alternative to Hegel, as did Balibar and others, with the multitude and so on. Bodei looked at Spinoza as the great, powerful attempt to consider no more the binary contrast between reason and passion, but to see, through intellectual love (*amor intellectualis*), how the highest knowledge is the ability to maintain the energy of passions, through the transitions.

> In the *transitio* toward greater perfection [. . .], each person shapes himself through intellectual and emotional learning that follows a model of consistent and constant imbalance in its progress. For Spinoza, "saying yes to life" is joy (not fought by a stern or envious reason) that feeds on all the energy of the passions transformed into positive feelings and that renders *amor intellectualis* similar to a harmonic orchestration of rationality and feelings, to the measure (*Takt* or "tact") fixed from time to time (in each person with respect to "particular things") by the power of his current *conatus*.
>
> To shake their passivity and not let men waste away in hardship, he uses the ascensional energy of feelings like *laetitia* and *amor*, no longer restrained (as in the Augustinian, Lutheran, or Jansenist theological traditions) by the necessity to obtain the extraordinary help of divine grace to defeat the enormous weight of original sin, or the insurmountability of evil, by human means alone. For Spinoza, "virtue" is no longer deprivation, repression, or self-censure, but rather *fortitudo* and *gaudium* (which, for him, is joy of a past thing that occurred beyond our hopes [. . .]). By means of the *transitio* to a greater intramundane perfection (but one that does not enjoy any ethical privilege compared to the totality of nature) the Pauline and Augustinian struggle between law and sin, between spirit and flesh, is abolished without resorting to asceticism or the intervention of supernatural powers. The tensions dissolve thanks to the intellectual love that, instead of blocking or repressing them, lets the natural forces of passion and the imagination develop until they find their own way toward their resolution in more satisfying conditions of existence. Life is more full of joy and has less need to transfigure itself in the

hereafter, to invoke a divine order so to avoid, in an Augustinian way, the "fear of becoming lost" that torments it.

The *transitio* is measured by the *conatus*, by the continuous quantity of movement of increased or decreased impulse or *cupiditas*—that is, of the appetite that is conscious of itself. The *conatus* is not, however, only ascendant (as some interpreters assert, projecting Nietzchean models onto it). It can also follow a descending course where the passions may prevail that are tied to *tristitia*—to which each is subjected by chance or by its passive surrender or acquiescence. The wise man, even with a rough or discontinuous "diagram" of the variations of his own power of existing, manages to maintain the high level of the power that has already been reached, or at least to persevere along the upward path.[3]

According to Spinoza, in fact, "*amor*" is not directed toward the whole or the general, but "toward the *res singulares*," that is, "individual things," understood in a not purely numerical sense, "in their concrete and visible expression with respect to the whole": "in this sense, the theory according to which *individuum est ineffable* is not true. Through this form of knowledge, one reaches the highest degree of 'effability': we can speak of a thing in the most articulate way because we love it singularly. We accept it with joy for how it is in the framework of the universal necessity specified and focused individually in every being."[4]

If for Spinoza the highest degree of knowledge remains linked to the knowledge of "res particulares," a synonym of wisdom, it is significant—Bodei noticed—that, despite every more obvious difference, "even Machiavelli thinks, like Spinoza, that understanding the 'essential truth of the thing' involves knowledge of the *res particulares* in their specificity":

this does not exclude, but even presumes, passage from knowledge and praxis through the universal, the overcoming (and not the abandonment) of both the confused, distorting viewpoint of the imagination and opinion, and the viewpoint that is transparent and well-articulated by types, norms, and laws: dictated by reason, but not yet experienced in concrete situations. Machiavelli obviously proceeds on the grounds of practical intelligence and not of *amor Dei intellectualis*. For Machiavelli, in fact, there is no need to be a 'wise man' in the full sense to know the *res singulares*.[5]

Anyway, this Machiavellian element seemed to him very important: one knows what one loves, and knowledge is not always the *vade retro* (going back) of passions, but the use of positive passions, precisely, of the joy, to grow.

The plexus of Spinoza's thought thus represents the bridge between ethics aimed at self-control and "political manipulation of the passions" and those that leave the field open to "the incommensurability of desire." In this way it helps to break down "the double wall that traditionally divides, on one side, the passions from reason and, on the other, the restlessness of the masses from the 'serenity' of the wise."[6]

Furthermore, he has put this into a relationship based on the contrast and contraposition with Jacobinism, with a kind of ellipsis—another image, an absolute metaphor—in which the relationship between reason and passions is overturned.

> The ellipse's second focus of concentration is given, in chronological terms, by the theoretical practices of French Jacobinism, through the use (completely backward relative to Spinoza) of fear and hope, which now, from the revolutionary vantage point of emancipation, are no longer seen as enemies but as auxiliaries of reason. They are not yet seen as instruments for subjugating the masses but as spurs of the autonomy of individuals and peoples. The paradoxical Jacobin "despotism of liberty"—as a vehicle of political and moral progress—institutionalizes these two passions (strengthening the hope or fear) and redistributes the roles of others in an attempt to rationalize them according to universal principals and make them become, over time, drivers of both spontaneous behaviors and reflections. With Jacobinism (which, however brief and fulminant its trajectory might have been, can be considered here almost as an archetype of modern political movements of radical emancipation) power changes into terror, clarified by a reason that is armed and supported by a collective will that is concentrated in the hands of a few men. Simultaneously, revolutionary hope transforms into a secular faith in the regeneration of future humanity and into religious faith that establishes, by decree, the existence of the Supreme Being

and the immortality of the soul. An otherworldly guarantee thus rewards the citizen's "virtue," remunerating his sacrifice to the general interest. The semi-spontaneous "great fear" in the summer of 1789 and the "great hope" that cut through all phases of the revolution were translated into political and religious forms at the same time. Unlike Spinoza, who derives politics from the essence of man insofar as it is *cupiditas* (of which the passions are an irremovable expression), the Jacobins want to compress and shape this essence across politics and "virtue."[7]

Jacobinism, however, reaches an "obsessive familiarity with death" that is not only a result, in revolutionary ethics and conduct, of the disposition to future sacrifices of oneself and of others, but also of the decision to use, in view of progress, "those demonic, turbulent, and uncontrollable passions that traditional wisdom had always held at a distance."[8]

Nevertheless, it was an attempt, as Leopardi said, to geometrize reason and therefore to put passions at the service of a political project. And, as Bodei clarifies at the conclusion of this book, after the great revolutionary terror, with Thermidor, together with the most abject fear, also ends the "great hope": "all the 'citizens' were put back in their places at least temporarily. Social hierarchies restructured themselves; expectations and desires were restored. Nothing, however—whether good or bad—could ever return to what it had been."[9] An analysis that continues also in the third part of the triptych, because *Personal Destinies*, also chronologically, starts from where *Geometry of the Passions* ends.

The Parabola from Two *Traguardi*: Personal Destinies

Personal Destinies, subtitle *The Age of Colonization of Consciousnesses* (2002), actually starts from the world of the Restoration, Schopenhauer, and Stendhal, and then develops until it reaches our present day. In general, it raises the question of how the Self is constructed according to the following two alternatives.

One is represented by Locke and leads to liberalism—as known—and in which the I/self is not something given, but a fact, in the sense that it is a construction (*factum*), which undergoes a transformation from a *fundamentum inconcussum* (unshaken ground) to a kind of thread that can be cut on one end by memory (the past) on the other by concerns/worries (the future). It is a line of dissolution toward an *x* that one can never grasp, which goes from Locke to Hume, up to Kant.

The other alternative is provided by Schopenhauer's "nihilistic" solution, according to which, at the bottom, within us, in what we feel the most, there is nothing; there is an anonymous voice that rumbles in a hollow sphere of glass. The individual and individuality here are an appearance; in a perspective that could then be extended by including the adverse effects that are recorded, for example, in Thomas Mann, another one of Bodei's favorite writers.[10]

In summary, he was interested in focusing on the fragility of the self, attacked by two points of view. According to Locke, the individual is something voluntary: you attribute rights to him or her, attach him or her to memory, but he or she always has the will to build him- or herself. Instead, the dissolving element in Schopenhauer and then in Nietzsche, for which we are plural, allows Bodei to come to the idea of the multiplicity of the self, which is one of his long-term research themes. He started studying it—he declared—at the beginning of the 1980s when he was very involved in the Pirandellian conferences in Agrigento, organized by the Pirandellian Studies Center. Through Pirandello, he discovered the *médecins philosophes* Théodule Ribot, Pierre Janet, and Alfred Binet. And thanks to them he became passionate about the history of the concept of "multiple personalities."

Once he earned the criterion to see how it was considered the fragility of the I/self throughout that time, he came to the second part of the twentieth century and to Claude Lévi-Strauss, who defined the self as a "pauvre trésor" and "insupportable enfant gâté" (a poor treasure and unbearable spoiled child).

The idea behind the research was that—on the contrary—such a model of the I/self was not to be abandoned. Though fragile, if you lose it, if everything becomes a fiction, a form of imagination, a mirror creation, an ethical problem arises. In this way, you end up becoming prey to forces you cannot control. It is the issue of understanding the so-called totalitarianisms, the cult of personality, in which Le Bon's study and the psychology of crowds becomes very important.

Bodei's interest about this rose from what he later called the "political sublime." How did it happen—he asks—that one could argue: "the Duce is always right"? How can it happen that you come to the idea of this boss who is unreachable and why you find there the centrality of believing? Here the resumption of myth becomes relevant, and through it the reference to Sorel. All of these elements, the historical-social factors such as the Weimar economic and political crisis, were not enough to explain why at a certain point you see that the so-called exceptional men, such as Hitler, Stalin, but also Roosevelt, and Wilson before him, appear. And many of them were people who read and commented on Le Bon. This is to say why the ideas of parliament, liberalism, democracy, of rational discussion in general, were replaced by the direct dialogue of the crowds with the leader, the *meneur des foules*, the crowd leader. The myth was created, obviously supported by a propaganda apparatus, according to which these are semi-divine beings. It is the case of the maxim, attributed to Himmler, which required the Kantian imperative to be adjusted to what the Führer said: "When you act, in short, ask yourself before doing anything if the Führer approves it."

The analysis of the configurations assumed by the I/self, conscience and personal identity take, as a whole, the form of a "parabola," in the double sense "of a geometric figure, which indicates the trace of a curve—with a starting point, a zenith, a decline—and of an exemplary story, which contains a teaching, theoretical and historical, on the mutual implications of the relations between the conscience and its political and historical horizons."[11] The initial stretch of the curve described in the first part of the book will thus be defined from the two *traguardi*, in the optical sense, that is, from Locke's and Schopenhauer's thoughts as "instruments intended to focus the view of an object between two points of aim." In this case, "they constitute the preliminary references for outlining two divergent lines of development: that of the individual and his autonomy and that of the elimination or denigration of the *principium individuationis*."[12] If the first trajectory is constituted by the progressive differentiation, enrichment, and problematization of individuality, the second trajectory, which from Schopenhauer will reach Le Bon, Gentile, and the totalitarianisms of the twentieth century, proposes to erase or reabsorb individual differences and, in the economy of the book, will be fully explained, as seen in great synthesis, in the second part on the colonization of consciences. On the other hand, what Bodei defines here as "strategies of individuation," the first part of the book, culminates in the chapter dedicated to the "individualism of differences," that is, to the thought of Georg Simmel.

The role played by Simmel in Bodei's reconstruction is diametrically opposed to that of Pirandello and involves freeing the individual from the "traps of life" and transforming "social conditioning into possible opportunities for personal growth." No longer being nailed to "a fixed role, as a member of a clan, a class or a profession," he or she now tends to differentiate him- or herself on the basis of belonging "to eccentric, open and distant social environments." In particular, the metropolitan individual is made up of a "variable interweaving of given realities and constructed possibilities," so that "while having in common with his peers the single digits of combination, the individual becomes all the more him/herself, the more he/she incorporates traits of universality shared with his/her peers, the more he widens the range of possible components of his/her own personality."[13] By virtue of these processes, the individual becomes autonomous, but the "lesser constraints" to which the modern individual is subject risk producing undesirable effects and leaving a growing margin for the deformation of individualism and selfishness. In opposition to a well-established philosophical tradition, for Simmel form is not connected to the universal, but to the individual, and his so-called "philosophical impressionism" turns out—notes Bodei—to be entirely consistent with his rigorous theoretical assumptions, precisely in relation to the individual: "this style of thought has its 'scandalous' point of strength precisely where it seems weakest: in the analysis of the residues refractory to any generalization, in what is irreducible as much to the pure interiority of individual psychology as to the exteriority of social relations."[14]

From this perspective, therefore, individuality is not subsumed under any law; it does not obey a totalizing logic or a purely conflictual logic, but is defined according to a paradoxical "individual law," as it is concretized in the unmistakable "face" (*Gesicht*) of each person, the precipitate of his past in the substantial form of his traits, showing the "succession of his life in a contemporaneity."[15] In a similar vein, Simmel interprets adventure as "impatient abandonment to chance" that attracts us because it "unites two contradictory aspirations: it makes one feel at ease in a foreign world and at the center when one is thrust into the periphery of life."[16] Thanks to adventure, the aspiration to live in virtual times and spaces is accompanied by "the obscure and paradoxical awareness that the elsewhere is already here, that the *ad-ventura*, the moving towards future things, is already contained in the present, in the lightning passage of experience," so that "the essential lurks in the inessential."[17]

Bodei also underlines how Simmel is "the only modern philosopher to highlight the gender difference in the formation of individuality and to philosophically examine the epochal novelty of the processes of emancipation of women," and that he saw "in the female world, and in the sphere of feelings that distinguish it, an eminent example of a new, arduous scanning of the possible."[18] At this height of his own reading of the philosophical path of the Berlin philosopher and sociologist, Bodei then discusses the "spirit in the machine," that is, the relationship between subjective spirit and objective spirit, in which "the more rationality migrates from subjective consciousness towards automatisms and material supports (as in the machine or in money), the more it tends to become meaningless and the more the individual sees his own faculties inexorably absorbed by autonomous devices."[19]

Unlike other philosophers of life such as Dilthey and Bergson who focus on a revitalization of the individual by tapping into the deposits of meaning or the depths of duration and otherwise in strengthening subjective interiority or spirituality at the expense of objectification, in order to cope with this "heavy subjective deficit of meaning," Simmel recognizes that the "transfer of subjective spirituality within objective and acosciential automatisms leaves, on the one hand, a wider space of possible freedom to individuals, while disclosing them, on the other hand, as abysses of tragedy (because the tragic does not come from outside, but arises from the dissent, almost Schopenhauerian, of human being and civilization with themselves)."[20] Even the relationship with temporality and openness to the possible assumes in Simmel a peculiar connotation that distinguishes it from philosophical tradition and common sense. In fact, he conceives the future as not clearly separated from the present, so we live in a "border zone" that includes both, and the will can overcome their opposition by erecting a bridge that unites them. Although the rigors of the new political phase of incubation of totalitarianism and the two world wars favored an authoritarian logic of hierarchical subordination rather than the autonomy of individuals, by the 1960s the "differentiated flowering of individuality" proposed by Simmel would eventually find a "renewed relevance."[21]

Strategies of Individuation

As for "strategies of individuation," however, all of Bodei's research can be considered included in this definition, which began in the mid-eighties, with the homonymous text published with some variants in different languages, and which would have found its starting definition in the first volume of the triptych dedicated to *Scomposizioni* ("Decompositions"), subtitle *Forms of the Modern Individual*, released in 1987 and, in an expanded edition as a sort of concluding summary of the whole enterprise, in 2016.[22]

The research's basic assumption is the crisis of dialectical thought, and the hypothesis providing the trigger is that the dialectic has been and continues to be "not only a theory of knowledge and a canon of interpretation of history, but also *a strategy of individuation, that is, a procedure for the building, enrichment and socialization of individuality*, the response to a double challenge dictated by the increased rate of *complexity and conflict* in social life and the consequent danger of disintegration of the personality."[23] Such a crisis coincided with the *"reformulation of several different theories of the 'subject' and with the appearance of rival theories about the constitution of individuality,"*[24] essentially hermeneutics and poststructuralist theories of difference and power that drew on Nietzsche and Heidegger, Gadamer, Ricoeur, Derrida, and Foucault, but also the communicative action of Habermas and the theory of plurality of the lifeworlds.

The dialectic is taken here in its ideal typical sense as a strategy that uses contradictions as a function of the development and expansion of individuality. Acceptance of splitting, risk, and suffering are the prerequisites for returning to the self in a more conscious and stronger form than before. Following Hegel's *Jaener Wastebook*, "A mended sock is better than a torn sock: this, however, is not true for self-consciousness."[25] Therefore, each time an obstacle is overcome the identity is strengthened: "By itself, identity is empty, inactive and worthless in its *immediacy*. It must continuously go beyond itself through this very contact or clash with the world. In fact, that which is natural, which has not been worked on, nor undergone man's intervention, and has remained untried, is deemed unworthy of *civilized* man."[26] Dialectical thinking implies the incorporation of otherness in a domesticated form, acclimatizing individuality to change, to conflictual expansion, according to a pathos of contradiction for development, based on the model of vaccine immunization. The protagonist of the dialectic—like the characters in the *Morphology of the Fairy Tales* analyzed by Propp—is the one who is capable "of stepping beside himself in alienation": and who "after gaining strength in the struggle with powers only initially alien, ends up *assimilating* them and becoming *immune*."[27]

The overview presented at the time of the writing of this research program is defined by the impossibility of constructing the subject in pyramidal form, as it was for Goethe, by a loss of a center and by conscious disintegration, which allows the individual to imagine him- or herself as equipped with different possible biographies, with a modular and decomposable consciousness, endowed with a propensity for porosity, while the traditional sources of authority find themselves weakened in their credibility. Although regressive versions of the "metaphysics of development" that supports it have also been provided and it has been radically delegitimized by methodological individualism centered on the *"rationality, intangibility and priority of individual choices,"*[28] it is nevertheless difficult—Bodei concludes—to believe that the dialectical project in its various forms has been canceled. In fact, it continues to maintain a value as a "bridge thrown towards solutions capable of unblocking situations of *impasse*, therefore as an *ars inveniendi* rather than as a teleologically oriented process."[29] In the field of personal identity construction, it continues to prove effective, even in the wake of Piaget's *Les forms élémentaires de la dialectique* (1980), in "exploring new possibilities by focusing on marginal anomalies" and in "*piloting transformation crises*, promoting the abandonment of psychologically inert stages and increasing the will to grow, as well as the 'autopoiesis.'"[30] It loses its absolute primacy, but retains the ability to resist "against the violence and seduction of the existent under any guise, from the *neo-positivistic primacy of the 'datum,'* to the *undisputed acceptance of existing power.*"[31] For the tasks to come, we shall have to test the strength of the dialectic of not separating *polemos* from *dialogos*, the instrumental action from the communicative action, the reasons of reality from those of possibility, in order to "make a virtue of necessity and *translate contradictions into opportunities* for change and development."[32]

The Pyramid and the Prism: Decompositions

With the "Strategies of Individuation," we are faced with the idea that there is subjectivity, as Rilke says, that each of us has within him- or herself something like an olive seed and that the great personalities have big ones and the modest personalities have little ones, and when they are young it's just about educating them. Educating, from the Latin word *e-duco*, to pull out what is inside. In order to study this issue, Bodei started from a constructivist idea, namely, that on the basis of natural factors, the brain, the heart, the various civilizations, but especially the various philosophical-political structures, build or propose to build individuality, even if in different ways. And in his *Scomposizioni* (Decompositions), he wondered how in the *Goethezeit*, that is, in the time of Hegel, Goethe, Hölderlin, Novalis, Fichte, and so on, this model of individual building and self-growth was prefigured. He called it the "pyramidal individual." What through the experience, pain, and contradictions—it has used the dialectical model in this sense—grows on itself and through contradictions it develops. He sought to understand the core of dialectics in the form, say, of "development by contradiction." But showing in the end how this pattern was eroded later, because we are faced with contradictions without development and development without contradictions. So is this idea of *Bildung* in Goethe, through *Wilhelm*

Meister and *Faust*, also in Hegel, to whom he attributed much importance. For Hegel, above all in his *Phenomenology of the Mind* (or of the Spirit, *des Geistes*), the journey of discovery, and then the broadest, systematic theory, with the philosophy of history and the philosophy of the absolute spirit, is that one for whom the individual fits in the historical flow without having that attitude Hans Blumenberg describes in *Shipwreck with Spectator*. Such attitude is often attributed to Hegel, mentioning the *Schlachtbank*, the butcher's bench, and the sentence sounds like: "history is nothing but a butcher shop." Nevertheless adding—and this is truly Hegelian—"and the pages of happiness are white pages," as Hegel wrote in his *Philosophy of History*. Here is the conflation, in the first case, what Hegel says indirectly thanks to Lucretius, showing how the spectator sees the shipwreck from the seashore. It remains that history is a *Schlachtbank*, but it is also something else, which has to be thrown in the history, very different from the spirits who are afraid to enter the *Wirklichkeit*, the reality as effectuality or effectiveness. Diving into the *Wirklichkeit* thus becomes very important to him.

The first step of this research project takes shape in the volume *Scomposizioni* and, at this level, "Strategie di individuazione" ("Strategies of Individuation") becomes the title of the concluding chapter of the analysis dedicated to Hegel as the culminating point of the process by which the true and the whole no longer coincide with the dimension of the self-conscious subject as such, but refer "diachronically to the long history of the 'spirit' (or civilization) of which the individual is part and, synchronically, to a systemic subject, to the *tableau* of intelligibility of the articulations and specifications of his own epoch."[33] The chapter concludes by reiterating the reasons for the crisis of the dialectical model and claiming for it, however, the dual character of acclimatization of thought to change and to overcome the necessary differences in level that every process of growth exhibits, and of affirmation of the need to submit to the severe discipline of contradiction, in an ethical sense too. The next chapter, "Domande ineludibili" ("Inescapable Questions"), results from a rehash and enlargement of the text of the previous edition and thus concludes the book, but also, chronologically at least (2016), the entire triptych.

The new edition of the book was confronted with a major historical change, namely, the growth of the uncertainty of the future and the increased awareness of the vulnerability that marks the existence of a large part of humankind.[34] *Scomposizioni*, as is well known, starts from the prismatic decomposition throughout Goethe's age of the elements present in Hegel's famous fragment *The ever-growing contradiction . . .* and, in philosophical terms, the "reagent" through which the specificity of Hegel's dialectical thought exposed in the book becomes evident is constituted, once again, by Georg Simmel's thought.[35]

The great turning point made by Simmel with respect to the Hegel of the *Phenomenology of the Mind*—notes Bodei—is represented by the fact that the "transformation of substance into subject" now becomes unfeasible. The substance, in fact, is now rationality that has become objective and has been deposited in entities independent of individual consciousness, institutions, machines, codified knowledge. Self-regulated mechanisms can also pass through individual consciousness: "but only in the form of anonymous automatisms, rejecting the intervention of a thought not previously bent to rigid forms, to a tested technique and not routed on paths already programmed and preordained."[36]

The continuous cycle of reconversion of objectivity into subjectivity and of the latter back into objectivity is now broken by the elimination of the "absolute spirit," as an "overview of the progress tasks of human civilizations," while "life" detaches itself from its "stiffened forms."[37] It follows, on the one hand, that "rationality tends to become devoid of meaning and meaning devoid of rationality" and, on the other hand, that "the individual tends to be emptied of his previous prerogatives and sees his faculties inexorably absorbed by mechanisms devoid of consciousness."

So the individual abandons his "exorbitant claims to be the depositary of a universal rationality based on consciousness" and takes leave of the "Ptolemaic illusion" of being "at the center of the universe of meaning": "no alliance between the learned and the masses is any longer envisaged to break the 'positivity' of the existing and to create a new ethicity."[38] What remains is the "infinite task" of "patiently weaving into the rope of humanity [. . .] all the various differences without pretending to ignore or reset them, until history has 'digested' and integrated them."[39]

Theoretical Keys: Coming Back to Destinies

Returning to our starting point after enriching it with its many implications, if we try to describe the theoretical core of the rich material in *Personal Destinies*, we could say that, in a phase of depowering the consciousness and the subject, we must try to understand along which new paths we can rethink the relationship me-us I/We, subjectivity-objectivity, continuity discontinuity, identity-difference, unity and multiplicity. Knowing that each of these categories appears, at the same time, incompatible and indispensable and exposed to the multiversity of interpretations and theoretical solutions.

Bodei suggests for these three theoretical keys, "three schemes of analogy, to be integrated into a single model and to implement, substantiate and specify analytically, referring to the entire process and story" described in the book. The first scheme sees personal identity as "condensation." A concept that is reworked from the Freudian notion and refers to "the psychic mechanism by which different figures overlap, without blurring, on the same image, as happens by taking several photographs on the same photographic plate." Here condensation becomes the superposition of different I/Self "conceived synchronously as psychic coordination poles, endowed with a certain permanence, which each acquires throughout life." On the diachronic plane, instead, condensation is seen as "a metaphorical transformation of the selves that have passed over and flock to the present self": "the path is precarious, yet [. . .] we manage to balance continuity and discontinuity and to find the tortuous path that leads back to all our successive psychic incarnations in a single lifetime."[40]

The second scheme of analogy concerns the constant variation of our "barycenter" and the synthetic role of self-consciousness as a place of restatement and reformulation of the many experiences and thoughts of the self. Such a work of punctual and temporary rearrangement is produced in waking and dreaming, in a conscious and unconscious way, both in the horizon of the present and along the axis of memory and expectations. Unlike the idealistic model of empty, specular self-consciousness, here a "full" consciousness is given "that finds itself, from time to time, being brought back to the center of gravity of its contents of the moment, holding the overall weight and giving them adequate form."[41]

The third scheme deals with the concepts of "heterotopia" and "heterochronia," following Michel Foucault but transposing beyond the original scope the two concepts. In fact, the two concepts designate the juxtaposition of incompatible yet complementary times and spaces. Times and spaces that are virtual yet real, as in the mirrors or in the unfolding of theatrical or cinematographic scenes, that from a spatial and temporal elsewhere refer to a present place and time. Similar characteristics can also be attributed to personal identity, which in itself is not an illusion turned with Lacan into a "fleeting illusion designed to disprove the Cartesian certainty of the *cogito*," nor is it reduced to "something concrete, tangibly real, to body, brain, neural network": "identity is—simultaneously and in the form of the collaborative antagonism of the *nec tecum, nec sine te* [not with you not without you]—consciousness and brain, mind and 'flesh,' universality and individuality, us and myself, something that is out of the world and something that is in the world. All the elements of these pairs coexist in their mutual disjunction and in their inescapable relationship of complementarity, of concave and convex."[42]

In the "self" there is thus the universal element of unity with oneself and, at the same time, the element of absolute singularity and determined being, so that personal identity accompanies us inadvertently as a "bland taste" (Jean-Paul Sartre) or the "discreet presence of an acquaintance, of a known person" (Bertrand Russell): "it is an obscure vital, coenesthetic, body-related feeling, whose 'intermittent' nature Ribot had noted, but which had already been philosophically discovered in antiquity by Aristippus, in the form of 'internal contact' (*tactus intimus*, in Cicero's translation). Only when we look at ourselves as if we were outside of ourselves, do we realize what we are."[43]

Thanks to the combined action of these three paradigms, it is possible to renounce both the reduction of consciousness to a mere prereflexive *cogito*, and the closure in the cage of reflection, as in the theory attributed to early Fichte and German Idealism in general. Personal identity can be looked at in two ways, as spontaneously anchored to the center of us, in which the oscillations are dampened and all the translations of the self are recomposed; or as a void, a cast left by a presence that continuously subtracts itself but keeping in gestaltic tension the complementarity of the two gazes. It thus becomes possible to perceive our life "as a whole that has a 'metaphorical history,' tormented and syncopated, reflexively reconstructible in a fairly coherent manner thanks to universal categories, but firmly anchored to the existence of a body, which—unlike all the others—I perceive as exclusively mine."[44]

In the shared experience, we feel the *ubi consistam*, which redistributes thoughts, memories, affections and perceptions around a central and mobile point, able to overcome the caesuras of oblivion. We thus know that we are the same as we were yesterday, and only when we watch ourselves living from the outside and suspend the sense of natural evidence do we end up detaching ourselves from the immediate evidence of the centrality of the self. Considering the two initial positions of *traguardi* as extreme edges of a band of oscillation placed between absolute affirmation and absolute negation of the *principium individuationis*, both positions end up recovering a theoretical side of legitimacy, although each excludes the claims of absoluteness of the other. The use of the two *traguardi* and of the heterotopic-heterochronic model does not imply an amorphous refusal to take a position, but rather implies becoming aware that "one is all the more free and creative the more one is able to draw on the deposits of collective meaning, to interpret, learn and enrich the codes and rules, to elaborate and make explicit the still unexpressed possibilities."[45] It is necessary to avoid, in an ethical and political sense, the one-sidedness of the theorists of tradition and communitarianism that exalt the bonds of the we at the expense of the individual and, likewise, that of the theorists of liberalism who consider the individual as pre-existing society. By honoring the reality principle and recognizing conditioning in the conditional form of "if . . . then," each of us enacts, however, a kind of "individual law" and "must introduce into the world the incalculable but universalizable *novum* of our own autonomous action, giving a response to the starting contexts that is not contained in the contexts themselves."[46]

The conclusion that Bodei draws from this series of fine-tuning of the different schemes of analogy is that one cannot get out of the path indicated by the two pathfinders, Locke and Schopenhauer. It is not possible to undo, on one hand, the persistence of a consciousness "capable of preserving itself in the time of caducity" and, on the other hand, the presence of anonymous and eternal powers that are insensitive and above time. Hence the ethical concern on which the book concludes: "The course of events cannot be abandoned to chance [. . .]. Especially before the emergence of announced disasters, it is necessary for each person to impart to the personal and collective life an orientation and a direction, which opens a path between necessity and freedom, between computability and incalculability, continually comparing the court of its conscience with the court of the world, knowing the merciless hardness of the latter without abandoning the hopes of the former, maintaining the energies of an interiority that does not suffer from the diseases of the substitution with the real and the anchoring with a reality that does not become impermeable to the efforts of reason to understand and practice to change it."[47]

Conclusion: Oxymoronic Logic and Open Questions

With the achievement of the perspective of a personalization of destinies, the strategy of the gaze is carried out, which among the fires of the ellipsis, parabolas, goals, triptychs, pyramids, and prisms compares the optical-geometric devices of detection with the genesis and crisis of subjectivity as personal identity and process of individuation, irreducibility of the individual and paradoxical aspiration to individual law. And it is carried out according to that sort of antinomian propensity and oxymoronic logic that Bodei first recognized as the long-term inspiration of his own philosophical endeavor, at the moment of retrospectively reflecting on the approach that had made it possible, summarized in the Latin formula from a poem by Catullus "*nec tecum nec sine te*" (not with you nor without you [implied: *vivere possum*] can I live). Let's say in the capacity consider the tensions (*tensioni*, the German *Spannungen*), the historical and conceptual conflicts as a form of antagonistic complicity, as a form of *logos* intrinsically tied, but also intrinsically stranger, to the *polemos*, and already present in the very titles of his books, as he noticed.[48]

It will then be a matter of seeing, in conclusion and at least for hints, how such a theoretical device then maintains its openness and capacity for investigation, both in the strict form of the questions that in the path followed so far remain unanswered or that the subsequent developments of the state of the world have taken it upon themselves to reopen. Or as themes that jut out toward other developments and find their reformulation in subsequent or parallel works of Bodei, and until the end have engaged him in the effort to keep philosophy the task of scrutinizing the physiognomy of its own epoch in search of the effectivity of the possible, leaving to those who remain the burden of continuing the legacy, from the perspective of an irreversible discontinuity.

Taking up some of the central points of *Destini*, such as the possible lives, the balance between I and We, and the very notions of destiny and oxymoronic logic, it becomes possible to focus on the problematic nodes and identify the successive elaborations to which they are subjected in Bodei's work.

The philosophies of Nietzsche, Bergson, and Simmel, side by side with the literary works of Proust and Pirandello, direct the individual toward the exalting or upsetting perspectives of enhancing one's self, or living in reality and imagining other lives, to sneak away from a destiny marked in advance, to guard within oneself as sketched multiple personalities a wealth of possible developments, not blocked, at least in desire, from the choices made in the past. The "mystery" of our fragile permanence in time, through the continuous changes that we undergo, thus opens up to the dimension of latency. *Latency* means something possible that is nevertheless already present in reality, or being of the "not yet" (*noch nicht*), which, on the other hand, puts us in relation with the forces by which we are shaped. This is the auroral scenario that unfolds at the opening of *Imagining Other Lives*, the 2013 book that compares reality/ies, projects, desires of "imagined lives" and of the interweaving between imitation and creativity through which each one elaborates and unravels every day his own personality: "We often tend to forget that we are guests of life. We are born without wanting to be and knowing it and in a certain time and place and, without wanting to be and knowing it, the body that we have received as a biological inheritance spontaneously unfolds its wonderful and, sometimes, terrible processes [. . .]. The fact that we depend on unconscious powers or powers greater than ourselves that operate without our consent and that partially mark our destiny does not mean that we must passively surrender to them. [. . .] In order to escape the narrow horizons within which our lives would be confined, we use the imagination as an antidote to the poverty and finiteness of every individual experience."[49] That is, the heterotopic dimension of imagination comes into play, a kind of oscillation between what is real and what is imagined, what is present and what is not, as in the space of cinema or theater, which maintains the copresence of opposite terms and makes possible the aesthetic-perceptual expansion of things beyond their reduction to any exchange, use, or symbolic value. Like it has been noticed in *The Life of Things*, starting from the observation that in the form of technological objects, of consumer goods, of personal effects, of household furnishings and items, of the street and the city, or in the more ambiguous guise of artistic objects or marginal, obsolete presences, objects and things proliferate out of all proportion in every aspect of our life, to culminate in an idea of works of art from the point of view of the coincidence between the things of everyday life and the accomplished unfolding of their qualities, between the transient and the eternal.[50] A kind of heterotopic oscillation that also makes possible the aesthetic relationship with the world investigated in *Le forme del bello*, that goes as far as the processes of aestheticization and of assumption on the part of the object of an erotic connection so strong as to lure and transform into a "sentient thing" the subject who is fascinated by it, and which proceeds according to a dual process of attraction. This process transfers to the object a power "analogous to that of the Latin *venustas*," and of habit, which by enveloping the latter with "prefabricated dreams" attributes to the subject an "ephemeral and façade identity" and takes away from the beauty its "auratic character of dazzling, moving and rare apparition," thus establishing a sensual alliance with the object rather than a rational one.[51]

A second aspect to be highlighted is that of balancing the self/I with the We. Following *Destini*, only thanks to Leibniz and Spinoza's *res singulares*, the individual acquires full ontological consistency and begins to have a value in him- or herself. What is different—historically and theoretically—is the sense of the self as individuality and equilibrium or balance *We-I* (the balance *Wir-Ich* also described by Norbert Elias). From the Middle Ages, and above all between Montaigne and Kant, this balance moved in Western culture from the primacy of the Us to that of the Self, to move again until the mid-twentieth century to the authoritarian restoration of the political supremacy of the Us. Bodei's theoretical proposal at the height of the 2002 book was centered on the observation that "we are very eager to keep alive the aspiration of an identity that is, at the same time, strong and free, consistent and open to further developments, able to oppose the cult of a rigid ego and, at the same time, to the gregarious or dissipative drives of a mass civilization that tends to chloroform existence."[52] This is why: "we need to rethink the status of identity and conscience in pluralist societies that have raised and moved elsewhere the theoretical hubs on which the individual's existence (God and the immortal soul) revived and threw the greasy bearings of tradition, a sort of autophagy. [. . .] The struggle between the push towards reflexive autonomy and the push towards the abdication of the subject to any conscious and responsible link between the I and the We remains as open as ever today."[53] Books such as, among others, those dedicated to the "generations" and to the "ages of life, ages of things" (2014), to the "limits" (2016), but also the updated new edition of *The Philosophy of Twentieth Century and Beyond* (2015), actually developed this direction of research.[54] On the whole, it is a pendular movement that brings to the forefront the direction of plurality, sharing and belonging, also as a reaction to the push toward proprietary and ontological individualism that the triumph of the neoliberal hegemony had brought with it up to the threshold of the new millennium. In the first case, we are talking about the sharing that each generation makes of its time, recovering the past and projecting into the future, with the associated transmission of material and immaterial goods from one generation to another. An inheritance that also involves principles and symbols that are perpetuated in the form of gift and restitution. In the second case, in the face of the drive to sweep away every limitation inherent in the processes of globalization and the progressive abolition of the inhibitions to earthly achievements connected with them, it is a question of the re-emergence of the attitude and the ethical drive to recognize and distinguish the limits in the relationship with nature inside and outside individuals, with economic development and with the consumption of resources that it entails. In the third case, finally, the representation of theoretical scenes and conceptual frameworks to which the story of twentieth-century thought is brought back, shows at the beginning of the new century a reformulation of the agenda of philosophical problems in which the recomposition of partial conjectures, rationally and empirically screened in their degrees of probability finds its meaning. And where it is no longer possible to postpone the ethical assumption and the public discussion of the responsibilities toward the consequences deriving from the new digital and biotechnologies, from the transformations of our biological base that they induce, from the dramatic impact of climate change and, in general, from the whole framework of problems that, as inhabitants of the earth, we share.

The third aspect, which starting from *Destini*, it is possible to enucleate and emphasize is the notion of "destiny" itself. The problem of fate and destiny is one of the problems—in the sense of the Greek "problema," the stumbling stone—which gives origin to the research in the book and for which it is titled. When Descartes asks "Quod vitae sectabor iter?" (What path shall I take in life?), he is quoting a verse of Ausonius, a Gallic poet. The idea is always that, we know we are deadly, we are mortal: fortunately, we do not think about it, but as *navigatio vitae* (navigation of life) happens on unpaved routes, we are exposed. Of this, Bodei told us that he had discussed for a long time with the British philosopher Bernard Williams: relying too much on the Kantian idea of autonomy, on the assertion of being autonomous, we forget the teaching of the Greeks, that is the *Ananke*, where there is *Tyche*, fortune, there are all these external forces that affect us. At any moment, there may fall a tile on the head. It is "misfortune" (Simone Weil). To be aware of this fragility, not of the good, but of the fragility of our existence, of being exposed. A little from Jaspers, too. Certain existentialist "exaggerations," it was too early to abandon them—Bodei argues—like leaving Sartre. The living nucleus of these existentialist considerations, which are basically of Heideggerian root and date back to *Being and Time*, is our exposure to waves: thrown into the waves of time, Augustine said. Much better than the *Geworfenheit* (thrownness), where one is knocked down there, it looks like rubbish. We have fallen into the waves of time and have to learn to swim if we want to use these nautical expressions, or to sail. *Navigare necesse est*, according to the words Plutarch attributed to Pompeius. In order to merit one's own birth, as his book on imagined lives will make clear, each one must become a contemporary of him- or herself, must learn to orient him- or herself with sufficient awareness above all in choosing which road to take in life, knowing, as Bergson wrote, that "the road we travel in time is covered with the rubble of all that we began to be, of all that we could have become." Each of us is exposed from the beginning of our *navigatio vitae* to unknown vicissitudes, along untraced routes, under the constant threat of storms, rocks, shallows and calm, possible shipwrecks. The powerful nautical metaphor pushes Bodei to resort to the acceleration that these risks have found in recent decades, when humanity has become "capable of self-suppression either with weapons of mass destruction or by altering the conditions necessary for its survival—climate, reproducibility of resources, pollution of air, water, soil—we must be lucidly prepared."[55] For this reason it is necessary to know that in the *navigatio vitae* "we are not alone in the open sea, but we are supported by institutions, traditions, ideas, and affections that change, but that preserve, for most individuals, constant elements."[56] However—opening up to the series of questions that finally Bodei's long reconstruction of the strategies of individuation, of the genesis and crisis of the subject, and of modern and contemporary individuality open up and leave us in charge—is it still possible, outside of the necessary outcome of the dialectical movement of exiting from oneself to re-enter it increased, to sustain, with the adage of Erasmus, "Naufragium feci, bene navigavi" (I did shipwreck, I sailed well)? Remaining in the metaphorical field of *navigatio*, is it still possible to access in this way a sort of "enlightened catastrophism"?

And, to remind of a fourth and final element that comes to us from *Destini*, does the oxymoronic model of dialectics, based on the antagonistic complicity of opposites[57] already operating in *Scomposizioni* as a pyramidal construction of the personality, still act as an articulate scheme of thought? Is it still true that one has to lose oneself to find him- or herself, to get away to return, to contradict oneself to develop? From the age of Goethe to that of Nietzsche, the engine of history is the *polemos* that strengthen the *logos*, through the experience of absolute devastation. It is still possible today to argue, following the line by Hölderlin, that "Wo aber Gefahr ist, wächst Das Rettende auch" (But where there is danger, what saves us also grows)?

Already the conclusion of the new edition of *Scomposizioni* (2016) dwells on the Stoic metaphor of the threads that are woven into the rope: "There remains the infinite but indispensable task of patiently weaving into the rope of humanity (which is all the more robust the more threads, the more partial stories, it manages to weave together) all the various differences without pretending to ignore or reset them, until history has 'digested' them and integrated them."[58] Although here again, in the metaphorical of *manducatio spiritualis*, a risky but in some form teleologically resolution-oriented process appears to be at work.

Beyond the threshold of the triptych that I have tried to outline in this contribution, the metaphor of the rope returns in the conclusions of the last book published by Bodei in his lifetime, on domination and submission (2019), precisely to describe the possibility of the individual to "recompose oneself," or "pull oneself together," and rediscover the possible connections between one's present, past, and future: "The fruitful present should resemble the unraveling of an 'hawser,' the nonpointal or episodic presence to oneself, capable of inserting the three dimensions of time, along nonlinear interweavings that form, however, wrapping themselves to form the hawser, a succession relatively coherent in their torsions."[59] Although Bodei himself observes, in a footnote to the text, that "the limit of the Stoic proposal is that the model suggested by the hawser is valid only on the individual level," nevertheless there remains room to propose, echoing the Foucaultian path of self-care, a thinking as meditation and reflection able of "periodically interrupting the spontaneous flow of chronological time and carving out a space of qualitative time in order to 'put back together' our fragmented thinking and our unbalanced living."[60]

Anyway, coming back finally to the results of Bodei's scrutiny of the individuation complex, and in the light of today's developments, we might ask: Is the individual still alive? Can he or she survive the overwhelming weight, for example, of the enormous power concentration that derives from the centralized control of big data? Or in the face of the human being's alteration of the features of the whole natural cycle that pushes us to talk about Anthropocene or Capitalocene? When was it given to individuals to control their ecological footprint? For these reasons one could also speak of the "death of the individual." That is to say, at the beginning of the new century, under the unsustainable pressure to which the forty-year period of neoliberalism has subjected individuals to the impossible task of solving systemic problems individually, and the preponderance of objectified culture over subjectified culture has been enhanced by technological and digital developments, as well as, on the whole and in a philosophical mood, considering that the interweaving between the processes of subjectification and those of subjugation is shown to be ever tighter, couldn't the problem that Georg Simmel tried to solve at the beginning of the last century in his famous conference on *The Metropolis and Mental Life* be proposed again in a new form? That is: "The deepest problems of modern life flow from the attempt of the individual to maintain the independence and individuality of his existence against the sovereign powers of the society, against the weight of the historical heritage and external culture and technique of life. This antagonism represents the most modern form of the conflict which primitive man must carry on with nature."[61] Namely, the stimulus of an author who, as we have seen, has played an important role in the contemporary exploration of the problem of the individual and individuation that has inspired Remo Bodei's research, and whose starting point could be a kind of recurring sting to be reactivated in search of a solution to match the changed conditions? Nothing but a few of the inescapable questions, "domande ineludibili," that were discussed on that numinous afternoon under the Pacific's highest sky and are still there for the philosophical enterprise of those who remain.

Acknowledgments

I am very grateful to professor Massimo Ciavolella and Professor Efraín Kristal for their invitation to join this conference and, through them, to all the institutions at UCLA that allowed this celebration of Remo Bodei. This contribution is published after the dear friend and master left us; for a broader view of the work of the Italian philosopher, I refer to my other contributions and to the collections dedicated to him in which they appeared: "A Philosophy of Impure Reason: Ethos Between Rationality and Passions in Remo Bodei's Italy (1943–2006)," in L. Ballerini, A. Borsari, M. Ciavolella, eds, *Navigatio vitae: Saggi per i settant'anni di Remo Bodei*, 17–24; "Le forme del bello: trasformazioni dell'estetica," in F. Vercellone and E. C. Corriero, eds, *Cristalli di storicità. Saggi in onore di Remo Bodei*, 105–22 (at 203–34, an updated bibliography of Bodei's work); "Il tempo dell'inatteso: Sull'impresa filosofica di Remo Bodei," *Iride: Rivista di filosofia e discussione pubblica*, 19–34 (monographic section: "Per Remo Bodei," 5–45); "Natura e animalità: oltre il dominio?," *Teoria Politica*, 415–24 (monographic section: "Per Remo Bodei. Letture di Dominio e sottomissione" [For Remo Bodei. Reading Dominio e sottomissione], 381–439). Many thanks to Paul Vangelisti, Tomaso Cavallo, and Heather Renee Sottong for reading the final version of the text and for their suggestions.

Notes

1. R. Bodei, *Destini personali. L'età della colonizzazione delle coscienze* (when not explicitly referring to printed English translations, texts quoted from editions in other languages are to be understood as translated by the author of this article). See also, R. Bodei, *Scomposizioni: Forme dell'individuo moderno*, Einaudi, 1987, 2nd rev. and enlarged edition, Il Mulino, 2016, and *Geometria delle passioni: Paura, speranza, felicità: Filosofia e uso politico*, English translation by G. W. Doebler, *Geometry of the Passions: Fear, Hope, Happiness: Philosophy and Political Use.*

2. In this and in the other cases in which the information reported does not refer to a printed text, the reference is to this author's still unpublished biographical-theoretical interview book with Remo Bodei.

3. R. Bodei, *Geometry of the Passions,* 282–83.

4. R. Bodei, *Geometry of the Passions,* 286.

5. R. Bodei, *Geometry of the Passions,* 290.

6. R. Bodei, *Geometry of the Passions,* 22.

7. R. Bodei, *Geometry of the Passions,* 23.

8. R. Bodei, *Geometry of the Passions,* 398.

9. R. Bodei, *Geometry of the Passions,* 467.

10. See R. Bodei, "La cognizione del dolore: Il tragico nel romanzo di Thomas Mann," in R. Bodei, F. Moretti, G. Guglielmi, M. Cavazzuti, *La conoscenza letteraria II,* 5–41. For a retrospective synthesis of the path taken in *Personal Destinies,* see *Scomposizioni: Forme dell'individuo moderno,* 2nd rev. and enlarged edition, Il Mulino, 2016, 17–20.

11. R. Bodei, *Destini personali,* 12.

12. R. Bodei, *Destini* personali, 37.

13. R. Bodei, *Destini personali,* 169.

14. R. Bodei, *Destini* personali, 352.

15. R. Bodei, *Destini personali,* 171.

16. R. Bodei, *Destini personali,* 173–74.

17. R. Bodei, *Destini* personali, 174.

18. R. Bodei, *Destini* personali, 179. See also 180–83.

19. R. Bodei, *Destini* personali, 184.

20. R. Bodei, *Destini personali,* 185.

21. R. Bodei, *Destini* personali, 186.

22. R. Bodei, *Beyond Dialectical Thinking:* "Political Logics and the Construction of Individuality," translated by Peter Carravetta, in *Graduate Faculty Philosophy Journal,* 123–40; "Stratégies d'individuation," translated by Charles Alunni, in *Critique,* 119–38; "Strategie di individuazione," in *aut aut,* 93–109. R. Bodei, *Scomposizioni. Forme dell'individuo moderno.*

23. R. Bodei, *Strategie di* individuazione, 93.

24. R. Bodei, *Beyond Dialectical Thinking*, 123.

25. R. Bodei, *Beyond Dialectical Thinking*, 127.

26. R. Bodei, *Beyond Dialectical Thinking*, 124.

27. R. Bodei, *Beyond Dialectical Thinking*, 125.

28. R. Bodei, *Beyond Dialectical Thinking*, 137–38.

29. R. Bodei, *Strategie di individuazione*, 108–9.

30. R. Bodei, *Strategie di individuazione*, 108–9.

31. R. Bodei, *Beyond Dialectical Thinking*, 139.

32. R. Bodei, *Strategie di individuazione*, 109.

33. R. Bodei, *Scomposizioni*, 347 (for the chapter, see 347–79).

34. See R. Bodei, *Scomposizioni*, 401–9.

35. See R. Bodei, *Scomposizioni*, 382–87. In the 1987 edition, Simmel is never mentioned. A specific analysis should be dedicated on another occasion to the detailed reconstruction of the growing weight assumed by the Berlin philosopher in Bodei's work.

36. R. Bodei, *Scomposizioni*, 386.

37. R. Bodei, *Scomposizioni*, 386–87.

38. R. Bodei, *Scomposizioni*, 387.

39. R. Bodei, *Scomposizioni*, 408.

40. R. Bodei, *Destini personali*, 281.

41. R. Bodei, *Destini personali*, 281–82.

42. R. Bodei, *Destini personali*, 282–83.

43. R. Bodei, *Destini personali*, 284.

44. R. Bodei, *Destini personali*, 285.

45. R. Bodei, *Destini personali*, 289, and see 286–89.

46. R. Bodei, *Destini personali*, 290.

47. R. Bodei, *Destini personali*, 290.

48. See R. Bodei, "A un altro me stesso," in *Annuario filosofico*, 15: "I have realized after the fact that almost every title of my books reflects unconsciously such a tension between a so-called 'cold' element, a logical and abstract one, and a 'warm,' red-hot, emotionally marked element—see titles like: *Geometry of the Passions, Ordo amoris* [The order of love], *Logics of the Delirium, Personal Destinies*" (the text was written at the very moment he was leaving his professorial position at the University of Pisa to move to UCLA; English translation, R. Bodei, "Understanding myself," in F. Vercellone and E. C. Corriero, eds, *Cristalli di storicità*, 17–25). In order to frame wholly the approach here mentioned, a kind of "hospitable or impure reason" also related to the specific features of the Italian philosophical tradition, see my "A Philosophy of Impure Reason."

49. R. Bodei, *Immaginare altre vite: Realtà, progetti, desideri*, 9–13. The specific form of the possible to which the book refers is that which is obtained in this way: "mentally overturning the idea according to which first the 'real' is given,

from which then the possible emerge as its depotentiated rejects, it seems, in this case, more fruitful the hypothesis of starting from the possibles in order to make them then pass through the test of their compatibility," 18.

50. R. Bodei, *The Life of Things, The Love of Things.*

51. R. Bodei, *Le forme del bello.*

52. R. Bodei, *Destini personali*, 276.

53. R. Bodei, *Destini personali*, 276.

54. See R. Bodei, *Generazioni: Età della vita, età delle cose*; R. Bodei, *Limite*; R. Bodei, *La filosofia del Novecento (e oltre).*

55. R. Bodei, *Immaginare altre vite*, 23.

56. R. Bodei, *Immaginare altre vite*, 23.

57. On the contrary, could it perhaps be better understood as antinomic—both contradictory alternatives remaining and the movement coming from their dynamic interaction?

58. R. Bodei, *Scomposizioni*, 408.

59. R. Bodei, *Dominio e sottomissione. Schiavi, animali, macchine, Intelligenza Artificiale*, 378–79.

60. R. Bodei, *Dominio e sottomissione*, 379.

61. G. Simmel, "The Metropolis and Mental Life" (1903), translated by Kurt Wolff, in *The Sociology of Georg Simmel*, 409.

Bibliography

Bodei, Remo. "A un altro me stesso." *Annuario filosofico* 20 (2004).

Bodei, Remo. "Beyond Dialectical Thinking: Political Logics and the Construction of Individuality." Translated by Peter Carravetta. *Graduate Faculty Philosophy Journal* 10, no. 1 (1984): 123–40.

Bodei, Remo. *Destini personali: L'età della colonizzazione delle coscienze.* Feltrinelli, 2002.

Bodei, Remo. *Dominio e sottomissione: Schiavi, animali, macchine, Intelligenza Artificiale.* il Mulino, 2019.

Bodei, Remo. *Geometria delle passioni: Paura, speranza, felicità: Filosofia e uso politico.* Feltrinelli, 1991.

Bodei, Remo. *Geometry of the Passions: Fear, Hope, Happiness: Philosophy and Political Use.* Translated by G. W. Doebler. Toronto University Press, 2018.

Bodei, Remo. *Generazioni: Età della vita, età delle cose.* Laterza, 2014.

Bodei, Remo. *Immaginare altre vite: Realtà, progetti, desideri.* Feltrinelli, 2013.

Bodei, Remo. "La cognizione del dolore: Il tragico nel romanzo di Thomas Mann." In R. Bodei, F. Moretti, G. Guglielmi, and M. Cavazzuti, *La conoscenza letteraria II*, 5–41. Quaderni della Fondazione San Carlo, 1984.

Bodei, Remo. *La filosofia del Novecento (e oltre).* Feltrinelli, 2015.

Bodei, Remo. *Le forme del bello.* il Mulino, 1995.

Bodei, Remo. *Scomposizioni: Forme dell'individuo moderno.* Einaudi, 1987, 2nd rev. and enlarged edition, Il Mulino, 2016.

Bodei, Remo. "Stratégies d'individuation." Translated by Charles Alunni. *Critique* 452–53 (January–February 1985): 119–38.

Bodei, Remo. "Strategie di individuazione." *Aut Aut* 206–207 (March–June 1985): 93–109.

Bodei, Remo. *The Life of Things, The Love of Things.* Translated by Murtha Baca. New York: Fordham University Press, 2014.

Borsari, Andrea. "A Philosophy of Impure Reason: Ethos Between Rationality and Passions in Remo Bodei's Italy (1943–2006)." In *Navigatio vitae: Saggi per i settant'anni di Remo Bodei.* Edited by Luigi Ballerini, Andrea Borsari, and Massimo Ciavolella. Agincourt Press, 2010, 17–24.

Borsari, Andrea. "Le forme del bello: trasformazioni dell'estetica." In *Cristalli di storicità: Saggi in onore di Remo Bodei.* Edited by Federico Vercellone and Emilio Carlo Corriero. Rosenberg & Sellier, 2019, 105–22.

Borsari, Andrea. "Il tempo dell'inatteso: Sull'impresa filosofica di Remo Bodei." *Iride: Rivista di filosofia e discussione pubblica* 33 (2020): 19–34.

Borsari, Andrea. "Natura e animalità: oltre il dominio?" *Teoria Politica* X (2020): 415–24.

Simmel, Georg. "The Metropolis and Mental Life" (1903). Translated by Kurt Wolff. In *The Sociology of Georg Simmel.* Free Press, 1950.

Contributors

Andrea Borsari is a full professor of aesthetics at the University of Bologna. He directs the series La vita e le forme and serves as the deputy director of *Iride: Rivista di filosofia e discussione pubblica*. He has taught as a visiting professor at numerous universities across Europe and beyond. His notable publications include *Mondo, cose, immagini: Sulle forme dell'esperienza estetica* (2018); *Mimicry: Estetica del divenire animale* (2018); and, as editor (both independently and in collaboration), *Philosophical Anthropology and Critical Theory* (2022); *Aesthetics of the Anthropocene* (2022); *Continuità e discontinuità nelle forme della cultura* (2023); *Temporary: Citizenship, Architecture and City* (2024); and *Urban Aesthetics* (2025).

Peter Carravetta is a professor of philosophy at SUNY at Stony Brook, known for his significant contributions to cultural criticism and the philosophy of interpretation. He has authored nine books, including *The Elusive Hermes: Method, Discourse, Interpreting* (2012); *Language at the Boundaries: Philosophy, Literature, and the Poetics of Culture* (2021); and *The Humanist Project: Will, Judgment, Society from Dante to Vico* (2024). He also founded and directed *DIFFERENTIA: Review of Italian Thought* (9 vols., 1986–1999) and translated *Weak Thought* by G. Vattimo and P. A. Rovatti (2012). His current research focuses on the theme of migration.

Paolo Cherchi is a professor emeritus at the University of Chicago, where he taught Medieval and Renaissance Italian Literature from 1965 to 2003. He also held the position of Professor of Italian Literature at the University of Ferrara from 2003 to 2009. Cherchi has authored more than 550 scholarly works, including articles, books, and edited volumes. In the past two years, he has published eight books, including *Le concordanze delle storie: Il modello* *degli antichi dall'Umanesimo all'Illuminismo* (2023); *Pagine sarde*, edited by Dino Manca (2023); and *Le 'meraviglie' di Eco* (2024).

Massimo Ciavolella taught at Carleton University (Ottawa) and the University of Toronto before coming to the present position as Franklin D. Murphy Professor of Italian Renaissance Studies and Comparative Literature at the University of California, Los Angeles. He has published extensively on medieval and Renaissance Italian literature and on Medical Humanities.

Gianpiero W. Doebler, PhD, is a translator specializing in texts using older forms of Italian and in poetry. Recent projects include works by Vittorio Alfieri (*Life*), poet Angelo Lumelli, and artist Gastone Novelli. Forthcoming is his translation of Matteo Ricci's *On the Entry of the Company of Jesus and of Christianity into China*.

After teaching philosophy at Boston University and the University of Pisa, **Alfredo Ferrarin** currently teaches at the Scuola Normale Superiore in Pisa. He has published nine monographs, including *Hegel and Aristotle* (2001), *The Powers of Pure Reason* (2015), and *Thinking and the I* (2019). His forthcoming book is *A World Not of This World: The Reality of Images and Imagination* (2025). Ferrarin specializes in the history of philosophy, with particular expertise in Kant, Hegel, Aristotle, Hobbes, Husserl, phenomenology, and the philosophy of imagination.

Efraín Kristal is a Distinguished Professor of Comparative Literature at UCLA. He was a Fellow at the Institute for Advanced Studies in Berlin, and of the Centre for Literature Philosophy and the Arts at the University of Warwick. He specializes in Latin American literature, translation studies, and philosophical approaches to the arts. He has published several single-author and edited volumes, and over one hundred articles, including the essay on philosophical and theoretical approaches to translation for the *Blackwell Companion to Translation Studies*, and an essay on Jorge Luis Borges and philosophy for Jeffrey R. Di Leo's *Philosophy and World Literature*.

Olimpia Pelosi is an associate professor of Italian Studies at the State University of New York at Albany. She has published extensively on authors of the Italian Renaissance and the Baroque eras, such as Francesco Colonna, Gaspara Stampa, Michelangelo Buonarroti the Younger, and Maria Domitilla Galluzzi. She has also written essays on modern Italian authors, often examined through the comparative critical lens. She is currently working on a book-length project on women sonneteers of the Italian and the French Renaissance.

Heather Renee Sottong is assistant professor of Literary and Cultural Studies at FLAME University in Pune, India. She was a student of Remo Bodei's while working on her doctorate at UCLA. Her research focuses on the Italian diaspora in Argentina and the literary appropriation of Dante in the Americas. Her monograph, *Transnational Dante: Inventing Argentine Cultural Identity*, explores how Dante was repurposed by Argentine politicians and authors who were concerned with the construction of Argentine national identity in the late nineteenth and early twentieth centuries.

Christoph Wulf, PhD, is a professor of anthropology and education at Freie Universität Berlin. He is known for developing the concepts of continental anthropology and continental educational anthropology, as explored in *Anthropology: A Continental Perspective* (2013). His current research centers on the Anthropocene. Wulf's work has been widely recognized, with his books translated into twenty languages. He also serves as the vice president of the German Commission for UNESCO.

Index